What's Your Competitive Advantage?

Pearson

At Pearson, we believe in learning – all kinds of learning for all kinds of people. Whether it's at home, in the classroom or in the workplace, learning is the key to improving our life chances.

That's why we're working with leading authors to bring you the latest thinking and best practices, so you can get better at the things that are important to you. You can learn on the page or on the move, and with content that's always crafted to help you understand quickly and apply what you've learned.

If you want to upgrade your personal skills or accelerate your career, become a more effective leader or more powerful communicator, discover new opportunities or simply find more inspiration, we can help you make progress in your work and life.

Every day our work helps learning flourish, and wherever learning flourishes, so do people.

To learn more, please visit us at **www.pearson.com/uk**

The Financial Times

With a worldwide network of highly respected journalists, *The Financial Times* provides global business news, insightful opinion and expert analysis of business, finance and politics. With over 500 journalists reporting from 50 countries worldwide, our in-depth coverage of international news is objectively reported and analysed from an independent, global perspective.

To find out more, visit **www.ft.com**

What's Your Competitive Advantage?

7 Strategies for running a more profitable business in a complex world

Cliff Bowman and Paul Raspin

Harlow, England • London • New York • Boston • San Francisco • Toronto • Sydney
Dubai • Singapore • Hong Kong • Tokyo • Seoul • Taipei • New Delhi
Cape Town • São Paulo • Mexico City • Madrid • Amsterdam • Munich • Paris • Milan

Pearson Education Limited
KAO Two
KAO Park
Harlow
CM17 9NA
United Kingdom
Tel: +44 (0)1279 623623
Web: www.pearson.com/uk

First edition published 2019 (print and electronic)

© Pearson Education Limited 2019 (print and electronic)

ISBN: 978-1-292-25939-0 (print)
      978-1-292-25940-6 (PDF)
      978-1-292-25941-3 (ePub)

British Library Cataloguing-in-Publication Data
A catalogue record for the print edition is available from the British Library

Library of Congress Cataloging-in-Publication Data
A catalogue record for the print edition is available from the Library of Congress

10 9 8 7 6 5 4 3 2 1
22 21 20 19 18

Front cover halftone texture © Aerial3/iStock/Getty Images Plus

Print edition typeset in 9.5/13pt ITC Giovanni Std by Pearson CSC
Printed by Ashford Colour Press Ltd, Gosport

NOTE THAT ANY PAGE CROSS REFERENCES REFER TO THE PRINT EDITION

To Courtney, James and Scarlett (Paul)

Contents

About the authors

Cliff Bowman BA, MBA, PhD is Professor of Strategic Management at Cranfield School of Management. His research interests focus on the creation and capture of value, complexity, dynamic capabilities, strategy processes and the development and leveraging of strategic assets. He has undertaken consulting assignments for a wide range of organisations and is the author of twelve books and sixty articles. Cliff is a past Chairman of the European Case Clearing House, was Faculty Dean of Cranfield School of Management from 1998 to 2006, and holds two non-executive director positions.

Dr Paul Raspin BCom, MEc, ACA, PhD Paul is the founder and managing director of Stratevolve, a strategy consultancy that works exclusively with senior executives and management teams to identify how to gain competitive advantage and create and capture significant value. In addition to his strategy consultancy role, Paul is an active researcher and author on the subject of strategy management and corporate finance. He is a senior visiting fellow at Cass Business School where he teaches strategy and finance to senior executives on the Executive MBA course. Prior to Stratevolve, Paul worked at Andersen for 12 years in the assurance, corporate finance, and strategy consultancy practices across offices in Australia, USA and UK. During this period, Paul led numerous strategy advisory and strategic change projects across multiple industries including financial services, retail, manufacturing, healthcare, telecommunications, transportation, and professional services. Prior strategy project briefs include growth strategy, valuing strategic options, customer centric strategy, disruptive technologies, and innovating business models.

Publisher's acknowledgements

Text

10 Oxford University Press: Boulton, J., Allen, P. and Bowman, C. (2015). Embracing Complexity. Oxford: Oxford University Press. 64 Prentice-Hall: Mintzberg, H. (1979). The Structuring of Organizations: A Synthesis of the Research. Englewood Cliffs, New Jersey: Prentice-Hall. 100 John Lewis & Partners: © J. Spedan Lewis, 1925 137, 138 Long Tall Sally Clothing: © 2018 LONGTALLYSALLY.COM 143 McGraw-Hill Education: McGregor (1960) 'The Human Side of the Enterprise', McGraw-Hill Education. 170 University of Chicago Press: Polanyi, M. and Sen, A. (2009). The Tacit Dimension. Chicago, USA: University of Chicago Press.

Photos

Cover Getty Images: Aerial3/iStock/Getty Images Plus/Getty Images 04t Gary Dewar: Author headshot © Gary Dewar 04b Antony Jones: Author headshot © Antony Jones

Part

1

Value-creating strategies

Chapter

Creating value

We live in a complex world, no one can predict the future and we can't anticipate the ultimate impact of any actions we take. These realities make the task of successfully leading a business incredibly challenging. In this book, we set out an approach to this challenge that *works with* the realities of a complex world. Our seven *competitive strategies* set the broad direction the firm should head in and the *change processes* that work with this reality. These processes rely on high-quality feedback which enables us to adapt to unfolding circumstances.

Our approach builds on research into how *value* is created and captured to develop a practical approach to guiding a business in turbulent times. Value has different meanings. A product has *use value*; it is a useful thing to the customer. Money acts as *exchange value* which enables us to trade goods and services. Value from a firm's point of view is the *profit* that is created by making and selling products and services. Our seven strategies are ways to create profit from providing use value to customers in a cost-efficient way. We explore these different forms of value in depth in Chapter 2.

We draw selectively from economics, strategy, organisation theory and complexity science in building this approach, which takes full account of the complex and unpredictable world we live in. We look at the firm as a value creation *system* and we explain seven strategies that can deliver competitive advantage. Each *strategy* has an associated set of *capabilities* which deliver customer value efficiently. These capabilities are supported by enabling *practices* which *shape the structures, systems* and *culture* of the business. Having selected a particular strategy, the associated capabilities and practices should inform the selection of specific *initiatives*. And these initiatives start to shift the value system in the direction indicated by the chosen strategy.

Thus, the role of the competitive strategy is to provide a clear overall direction for the business in a way that allows for adaptation and change as the future unfolds. The strategy provides guidance for where we wish the value system to be headed; it is neither a straightjacket nor a detailed blueprint for how the business should look at some future time. The competitive strategy provides a focus which can 'pull' the system towards the future. This focus increases the chances that, whatever changes we introduce into the system, they will 'fit' with each other, that is, we will have coordinated actions going forward.

Every business has its own particular history which shapes how it looks today. What works in one firm may well not be effective in another. Whilst there are some general principles that underpin how value is created and captured, each firm's circumstances are unique, and the best we can do is to try to understand the peculiarities of the context we are in and proceed to adapt the value system with caution. Key to the introduction of any change designed to create competitive advantage is *feedback*. In a complex system, you cannot predict the effect of any change you make, so you need continual and appropriate *live information* from the system to enable you to make necessary adjustments.

A competitive strategy acts to shape the *direction* of change in the system. It guides the selection of change initiatives, and as a consequence, the chosen initiatives are more likely to provide additional synergies between them. These synergistic outcomes embed the strategy into the system. Our competitive strategies address not only the direction of travel but also inform the processes of organisational change.

In this book, we set out the underlying concepts and logic that led us to focus our attention on seven competitive strategies. Some of these strategies have been explained by previous contributors to the strategy field and will be familiar; others have been developed through the course of our research. Our approach is based on how value is created and captured and how these processes unfold in a complex reality. We begin with brief summaries of the seven strategies.

Seven competitive strategies

We have focused our attention on seven strategies: *Specialisation, Adaptive, Low cost, Innovation, Excellence, No Frills* and *Targeting* (these spell out an easy to remember mnemonic: *SALIENT*). These seven strategies have been derived from prior contributions to competitive strategy and the theory of value creation and capture that we set out in the following chapters. We explain how the strategies were derived in Chapters 2 and 3. We now briefly summarise each strategy.

In Figure 1.1 we set out our seven strategies. Each strategy creates competitive advantage in a particular way and each indicates different degrees of change in the customer needs being met and the products being supplied. (Note that throughout the book we use the term 'product' to refer to any product or service.)

Specialisation

With *specialisation* we choose to focus on a single product or product group and compete through superior product performance. Growth comes primarily from expanding the range of markets we serve. We can see from the figure that with specialisation the product remains the same but we seek out new customers and different needs that our products can meet.

A perfect example of specialisation is WD40, which is now in four out of five American households. WD40 has specific and unique

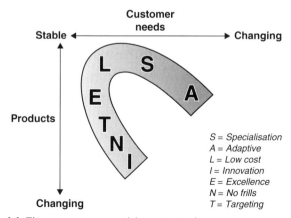

Figure 1.1 The seven competitive strategies

qualities that continue to attract a broad range of customers – home owners, mechanics, aeroengineers – and is an outstanding example of specialisation and market dominance built around a niche product. A successful specialisation strategy builds entry barriers that deter other firms from competing.

Adaptive

The intention of the *adaptive* strategy is to increase the system's ability to respond to changing circumstances, particularly to *changing customer needs*. As indicated in Figure 1.1, we would need to *adapt* the products we offer to meet these changing needs.

Zara, the fashion clothing retailer, is a stellar example of a firm pursuing an adaptive strategy. Zara has a highly developed capability to adapt and adjust to unfolding fashion trends and changes in customer needs. The distinctive feature of Zara's business is that clothing is only manufactured where there is customer demand.

Low cost

The *low-cost* strategy aims to deliver *equivalent* product quality compared to competitors but with a continual and relentless focus on *cost reduction*. The low-cost strategy is particularly effective in markets where products have long life cycles and customer needs are relatively stable.

A striking example is Bavaria Yachts. This unconventional German boat builder has emerged as one of the largest and most successful boat building companies in the world. A combination of German engineering precision, automation, use of robotics and adapting efficient manufacturing techniques from the automotive sector has seen Bavaria Yachts deliver equivalent quality yachts at significantly lower costs than its rivals.

Innovation

Here the focus is on competing through *product innovations*. The *innovation* strategy is suited to circumstances where customer needs are relatively stable and there is scope to meet those needs in novel and superior ways. Typically, it costs money to innovate, so this strategy shifts the system to serve customers whose needs are evolving, who value new product solutions and are prepared to pay a premium price to acquire them.

SpaceX is an exemplar of an innovation strategy. To meet Elon Musk's vision of interplanetary space travel to Mars, he concluded that he would need to found a company to develop a reliable and re-usable rocket that would transform the economies of space travel. Developing such a rocket led SpaceX to vertically integrate its manufacturing of rocket engines, rocket stages, spacecraft, avionics and software. This innovation was a significant and innovative departure from the space industry norms and has put SpaceX on track to reduce the cost of space flight by a factor of 10.

Excellence

Excellence involves the continuous incremental improvement of product or service quality. Similar to the *low-cost* strategy, it fits situations where customer needs, products and technologies are relatively stable. The *excellence* strategy embeds *professionalism* in the system.

From having zero presence in the luxury car market, Lexus has established itself as a major player. Lexus has achieved parity with many European luxury vehicle manufacturers on key quality dimensions. This impressive accomplishment is the outcome of a deliberate and sophisticated engineering project that focused on the relentless pursuit of excellence.

No frills

In contrast to *low-cost* and *excellence* strategies, the no-frills strategy involves shifting the system to serve price-sensitive customers with a *stripped-down alternative product or service*. This may require us changing the customers we serve, the products we sell and the processes we use to make them. Thus, whilst the customers' needs may not change much, our products have to change to be able to meet these basic requirements at a competitive price.

ALDI is a prime example of pursuing a no-frills strategy. This successful grocery retailer has a deep understanding of what price-sensitive customers are looking for and provides just those products and services that their customers value and will pay for. Any supply chain costs that don't directly contribute to deliver customer value are stripped away resulting in the efficient and cost-effective delivery of customer value.

Targeting

Here the business targets a *specific market segment* and serves the needs of these customers more effectively than less focused rivals. Whereas with *specialisation* the focus is essentially on the product, then looking for markets that value the product, with *targeting* the focus is on the customer and developing products or services that meet their needs. Like the *no-frills* strategy, the target customer's needs may be relatively stable, but our products have to be developed and refined to meet their particular requirements.

Few firms can claim to be pursuing as clear a targeting strategy as Long Tall Sally. This retailer produces clothes exclusively for taller women where style starts at 5′ 8″ and shoe size 7. The core of Long Tall Sally's success is staying focused on a very specific segment of tall women; understanding what it means to be a tall woman and using these insights to be their first choice for fashion clothing.

Capabilities

Value is created by *people* working with other assets, like equipment, systems, brand names and bought-in components. A firm's capabilities are the *collective know-how* of managers and employees. Capabilities are built up over time: experience and feedback from the system shapes these emerging capabilities.

Capabilities cannot be 'willed' into existence by a management decision or strategy. They can only be *enabled to develop* by changes to what we refer to as *practices*. Practices are the ways in which we structure or organise work, the types of *systems* we deploy and the *culture* of the organisation. Practices can be changed, which may enable the development of the capabilities required to pursue a particular strategy. For example, we could change the way we recruit staff so as to increase the range of experience we can call on. This change to the recruitment system may enable us to become more *innovative*. Or we may decide to reorganise and group staff so that people can interact more swiftly and spontaneously. This change may enable us to respond more effectively to changing customer needs, that is, be more *adaptive*. Or we may try to capture and codify some 'best practice' that has emerged in one part of the business and seek to transfer these methods to other staff. This transfer of knowledge might help us improve efficiency in pursuit of a *low-cost* strategy.

If a strategy is successfully introduced, it will augment the firm's existing capabilities. The current business may have evolved capabilities to deliver standard products efficiently; the adoption of, for example, an *adaptive* strategy would *augment* these embedded capabilities enabling the firm to be able to more rapidly respond to changing customer needs. This may in turn allow the firm to premium price or secure more customers. All firms have more capabilities than liabilities; otherwise, they would soon go out of business. The successfully embedded strategy adds to these value-creating capabilities.

The strategy guides the firm's value system in a particular direction. Any strategy choice is potentially feasible. Thus, a firm that is currently competing through being cost-efficient could either strive to be even more efficient by embedding our *low-cost* strategy, or the firm could build on the existing capabilities and layer an additional capability by *targeting* the needs of a particular type of customer, for example, customers that have limited ability to hold stock. By developing new ways to deliver smaller quantities more frequently, we may be able to charge a price premium to these clients. Thus, to gain advantage in a market where all competitors are striving to cut costs, a strategy that *augments* these embedded cost-efficient capabilities with an ability to focus on the needs of, in this case, low-volume customers, might offer an advantage.

In Chapter 3, we explore the firm's value system which is made up of three interlinked processes: the processes whereby inputs, human and otherwise, enter the system which we label *sourcing*; the processes that transform inputs into products or services, which we call *operations*; and the processes involved in converting these products into cash, which we summarise as *selling*. Firms survive and prosper if they have superior *sourcing, operations* and *selling capabilities* and these capabilities will be enabled or hindered by the firm's structure, systems and culture.

From strategy to action

The chosen strategy is just an idea. Before it has any effect on the system, it must be translated into *action*. We suggest this translation works through four levels, where the scope shifts from a broad direction, indicated by the strategy, through to highly specific actions.

Figure 1.2 illustrates this shift from the chosen competitive strategy through to specific actions. The process moves through these stages:

1. Selecting *existing capabilities* that need to be enhanced and/or *new capabilities* that need to be introduced into the sourcing, operations and selling activities

2. Identifying enabling **practices** that will help and support the development of the required capabilities; the practices will affect the *structure, systems* and *culture* of the business

3. Developing specific **initiatives** to install those practices and to directly build the required capabilities

4. Moving from initiatives into **actions** that directly impact the system. These actions must also generate feedback to enable us to track the effects of the changes introduced.

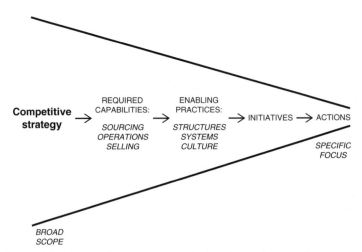

Figure 1.2 Moving from strategy choice through to action

This last step is critical: if there is no change in what people *actually do*, the strategy process will have no positive impact on the system.

A clearly stated competitive strategy can build a *coherent collective intention*, which can help to integrate the efforts of all the members of the firm. It can create some consistency of intent over time and it indicates the kind of actions and outcomes that would 'fit' with this direction, as well as signalling those actions that don't 'fit'. It legitimises certain actions and enables and supports local initiatives informed by and in line with the collective intent set by the strategy.

The strategy approach we set out works with the complexities of the real world. In the next section, we explain what it means to inhabit a complex world and how our approach to competitive advantage works with this reality.

We live in a complex world

Complexity means that there are many variables in the system, and these variables interact in ways that cannot be predicted. One consequence of complexity is that we can't forecast the future, which of course makes it difficult to formulate an appropriate strategy for any business. The firm is an 'open' system, which interacts with suppliers and customers; they are just as much a part of this system as managers and staff.

But managers are expected to *control* organisations. They are supposed to 'run' the business. However, complexity means that you can't actually control any organisation, and we contend that a good deal of inefficiency and personal stress results from pretending we can control an organisation, when in reality we can't. Indeed, the task of managing becomes even more difficult where we act on the assumption that things *can* be controlled. The actions we take, based on this false assumption, cause unintended consequences, which lead us to escalate our attempts to 'control' and exacerbate the problems. We might be able to control some events and processes 'inside' the organisation, but we have no control over customers and competitors. So what can be done?

We can *work with* complexity rather than pretend it isn't there. We can engage in this open system in ways that are more likely to be fruitful, rather than trying to control the uncontrollable. We can *enable the organisation to adapt* to changing circumstances.

Features of a complex system

Dr. Jean Boulton[1], a leading proponent of complexity thinking, puts it this way: 'When we say the world is complex we are saying it is:

- *Systemic*: the world cannot be understood by taking apart the bits and understanding them separately. Factors work together synergistically, that is, the whole is different from the sum of its parts.

- *Path dependent*: history matters and the sequence of events is a key factor in giving shape to the future.

- *Sensitive to context*: one size does not fit all, and the way the future emerges is dependent on the detailed and particular events and patterns of relationships and particular features of the local situation.

- *Emergent, uncertain but not random*: although the future does not follow smoothly from the past, neither is what happens random. The world is neither chaotic nor predictable but somewhere in between.

- *Episodic*: things are becoming, developing and changing, but change seems to happen in fits and starts. On the 'surface' patterns of relationships and structures can seem stable for long periods of time, although micro-changes may be going on under the surface.

- *Self-organising*: Radical change may happen suddenly, new patterns of relationships can self-organise and some completely new features of the system that could not have been predicted may *emerge*.'[2]

Complex systems *self-organise*. Think of how a market organises. No single individual decides what will happen; nevertheless, the effects of hundreds of actions, decisions and trades result in some form of coordinated action. The eighteenth-century economist

Adam Smith described this process as an 'invisible hand'. Similarly, any business self-organises because no person or group controls the entire system. We may decide to raise prices, introduce a new bonus scheme and source from a cheaper supplier, but the *effects* of these changes are not controlled by us; they are outcomes that are determined by the interactions of these changes with the wider system. Thus, the effects of these changes may be quite different to what was hoped for or expected. For instance, maybe the price increases resulted in a drop in sales, which we responded to with price cuts to below the previous level. The bonus scheme resulted in higher productivity, but due to the drop in sales, one result was bigger inventories of finished goods and whilst switching suppliers reduced operating costs to predicted levels, there was early evidence that the cheaper components were leading to more warranty claims.

The firm's value system

The value system consists of a large number of *variables* that interact with each other. Important variables would include skills, attitudes, routines, customer perceptions, equipment, information systems, leadership behaviour, government policies, brand loyalty and competitor actions. These interactions can be *synergistic* or *antagonistic* with respect to the generation of profits, and the nature of these interaction effects can be difficult to predict. These interactions are typically *nonlinear,* which is an essential quality of a complex system. The system is in a *continual state of becoming*; it is *emergent,* and it has no single definable end state.

The firm is definitely not like a machine. There aren't 'levers' that can be pulled to produce desired outcomes. As we have said, the value system includes suppliers, customers and competitors and no one controls what they do. Similarly, you can give orders and instructions to employees, but you can't predict how they will respond. We come across many examples where executives are frustrated that their strategies have not been implemented. Often they conclude that the problem is communication; if only staff understood the strategy, it would get implemented. Poor communication is often a problem; but in many cases, middle managers know full well what the strategy is. They just don't think it will work, they don't like the implications of the strategy for them personally or they fear the disruption caused by the required changes. In the complex system of any business, all an executive can know with any confidence is what he or she chooses to do; what happens as a *result* of their actions cannot be predicted or controlled.

A business can survive and thrive with a healthy positive flow of *cash*. Customers provide cash in return for products and services, suppliers receive cash for their productive inputs. Customers decide whether what we produce is valuable or not. Thus, the open nature of the *value system* means that no one is in control of the whole system. This lack of control is the source of business risk, which is an inevitable quality of any business. We can try to reduce these risks by, for example, locking customers or suppliers in to long-term contracts, by trying to eliminate competitors or by reducing dependence on people or resources that are in scarce supply. A good deal of strategy thinking can be viewed as attempts to reduce business risk. But the problem is there is always some risk in the system and, worse, when we try to reduce risks the actions we take can cause unintended consequences which produce new sources of risk.

The problem we are addressing in this book is that many of the prescriptions offered to managers to help them 'manage' more effectively are based on inappropriate assumptions about the way the world works. Here we acknowledge complexity, and we offer an approach that *works with* this reality rather than denying it. In developing our ideas about *competitive strategies*, we build on a wide range of prior theories, prescriptions and case studies to synthesise a workable approach to leading a business.

Strategy processes often proceed through a sequence of *formulation* where a plan or 'blueprint' of what the firm should like is devised, which is followed by an *implementation* stage where budgets are set, performance indicators are decided and targets and milestones are projected forward. This kind of strategy process is underpinned by implicit assumptions about how the world works, that it can be predicted, controlled and 'managed'.[3]

But because a firm is a complex open system, we don't believe it is a good use of time and resources to craft overarching strategies and follow these up with detailed implementation plans. The fact is, no one knows more than the system, and no one knows better than the system. Because no one can predict the future, there are far more examples of failed strategies than ones that were implemented as intended and that were also successful.

Change in complex systems

Figure 1.3 summarises the effects of a change introduced into a complex system. The action A 'invades' the system, for example, a new salesperson is recruited. This action impacts other elements in the system (B to F) either directly, as in A's impact on B and C or indirectly, the 'knock-on' effect of the change to B affecting D and F. The effect on the performance of the system as a whole is the outcome of positive and negative impacts on both the individual elements in the system (B to F) and the interaction effects (synergies, or not) between them.

The figure is clearly a very simplified representation of an actual organisation, but it shows how difficult it is to anticipate in

A new action 'invades' the system

ACTION

A

And changes other elements in the system

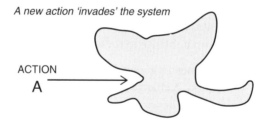

Which leads to positive and negative direct effects and interaction effects

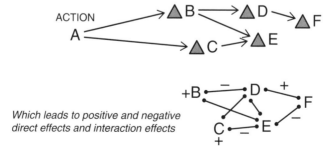

Figure 1.3 Change in a complex system

advance the effect or ultimate outcome of any change. Where changes are introduced by individuals with only a limited knowledge of the wider value system, for example, an executive appointed from outside, there is even less chance that they can anticipate the impact of any action they introduce.

We would expect that where the net effect of a change is clearly positive, then this change will persist. The system 'selects' the change and it is retained. But some changes that don't synergise with the system can still persist through the exercise of formal power, or where additional resources are deployed to support it, or where there is 'slack' in the system that can allow these practices to persist.

Internal and external 'fit'

The start-up firm faces the brutal reality of a competitive market. This is an extremely tough selection environment and only firms that adapt to 'fit' the market will survive. The founder of this business may have had a clear picture in their mind about what a successful business would look like, what products they would sell at what prices, etc. The emerging reality of trying to establish this business may mean that what the business actually looks like bears little resemblance to these images the founder initially held.

All businesses evolve through a sequence of variation–selection–retention. A change is introduced (the *variation*); if it 'fits' or synergises with the wider system, it will likely be *selected* and *retained*. In large, long-established businesses, there may be 'slack' in the system that enables poor practices and inefficient behaviours to persist. In benign organisational contexts, activities 'inside' the organisation can be buffered or insulated from external pressures from the environment. Even where these practices are not effective or efficient, 'slack' can allow them to stick around.

We have two kinds of 'fit': *internal fit,* which is the fit between the activity and other parts of the internal system; and *external fit,* which is the fit between the internal system and the wider external environment. The small start-up business will need to continually adjust its internal activities to maintain external fit and if it fails to adapt it will disappear. The larger organisation may be able to tolerate activities that don't contribute to external fit. For example, if it has a line of successful products, the revenue streams they generate may allow poor-performing products to survive and inefficient practices to persist.

Emergent strategies

When we explain the seven strategies to managers, they often remark that their business is currently pursuing one or other of the strategies. This may be by 'design', that is, the managers are deliberately trying to become *low cost* or to pursue *excellence*. Or it may be that competitive pressures have more or less driven the firm to become *low cost*, and hence, the competitive environment has *selected in* low-cost practices and *selected out* activities that add costs, like product innovation. The **emergent strategy is the outcome of management actions and choices, learning from feedback and selection pressures from the market.**

In some cases, managers explain that they do 'bits' of two or three strategies, or they seem to be trying to be *low cost* in one part of their operations and *innovative* in other parts. Others own up to just 'muddling through', without any clear focus on any strategy. Muddling through is not necessarily a '*laissez-faire*' approach. It may be that in changing contexts, the best we can do is adapt to unpredictable changes that the market environment throws at us.

Guided change processes

Our competitive strategy approach takes as given the complex nature of the social world and works with these realities. The approach allows for emergence and adaptation. The broad direction of the system can be decided, and this takes the form of a chosen *competitive strategy*. Then what happens subsequently is *shaped* by the strategy and the *emergent outcomes* of initiatives, trials, experiments and pilot tests. This ongoing process is informed by the strategy, but the resultant changes in the organisation are allowed to emerge, rather than them being specified, designed and predetermined.

The actions executives take can certainly change the system; our argument is that no one can predict the *outcome* of any action.

So the prudent way to approach change is to indicate a broad direction of travel, the *competitive strategy*, identify relevant change initiatives, try out an initiative, get feedback and then **escalate** the initiative, **adjust** it or **abandon** it.

This approach results in an **evolving portfolio of initiatives** that are guided by a clear *competitive strategy*. We explain how this can be done, and the likely benefits that should flow from this approach to the continual renewal of the business. The guidelines set by the strategy increase the chance that there will be emerging synergies. If these initiatives *synergise* with each other, they will have more impact. The effect of one initiative is amplified because it connects with and supports other related initiatives.

We depict the strategy change process in Figure 1.4. Having agreed on a competitive strategy, in this case the *low-cost* strategy, this choice triggers the selection and trial of a flow of initiatives, indicated by the arrows, intended to deliver continuous cost reductions in the system. Initiatives that don't align with the low-cost strategy would be discontinued, as indicated by the blocked arrow at Time 1. Over time, we would expect synergies to build up as the effects of previous initiatives interact with subsequent initiatives. The strategy is also a guide to decision making. At Time 3, we face a choice of doing A or B: if we are sticking with the chosen strategy, then we do A.

One key benefit that executives report from this approach to strategy is that it makes them more willing and confident to engage with *change*. The incremental but guided change process that is at

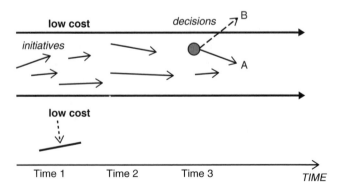

Figure 1.4 How the strategy shapes organisational change

the heart of our approach and the role of feedback gives them confidence that initiatives can be trialled at relatively low risk.

Eisenhardt and Sull have argued that firms should follow a set of 'simple rules' which guide decision making.[4] The attraction of reducing the problem of 'strategy' to a clear set of relevant and easily understood rules is clear, and given the complexity and uncertainty, these rules could usefully shape the emerging changes to the firm's value system. Our competitive strategies could be viewed as a particular form of 'simple rules'. In our case, the strategy indicates the direction of travel, and it also determines the selection of relevant practices and change initiatives. Thus, whilst the strategies impact the firm's value system in a different way to a set of rules, there are parallels between these two approaches to strategic change.

When considering a direction to take the business in, it makes sense to focus on the primary relationships with customers and suppliers. In particular, our competitive strategies emphasise the need to engage with and understand customers, their needs, their perceptions of products, and how these might be changing.

In summary, a competitive strategy defines the broad direction the system should take, allowing for unanticipated events and changes emerging in the future. The competitive strategy does not set out a blueprint of what the future of the system should look like; it provides guidance that *shapes* rather than *determines* the emerging system. We need to be cognisant of the nature of a complex world, recognise the emergent nature of change and work *with* these realities.

Competitive strategies and synergy strategies

Our competitive strategies are appropriate for single businesses, or strategic business units (SBUs) that are part of a larger organisation. In the final chapter we consider organisations that are made up of several SBUs. These *corporate* structures may have a set of similar or related SBUs, or they may consist of a portfolio of unrelated businesses. Multi-business organisations must have a reason for existing: why has this particular group of SBUs been collected together? Typically, the argument is that there are potential *synergies* that can be delivered by coordinating the SBUs in different ways. In Chapter 14 we explore the multi-SBU context and develop a set of seven *synergy strategies*.

To be clear, the *competitive strategies* we develop in the book apply to a 'stand-alone' business, for example, a small- or medium-sized enterprise, or the strategies apply to an individual business unit within a corporate structure. The *synergy strategies* are applicable to multi-SBU corporations. Whether the corporation is multi-*national* makes no difference to the argument we develop, although operating across borders can complicate the delivery of synergies.

In Chapter 2 we explain how the seven strategies were derived.

Chapter

Seven competitive strategies

Our seven strategies are developed from our understanding of what customers value and how they choose what products to buy.[5] The term *value* tends to be used rather loosely. We make a distinction between two forms of value: firstly, **use value** which is the usefulness or utility of a product or a service, and secondly, **exchange value** which is the price that somebody pays for this product or service. Use value is an entirely subjective judgement as seen by the person who buys the product, and exchange value is what they pay to acquire the product. We are interested in the creation of use values in ways that lead to the capture of exchange value. Although we focus our attention on value creation within the context of a *profit-seeking firm*, the ideas developed in the book can be adapted for not-for-profit organisations.

Critical to our understanding of value creation is the economists' concept of *consumer surplus*, which we explore first. We then develop the seven strategies as being different ways of delivering consumer surplus. Then we explore prior theories of competitive strategy and show how they link to our seven strategies. Finally, we consider the likely outcomes we would expect from the pursuit of each strategy.

Consumer surplus

Customers receive from the firm a delivered product or provided service (as we suggested in Chapter 1 we will use 'product' to mean product and/or service). In exchange for receiving this *use value*, customers give up *exchange value*, which is a payment for the product. We argue that the form of value that customers are interested in is *consumer surplus.* Consumer surplus is the difference between what the customer is *willing to pay for the product, less the price* they actually pay for it.[6]

Consumer surplus is a critical concept in our argument, so we need to be clear what it means. When we think we have bought a 'bargain', we think that what we have bought is worth more, in cash terms, than we paid for it. We naturally make these judgements, where we attach a monetary value to a product. Another way to think about consumer surplus is 'value for money', a phrase in common use. Here 'value' would be the use value of the product, and 'for money' would be price. Thus, consumer surplus would be another expression for 'value for money'.

For example, you arrive home late, hungry and discover there is no bread in the house. You walk to your local supermarket where you hope to buy a particular sourdough loaf they bake in the store. Usually when it's this late the supermarket has little fresh bread to sell. You spot that they still have one sourdough loaf left. You would be happy to pay $5 for the loaf; it's your favourite bread, you're hungry and you're delighted they have a loaf to sell. When you pick up the loaf, you notice that it has been marked down. The sticker price is usually $3, this has been over-written and the loaf is now priced at $1. The supermarket routinely does this as they know that they can't sell this loaf the next day because it's no longer fresh. Naturally, you are pleased; you seem to come out best in this deal.

Here the *use value* is the loaf. The *exchange value* is the $1 you pay for the loaf. Consumer surplus (CS) is the difference between what you think the loaf is worth to you ($5) and the price you actually pay ($1), that is, $CS = 5 - 1 = 4$. Consumer surplus is only realised in the transaction, it is generated through the exchange.

Another way of thinking about consumer surplus is a reverse or 'Dutch' auction where the seller, for example, the storekeeper, opens with a price (say $10) and asks for takers at that price, and then if no one buys he drops the price. When the storekeeper hits $5, you would buy the loaf, always assuming there are other potential customers in the store that are in the auction! If there are no other customers, you are likely to hold out for a lower price.

What if the store manager notices that you regularly turn up at this late hour looking to buy bread? And instead of marking down the price, he charges you $4. The amount you are willing to pay for the loaf is still $5, but in this case the store gets $4 not $1. Thus, price carves up the value of the exchange ($5) between buyer and seller. **The *value realised* through the exchange is split between the buyer and the seller.** A low price means that the buyer captures more value, and then more of this realised value takes the form of *consumer surplus*. With a high price, the seller captures more value, and hence more value is realised in the form of *cash*.

The dependence of the buyer on the one hand and the seller on the other on doing this deal at this time determines the price struck and hence who captures the 'lion's share' of value in an exchange. We explore the role of dependence and the power relationship between buyer and seller in Chapter 3. In order to sell anything, you need to be offering more consumer surplus than competitors. *The key point here is that firms win business by offering more consumer surplus than rivals.*

Consumer surplus and profit

Winning the business is only half the story, of course. In order to make money you need to deliver consumer surplus *efficiently*. Firms are systems set up to create a flow of profits, which are returned to the firm's owners. To generate a flow of profit, a firm needs to sell products, which it can only do if it offers more consumer surplus than rival firms. Product sales generate the flow of revenues into the business. If the firm creates products which are seen to deliver higher levels of customer-perceived use value (PUV), it has the option to either sell *more* products by keeping prices competitive or to sell *fewer* products at a higher price. Thus, revenues of $10m could be made up of a sales volume of 10m units at a price of $1, or sales of 5m at a price of $2.

There is a *dual requirement* in any successful business to look after the *customer,* by delivering consumer surplus and to simultaneously look after the *owners* who have invested in the business. These dual requirements should drive actions and choices. The interests of *customers* are met through the delivery of consumer surplus, and the interests of the *owners* are met by delivering a flow of profits. This means creating consumer surplus *cost efficiently.*

Managerial vs customer orientation

Firms are hierarchical structures. The power of managers ultimately derives from their ability to hire and fire subordinates. Whilst this is an inbuilt feature of all firms, there are aspects of the firm's hierarchical structure that can reduce performance. Just because managers have formal power over subordinates does not necessarily mean they have more or better quality information or insights into what customers value or how to improve the efficiency of the value system. The more complexity and diversity in the value system, the less likely it is that any particular manager will know enough to consistently be able to make decisions and choices that enhance the efficient creation of customer value.

Most firms have adopted control systems that involve the setting of quantitative targets and monitoring performance against these targets [key performance indicators (KPIs)]. Some aspects of the value system are relatively easy to measure, like sales volume, and KPIs tend to reflect these easy-to-measure outcomes. The 'balanced scorecard' is an attempt to broaden performance measurement to incorporate measures of, for example, customer satisfaction, employee engagement. But these performance management approaches are essentially driven from the top and are ways in which managerial control is exerted.

But as the success of the firm is fundamentally predicated on delivering value to customers and if consumer surplus is the necessary basis of value creation, then surely this imperative should be driving actions and decisions inside the firm? We are familiar with the phrase 'the customer is king'. This is undoubtedly true in all circumstances where the customers have a choice of what product to buy to meet their needs, that is, everywhere except a monopoly supplier. We believe this imperative should become the primary source of authority in the firm. Rather than 'do this because I'm the boss and I say do it', this should be replaced by 'we should do this because it delivers more customer value, or because it delivers customer value more cost efficiently'. The customer then is dictating how the value system should evolve and develop, not managers.

This is not a new idea. In an essay written in 1926, Mary Parker Follett addressed issues of authority in business management. She argued that the 'law of the situation' should replace managerial authority as a motive for action; the *situation* dictates what needs to be done, not the manager. She found that people respond better to situations than to top-down orders, and managers should give people the means and willingness to respond to given situations instead of merely giving orders: 'My solution is to depersonalize the giving of orders, to unite all concerned in a study of the situation, to discover the law of the situation, and obey that.' We are merely extending this argument to the continuing 'situation' of needing to deliver customer value efficiently.

Mapping perceived use value and price

In Figure 2.1 we represent a customer facing a purchase decision. PUV refers to the usefulness, benefit or satisfaction that this customer expects to get from the product. Price is what the customer pays for it.[7]

What the customer thinks the product is worth in money terms (their *willingness to pay*) is denoted by $PUV. Thus, $PUV is how much this customer thinks the product is worth, in monetary terms. Customers will choose products on the basis of the amount of consumer surplus they perceive.

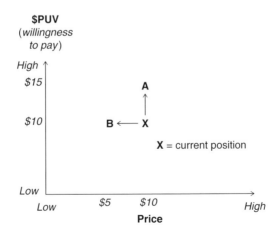

Figure 2.1 Price and PUV

29

In the figure the current position of the product is represented by X. Here the customer would be willing to pay $10 for the product, and the seller is charging $10. In this position, the customer gets zero consumer surplus, as what she thinks the product is worth is the same as the price being charged.

If the seller drops the price to $5 (point B), then the customer captures $5 of consumer surplus (CS: $10 – $5 = $5). Alternatively, the seller could improve the product in the eyes of this customer by, for example, adding features, changing its appearance, etc., a move to point A in the figure. Now our customer is *willing to pay* $15 for this improved product. If the seller still charges $10, then the customer again gets $5 consumer surplus (CS: $15 – $10 = $5). Thus, for the seller to get this customer's business, they either have to drop the price (to B) or add PUV (move to A). Either move delivers more consumer surplus, and at points A and B, the customer gets the same amount of consumer surplus.

This customer would be equally satisfied at either A or B. These points where consumer surplus is the same can be connected to form a line of equal amounts of consumer surplus, which we will refer to as a *consumer surplus isoquant*. We develop this idea in Figure 2.2.

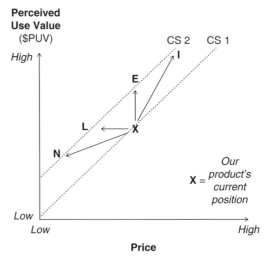

Figure 2.2 Moves that increase consumer surplus

Here we depict two consumer surplus isoquants CS1 and CS2. At any point on CS1, this customer gets the same amount of consumer surplus. At any point on CS2, the customer gets *more* consumer surplus than on CS1. As consumer surplus drives customer purchasing behaviour, to win business we need to figure out how to offer *more* consumer surplus than rival products.

The current product we offer to this customer is located at point **X.** We have at least four options that would result in us offering more consumer surplus. The move to **I** delivers substantially more use value to this customer. Even though at point **I** we are charging a premium price, the customer still gets more consumer surplus as the new product (I) is seen to be so much better than X. The move to **E** delivers more PUV at the price we currently charge. Again the customer is better off; she gets more consumer surplus, or more 'value for money'.

If we drop our price to point **L,** we would be offering the same amount of $PUV at a *lower* price than we currently charge, again delivering more consumer surplus. And if we move to **N,** we are offering less $PUV, but the price is low enough to still deliver this customer more consumer surplus than we currently offer.

These four moves are the basis of four of our strategies: *I = innovation, E = excellence, L = low cost* and *N = no frills.* All of these strategies assume that the customer represented in the figure has needs that remain fairly stable over time.

Our fifth strategy, **adaptive,** enables us to meet *changing* customer needs and thus deliver more consumer surplus through becoming more responsive to the changing requirements of our customer. The sixth strategy, **targeting,** represents a choice to focus on a particular customer *segment,* and by doing this, we should be better able to offer superior PUV, and hence deliver more consumer surplus. Finally, with **specialisation,** by focusing on a limited range of products, we are able to offer superior product performance compared to less focused rivals.

In Figure 2.3, we build on this argument and shift the focus from the position of a particular product and customer combination, to the broader position of the firm as a *value system* offering products to a segment of a market.

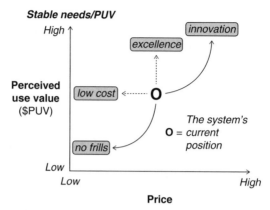

Figure 2.3 The innovation, excellence, low-cost and no-frills strategies

Innovation, excellence, low cost and *no frills* apply where customer needs and PUV remain stable, and they deliver advantage by offering customers more consumer surplus.

In Figure 2.4 the *adaptive* strategy delivers superior value to customers whose needs are *changing*. The penalty for not being able to respond to changing needs is falling sales and/or lower prices, indicated by the dotted arrow.

Targeting shifts the system to focus on and serve the specific needs of a particular segment. By meeting the particular needs of the target segment better than rivals, the firm may be able to premium

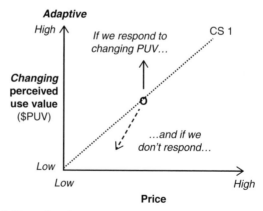

Figure 2.4 The adaptive strategy

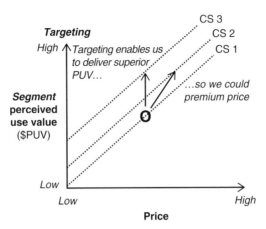

Figure 2.5 The targeting strategy

price (Figure 2.5). By adding PUV and leaving price the same, the target customer moves to a much higher level of consumer surplus (CS3). If you choose to premium price, she moves to CS2, where she gets more consumer surplus than being on CS1 but not as much as she would get if the price remained the same (CS3). This illustrates how the price charged *carves up* the value created between the seller and the buyer.

With the *specialisation* strategy, whilst the products remain the same, we are searching for different customers and different needs that can be served by these products.

Growth through specialisation can be achieved by extending the geographic scope of the markets we serve. Here we would be meeting similar customer needs as our 'home' market, the customers just happen to live in different countries or regions. Another option for growth is to search for different customers who may have different needs, but these needs can nevertheless be met with the same product.

Our favourite example of the *specialisation* strategy is WD40. In Figure 2.6 our product, WD40, is valued by home owners, car mechanics and aerospace engineers. We charge the same price per aerosol can (say $4) in all three markets. Home owners see WD40 as delivering far superior performance compared to rival products (X). Mechanics value the all-round capabilities of WD40 and are

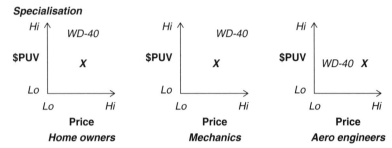

Figure 2.6 The specialisation strategy

prepared to pay a premium price relative to rival products, and the aerospace engineers have different needs but see our product as equivalent to other products and at $4 a can it is cheaper.

Whilst the seven strategies have been derived primarily from our understanding of consumer surplus, our thinking has been informed by prior work on competitive strategy, which we summarise in the next section.

Existing approaches to competitive strategy

Figure 2.7 summarises the most influential contributions to our understanding of competitive strategy. An inspection of these approaches reveals that whilst there are some similarities and alignment across them, none of them offer a comprehensive set of competitive strategy options.

Porter's generic strategies

The most influential writer on competitive strategy is Michael Porter. His books on *Competitive Strategy* and *Competitive Advantage* have shaped the way the field has evolved.[9] Porter identifies three 'generic strategies' which can defend the firm against the forces of competition. These are *cost leadership*, becoming the lowest cost producer; *differentiation*, premium pricing through offering a superior product; and *focus*, targeting a narrow market segment. As indicated in Figure 2.7, each generic strategy aligns with one of the seven strategies: cost leadership aligns with *low cost*; differentiation aligns with product superiority achieved through either *innovation* or *excellence*; focus aligns with *targeting*.

STRATEGY	Porter	Treacy & Wiersema	Kim & Mauborgne	Ansoff
Low cost	*Cost leadership*	*Operational excellence*		*Market penetration*
Excellence	*Differentiation*			*Market penetration*
Innovation	*Differentiation*	*Product leader*	*Value innovation*	*Product development*
Adaptive		*Customer intimacy*		
No-frills			*Value innovation*	
Specialisation	*Product focus*		*Unmet needs*	*Market development*
Targeting	*Market focus*	*Customer intimacy*		

Figure 2.7 Prior theories of competitive strategy[8]

Treacy and Wiersema's value disciplines

Whereas Porter bases his generic strategies on industrial organisation economics, Treacy and Wiersema's *Value Disciplines* are based on empirical work.[10] They identify three different customer segments who value different things. One segment values a standard product at a keen price, another demands the very latest product innovations and the third segment values a bespoke product or service. Their 'value disciplines' which serve these different segments are *operational excellence, product leadership* and *customer intimacy.*

Product leadership aligns with our *innovation* strategy. Operational excellence aligns primarily with *low cost*, as the focus of the 'discipline' is operational efficiency. Customer intimacy aligns with both our *adaptive* and *targeting* strategies, where the firm seeks to address the needs of a specific customer segment. In the case of *targeting*, the customers' needs are relatively stable, whereas the *adaptive* strategy enables the firm to respond to *changing* customer needs. One of the important contributions of Treacy and Wiersema's work is they have set out *practices* that are associated with each discipline. We build on their ideas in the case chapters.

Kim and Mauborgne's Blue Ocean Strategy

In Kim and Mauborgne's *Blue Ocean Strategy,* they argue that the route to success is to avoid competing in 'red oceans' and instead to seek out market segments with as yet unmet customer needs.[11] Their value innovation process involves reconfiguring the product to meet unfulfilled customer needs by posing these questions:

- What dimensions of the product might be *eliminated* that the industry has taken for granted?
- What dimensions might be *reduced* well below the industry standard?
- What dimensions might be *increased* well beyond the industry standard?
- What dimensions should be *created* that the industry has never offered?

Their approach to 'value innovation' clearly involves the development of different products. This aligns with our *innovation* strategy, and given that some product dimensions could be *reduced*, value innovation could also deliver our *no-frills* strategy.

In a similar vein, Clayton Christensen argues that there are segments of demand that are as yet unmet.[12] Thus, if a reduced product specification can be offered at a low price, many more customers could enter the market.

Ansoff's matrix

Igor Ansoff derived a very powerful way of categorising the product and market choices facing a business.[13] These are set out in Figure 2.8.

If we choose to stay selling our existing range of products into existing markets, how can the business grow? There are two routes to growth through *market penetration*: if the current markets are growing, we could grow along with the market growth rate; if the

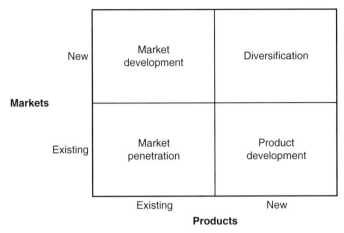

Figure 2.8 Ansoff's matrix

markets are not growing (or growing slowly), the only way for the firm to increase sales is to expand its market share. The latter option is the more aggressive growth option and will likely lead to retaliation.

Market development involves us taking our existing products into new markets. These new markets might be different customer segments, similar customers in different geographies or, for example, taking a product currently sold to industrial buyers and marketing it to consumers. Questions that need to be addressed with market development are: What makes us think we can sell our existing products into this new market? Do we have a product that will be competitive with existing rival products? How similar is the new market to the existing market? What additional capabilities would we need to successfully enter this market? Can these be built or acquired?

With *product development,* we stay in our current markets but look to grow by developing new products targeted at existing customers. Product development requires research and development capabilities that sit alongside the routine operations of the business. Firms that can grow through product development are simultaneously exploiting existing knowledge by producing products developed in the past, whilst simultaneously developing new knowledge. This is a difficult trick to achieve over sustained time periods, and some firms opt to focus on product development by outsourcing production, for example, Apple.

Diversification is the riskiest growth option as the firm is not leveraging any existing capabilities. A strategy of selling new products into new markets is often realised through acquisition. With an acquisition, whilst the acquiring firm has no relevant capabilities, these would be present in the acquired firm. The question then becomes one of synergy: how can the acquiring firm add value to the acquired firm? We explore *synergy strategies* in Chapter 14.

Ansoff's matrix sets out alternative choices about *where to compete.* Our competitive strategies address the question: *how should we compete? Low cost* and *excellence* are strategies that should enhance penetration into existing markets with existing products. *Innovation* typically involves developing new products to serve existing markets, and *adaptive* is a response to the changing needs of existing customers. *Targeting* is the choice to focus on a narrow range of customers which represents a new segment from the firm's point of view. With product *specialisation,* the firm would be taking a reduced range of products into new markets. *No frills* represents a diversification for the firm: serving price-sensitive customers with a no-frills product changes both the market and product. Figure 2.9 positions the strategies in Ansoff's matrix.

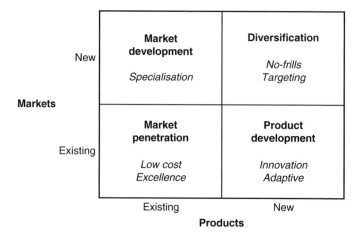

Figure 2.9 Locating the seven strategies in Ansoff's matrix

These prior contributions to competitive strategy are sound foundations that we have tried to build upon. What our strategy approach adds to this body of knowledge is:

1. an underpinning theory of value, which we elaborate in the following sections and Chapter 3,

2. a comprehensive menu of seven possible strategies, and

3. an approach to strategy-guided change (Chapter 4) that builds on insights from complex system thinking.

Strategy outcomes

If a strategy is successfully embedded, it should improve the performance of the system. If we assume that the firm is trying to deliver increased profit flow, this can result from either selling more, getting better prices, controlling production costs, benefiting from lower input costs or a mixture of these.

In the right side of Figure 2.10, we can see that 'value added' is the difference between what the customer is willing to pay for the product ($PUV) and the unit cost of making it. Price distributes this created value between the firm and the customer. A high price means that the firm captures most of this value; a low price means that the customer captures most of the value in the form of consumer surplus. Price and cost are represented by straight lines as

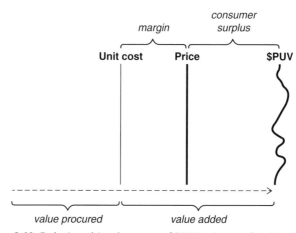

Figure 2.10 Relationships between $PUV, price and unit cost

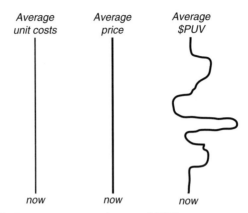

Figure 2.11 Current costs, prices and PUV

they are one-dimensional constructs; $PUV is represented by a wavy line to signify that there are multiple qualitative dimensions of PUV, for example, for a car these might be acceleration, comfort, road holding, styling and these can vary over time.

Willingness to pay ($PUV) less price gives us *consumer surplus* and this determines the volume of sales. If we premium price, we will sell fewer products but we make a bigger margin on each sale. Lower prices will lead to more sales as more customers are attracted to our $PUV/Price combination.

The value system can deliver a greater profit flow where unit costs can be reduced, prices can be raised and $PUV can be increased. We now explore the seven strategies and their outcomes in more depth. The initial starting position of the system is depicted in Figure 2.11.

Excellence

The *excellence* strategy has the intention of driving the value system through a stream of continual improvements in product quality, which feed through to customer $PUV. To sustain advantage, these processes of product improvement must be embedded and difficult for competitors to replicate. The strategy introduces a dynamic and continuous focus on understanding what customers value and converting these understandings into quality criteria. These 'internal' quality criteria need to accurately reflect customer $PUV and they should drive actions and choices in the value creation process.

Continuous incremental improvement in product quality fits a relatively stable context where customer needs are changing slowly or not at all, where it is possible to get high-quality intelligence from customers about their needs, and where a flow of improvements in quality can be sustained over time. The outcomes of a successfully introduced *excellence* strategy are depicted in Figure 2.12.

Over time, a series of initiatives continuously increase customer $PUV. The aim would be to deliver these enhancements whilst keeping unit costs stable. This can be achieved through a *learning* orientation. Stability allows for repeated performance of value-creating activities, which can enable the continuous building of *know-how*. Knowledge sharing can help to spread 'best practices', and a deep knowledge of customer needs can help to ensure that time and resources are not wasted on delivering product features that customers don't really value.

The continuous enhancement of customer $PUV coupled with stable prices should increase consumer surplus ($PUV – Price). This should lead to *increased sales volumes,* and if costs remain stable profit flow will improve (sales volume × margin). Higher sales volumes may deliver cost advantages through accumulated experience and/or economies of scale. Thus, it is possible for an excellence strategy to deliver both $PUV enhancements and to lower unit costs.

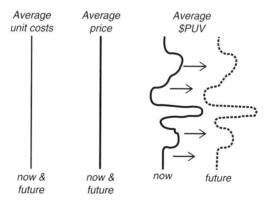

Figure 2.12 Excellence outcomes

Alternatively, the higher levels of $PUV could enable the firm to raise prices. The effect would be higher margins (Price – Unit cost) and if the sales volumes do not fall significantly as a consequence of the price hike, profit flow should increase.

Low cost

The *low-cost* strategy aims to deliver equivalent product quality compared to competitors but with a continual and relentless focus on cost reduction. Key to the success of this strategy is knowledge of customer needs, about what they *really* value in the products, which enables us to strip out unnecessary expenditures which don't deliver customer $PUV. Customer feedback is vital to ensure that cost-reducing initiatives do not damage $PUV. Whilst the low-cost strategy can be pursued by any business, it would be particularly appropriate where the product concerned is a standardised undifferentiated commodity. This can enable a focus on cost reduction rather than product improvement, and assuming the demand for the product will sustain, investments in assets and capabilities that can deliver enduring cost savings are feasible.

The expected outcomes from a *low-cost* strategy are set out in Figure 2.13. The focus is on delivering existing levels of customer $PUV at lower costs. Hence, $PUV should not change whilst unit costs are continuously reduced. Lower unit costs deliver a bigger *margin* (Price – Unit cost), and as consumer surplus ($PUV – Price)

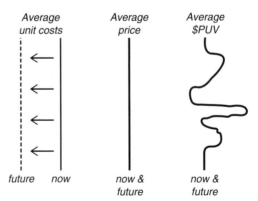

Figure 2.13 Low-cost outcomes

stays the same, then sales volumes should also remain stable. Stable sales volumes and bigger margins deliver increased profit flow.

If there are significant volume-related cost advantages to be had, for example, from accumulated experience, procurement and other scale economies, it may be appropriate to use a lower cost position to *reduce* prices. Then whilst margins might stay the same, that is, the lower unit costs are matched by lower prices, the enhanced sales volumes that should result from lower prices can generate more profits. Of course, the challenge to this decision to compete on price is that rival firms will be forced to drop their prices, which they can do, overnight if necessary. The low-cost strategy should, however, enable the firm to ride out the price war in better shape as the lower relative cost positions provide some margin, whereas higher cost rivals may find themselves operating with zero margins, or at a loss. The end game would be that the higher cost rivals exit the market, which would provide an opportunity to incrementally raise prices.

Innovation

Whilst the *excellence* strategy delivers a continual flow of *incremental* improvements, product *innovation* can 'jump' the system to a higher $PUV position. Product innovation generally involves the additional expenses of research, development and changing production systems; thus, higher PUV usually comes with higher unit costs. The pay-offs for innovation are the premium prices that could be charged.

For this strategy to succeed, the system must deliver *valued innovation*, not just different products. The outcomes of innovation processes must be perceived to be valuable by customers, so it is critical that throughout the phases of product innovation there is continual interaction with customers and potential customers. In particular, timely and accurate customer feedback can help steer the development of the innovation.

We focus on *product* innovation. However, the system can also 'jump' to a lower cost position through breakthrough innovations in production and service delivery processes.

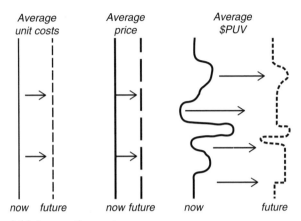

Figure 2.14 Innovation outcomes

The outcomes from a successful product *innovation* strategy are set out in Figure 2.14. The strategy changes costs, prices and $PUV. Product innovation will likely raise costs initially. But customers who value innovative product solutions will be prepared to pay a premium price to obtain them. The extent of the innovation is depicted by the size of the shift in the $PUV curve. The mix of higher prices, significantly higher levels of customer $PUV and increased costs should deliver bigger margins. Innovation is the *riskiest* strategy as this mix of cost, $PUV and realised prices is impossible to predict. The expectation would be that higher $PUV permits premium prices that *more than offset* the cost increases, but none of these outcomes is assured.

The risks of innovation are exacerbated by the time lags involved in research and development. Decisions to invest in researching new products taken in year 1 can only be based on information available at that time. If the development process spreads over five years, the innovation enters a very different and largely unpredictable market context in Year 5.

No frills

Our *no-frills* strategy is intended to shift the system to a low price, lower $PUV position. The intention is to serve price-sensitive customers with an acceptable, but basic version of the product or service. Critical to this shift is an understanding of what price-sensitive customers perceive as essential qualities, and which product or

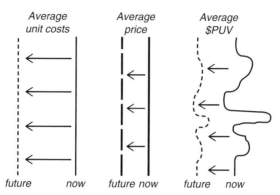

Figure 2.15 No-frills outcomes

service features are 'nice to have', but are non-essential. In this way we can strip out costs that deliver non-essential aspects of $PUV without damaging the essential core features.

The outcomes from a *no-frills* strategy are depicted in Figure 2.15. The no-frills $PUV offer is inferior to the 'standard' level. Price-sensitive customers would prefer the standard offer but can't or won't pay the prices charged for this level of quality or service. The stripped-down product offering can be delivered profitably where significant cost savings have been achieved through stripping out non-essential product features. The no-frills offer, a shift to serve a price-sensitive segment whose needs may be currently unmet, could lead to significant sales volumes. Thus, although prices and costs are lower, margins may be stable, and the larger sales volumes would deliver an increased profit flow.

Adaptive

The *adaptive* strategy is suited to uncertain market contexts. The other strategies assume that there is some stability and predictability in the wider system within which the firm is situated: customer needs and suppliers are fairly stable and the technologies used don't change significantly. But where there is uncertainty, dynamism and flux in the environment, the firm needs to be able to effectively respond to emerging but unpredictable events. *Adaptive* as a competitive strategy emphasises the need for flexibility, informed by an ability to sense weak signals of changing tastes and trends and to rapidly incorporate emerging technologies into the value creation processes.

The *adaptive* strategy can be considered as 'guided adaptation'. Uncertainty can take different forms; for instance, it could mean that customer tastes or needs are changing, but in ways that we cannot predict. Or it could mean that new entrants are coming into our market places who offer different product solutions to ours. Or technologies that we use are in a state of flux. Where the firm faces uncertainty, it needs to be able to react, respond or adapt to these unforeseeable changes. We can't know today exactly how to improve the efficiency or effectiveness of the system where we face uncertainty. What we need to build therefore is the capacity to sense early signals of what the future states of, say, customer tastes or needs would be and to build the capability to rapidly respond to those emerging trends when they become a little clearer, or more predictable.

If what customers value is changing over time, the system needs to be able to continually respond to these changing needs. The adaptive strategy can be delivered where the system has an amount of 'slack' in it; slack referring to underutilised resources. However, this is a relatively expensive way to deliver adaptability. Alternatively, and preferably, adaptability may be delivered with no slack. One way of achieving this would be to change the vertical scope of the system, by shifting from 'making' or providing certain product or services 'in house', to buying them from suppliers as and when they are required. This requires developing the procurement capabilities of the firm as well as the ability to integrate these procured inputs with the more permanent 'in-house' capabilities.

Targeting

Our sixth competitive strategy is *targeting*. Here we target a specific market segment and serve the needs of these customers more effectively than less focused rivals. The system shifts from offering products that meet a broad range of customer needs to developing products that meet more precisely the needs of a specific customer segment. By meeting these needs more effectively than rivals, the firm may be able to premium price.

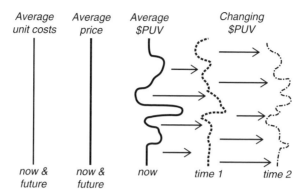

Figure 2.16 Adaptive outcomes

We can use a lock and key analogy to characterise the *targeting* strategy. In Figure 2.16, the role of the strategy is to steer the value system to more closely fit the specific needs of the customer segment: **to cut the key that 'fits' the customers' lock,** and thus unlock the potential value that is as yet unrealised. The benefits of targeting would be either superior sales volumes as the firm can now offer higher levels of $PUV to a specific segment, or premium prices. Key to the success of this strategy is a deep understanding of the specific needs of the target customers.

Specialisation

Our final strategy is product specialisation. We compete by focusing on a single product or product range, and delivering superior customer value through being lower price, or by offering superior

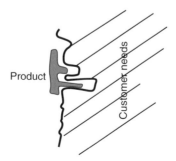

Figure 2.17 Targeting: Cutting the key to fit the lock

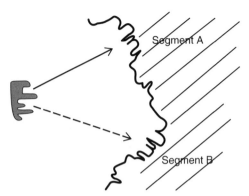

Figure 2.18 Specialisation: Finding the locks that fit the key

$PUV. With product specialisation, we are searching for the *locks that fit the key*, as in Figure 2.18. Growth would derive from finding new markets where the specialised products could compete. So where we currently serve Segment A, we would search for other market opportunities like Segment B.

Strategy choices and context

Each strategy tends to 'fit' a particular context. The *low-cost* and *excellence* strategies fit well with a stable context where the firm's value system co-evolves at an incremental rate with the market environment. The *adaptive* strategy fits a *changing* context and develops the firm's ability to rapidly respond to changing customer needs. Thus, the environment strongly influences the way the value system evolves.

In contrast, the *innovation* strategy *acts on* the context to change or disrupt it. The *no-frills* strategy is a conscious choice to move the system to serve a different, price-sensitive segment. *Specialisation* and *targeting* require there to be significant and enduring differences between the needs of different customer segments.

But no matter what we choose to do 'inside' our organisation, what materialises in the market place is ultimately in the gift of customers. The prices we can command, the volumes we can sell depend on how customers *perceive* our products and services. We explore PUV further in Chapter 12.

Dynamic strategies

Porter, Kim and Mauborgne and Treacy and Wiersema suggest specific ways in which a firm can gain competitive advantage, for example, through low cost, innovation, etc. Where markets are in a state of turbulence and flux, which Richard D'Aveni refers to as *hypercompetition*, sticking to one competitive strategy might not be the answer.[14]

In response to these challenging circumstances, some authors have suggested a dynamic approach to gaining and sustaining advantage. The focus shifts from identifying one way of competing and staying with this, to developing *dynamic capabilities* which enable the firm to continually refresh its ways of competing, in line with the changing competitive landscape. David Teece argues for a continuous process of market *sensing*, *seizing* opportunities and effecting the necessary *transformations* to the business. Rita McGrath explains how firms can compete through a stream of *transient* sources of advantage: where competition is such that a firm can only hope to gain advantages for a few years, or even months, to compete over the longer term requires the capability to deliver a succession of changing sources of advantage.[15]

Our competitive strategies incorporate circumstances where the market environment facing the firm is stable, and where it is in a state of turbulence. In **stable** circumstances, customer needs will not change significantly; the products supplied to meet those needs don't change much, neither do the technologies we use to make them. The *low-cost* and *excellence* strategies would fit these contexts, as would *specialisation* and *targeting*. Similarly, our *no-frills* strategy assumes that the needs of price-sensitive customers are stable.

The *innovation* and *adaptive* strategies would match circumstances where we face more **unstable** markets, where customer needs and product solutions are changing, and to sustain advantage requires the firm to continually adapt and innovate. But the strategies can be used to introduce some instability into the marketplace. If you successfully embed an *innovation* strategy in a context where most competitors are competing through cost efficiency, this will disrupt the market. Also you may find that there is a natural succession where one successfully embedded strategy provides a stable base to then explore a different strategy. As, over time, the new ways of working become established routines, managers' time and resources may be released to explore a new strategy, and thus capabilities become *layered* one upon the other.

Thus, the competitive strategies offer a comprehensive set of feasible directions that the system may move in. The strategies build on and incorporate prior contributions to the field and extend the menu of feasible options that could be explored. But critically, we recognise the uncertainties and complexity of the value system in our approach to managing change processes. Thus, a strategy is an *intention* to move the system in a particular direction; this intention cannot be simplistically realised through a formulaic and linear process of 'strategy implementation'. We have to recognise and *work with* the complex reality of the value system and be prepared to adapt and adjust our actions as we go. Competitive strategies are about the process of changing the system; they are not a simplistic idea of a *destination* for the system. The system is in a continual state of *becoming*, the strategy can only provide some shape and direction to this emergent process.

The Usain Bolt principle

The Usain Bolt principle: *When being chased by a grizzly bear you don't have to run as fast as Usain Bolt to survive, you just need to run faster than the other guy.* If you compete in a market where there is little product innovation, then even a small amount of product improvement can deliver competitive advantages. Take the case of a major European fertiliser manufacturer, which we will call Alpha. Competitors in this market typically focus on production efficiency and sell through agents and distributors. One consequence being that no one who made the fertiliser had any direct contact with the user, the farmer. Alpha introduced a small experiment which took some of the technical and production staff out to meet with the farmers. Prior to this initiative, Alpha had no idea how important consistency in pellet size was to the farmer. Consistency is vital to prevent blockages in the pellet spreading equipment and to ensure the correct amount of fertiliser is applied. Now through changes to the production process, consistent pellet size is delivered to the farmer, and Alpha's market share has increased.

The Usain Bolt principle means that incremental improvements in the firm's capabilities can deliver significant rewards. In markets

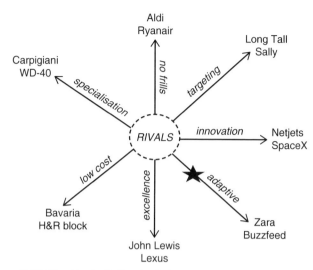

Figure 2.19 The Usain Bolt principle

where firms typically compete through product innovation, a firm can gain advantages by becoming more efficient. Or in a market where excellence is the norm, for example, professional services, advantage could be gained by becoming a little more adaptive and responsive.

In Figure 2.19, we represent the seven strategies. At the ends of the arrows we have some of the case study firms we use as exemplars of each strategy later in the book. These cases are examples of firms who have successfully pursued a particular strategy. In the centre of the figure are the close competitors to our focal firm. The Usain Bolt principle suggests that a position along any strategy which is closer to an exemplar firm, for example, Zara, would represent a source of advantage. Thus, if our focal firm can shift along the *adaptive* strategy to the position of the star, this would confer advantage. It isn't necessary to be as adaptive as Zara, just to be more adaptive than rivals.

Dealing with uncertainty

In this chapter we have shown how we have developed our seven competitive strategies from established theories of competitive strategy. The principles and ideas we outline are also consistent with some other recent publications. A case in point is a *The Lean*

Start Up by Eric Ries, a Silicon Valley entrepreneur.[16] He puts forward a number of key principles for start-up success based on his own experience, academic research into 'customer development' and with an eye to the Japanese concept of low-cost manufacturing.

The Lean Start Up principles concern the allocation of resources, especially those directed at product development, as efficiently as possible. More specifically, they show how to shorten product development lifecycles by a combination of experimentation and iterative product releases.

The core idea within *The Lean Start Up* is to get early customer feedback that accelerates learning and avoids major and expensive project failures. This emphasis on trials and experimentation, supported by rapid customer feedback cycles, is consistent with the approach we advocate for creating and capturing value.

Another recent publication that is consistent with some of our core concepts is *The Black Swan* by Nassim Taleb.[17] The black swan is a metaphor that describes an event that comes as a surprise and has a major impact. Taleb's work highlights the disproportionate role of high profile and hard-to-predict events, along with psychological biases that blind people to uncertainty. We find common ground with Taleb regarding two ideas in particular. Firstly, the idea that the future is unpredictable when it comes to events that matter. Secondly, rather than attempting to predict the future, organisations should build robustness against negative events and seek to exploit positive events. A point of deviation with Taleb's material and our thinking is that we put emphasis on understanding uncertainty with reference to complexity theory and we adopt a systems-based view of organisations. We also explore how existing environmental uncertainty can be accommodated through the use of properly structured trials and experiments, our *value initiatives*.

Given complexity and uncertainty and the difficulty of predicting the consequences of decisions, we often get asked: what do you see as the role of forecasting? In this area, some powerful insights have recently emerged through research conducted by Tetlock and Gardner, published in *Superforecasting: The Art and Science of Prediction*.[18] This body of work reports on findings derived from participation and experiments conducted within an IARPA (Intelligence Advanced Research Projects Activity)-funded forecasting tournament.

The study identifies some 'Superforecasters' who consistently perform better than the average intelligence community analyst. It then goes on to derive some traits that superforecasters seem to possess and the processes they adopt. The results are too extensive to recap here, suffice to say that utilising a blend of statistics, psychology, training and different levels of interaction amongst forecasters led to superior results.

One key point of interest for us was the frequency by which superforecasters updated their forecasts and their granular thinking that led to refined incremental adjustments of their probability estimates of various predicted outcomes. This activity is consistent with 'sensing' the environment, a key part of an emergent approach to change. Whilst we remain generally sceptical of the ability of executives to forecast significant meaningful events, we can appreciate how some practices can help firms to become more capable of sensing the early warning signs of external changes, which is a prerequisite for successful adaptation.

The ideas around the merits of firms conducting trials and experiments, building adaptive capabilities and continuously sensing environmental changes are not new, but are definitely popular as they propose to help firms to better cope with uncertainty. It seems clear to us that coping with uncertainty and building durable organisations is the single most significant challenge faced by firms today.

To translate the ideas we have developed in the book into actions which will ultimately shape the future of the business, we set out various application activities in the following chapters. These enable you to become familiar with the concepts in the book and to build confidence in using these ideas in your everyday practice. The first application gets you to think about what value means to your customers.

Application 1: PUV analysis

Central to the process of value creation is the customer, and critically, what the customer values. We have employed the term Perceived Use Value (PUV) throughout the book and here is an opportunity for you to start deploying this critical construct in your own practice.

We have developed this technique for over 20 years. We suggest initially you get a team of people to trial the technique; then to really get benefits from it we suggest replacing the team's view of customer PUV with real information from clients and customers. This can be gleaned through focus groups, or in B2B relationships simply asking your customers what they are looking for in the product or service you offer can yield useful insights. In Chapter 3 we suggest ways in which we can get a better understanding of customer PUV.

Step 1 Choose a product or service you currently offer

Step 2 Identify a target customer for this product

Step 3 Unpack the dimensions of PUV

Step 4 Share your dimensions of PUV

Step 5 Weight the PUV dimensions

Step 6 Rate three competing products across the five PUV dimensions

Step 7 Calculate PUV scores

Step 8 Plot products on the PUV/Price matrix

Step 9 What are the implications of this analysis?

Step 1: *Choose a product or service you currently offer.* Our advice is to choose one that could benefit from some investigation. Often managers choose a new product, or a proposal that they are currently working on, or a product that seems to be in trouble, or their biggest seller.

Step 2: *Identify a target customer for this product.* You need to be precise. If this is a B2C transaction, then be specific about the customer you are trying to model. For example, if you were a high street bank, the product you have chosen might be a fixed-rate mortgage. The customer is NOT 'anyone who wants a mortgage'. It could be a single woman aged 28, managing a branch of Costa Coffee, currently living with her parents in Solihull, who are providing a $20,000 deposit. She is looking to buy a one-bed flat for $190,000 in Coventry where she works.

If this is a B2B transaction, as far as possible identify the likely buyer, for example, the head of IT procurement at B&Q, and if you can name this person, even better. This specificity is vital as it moves us away from bland generalisations like 'customers only want X' or 'they won't pay more for a speedy response'. Well, some might, others may not.

Step 3: *Unpack the dimensions of PUV.* In Figure 2.20 the target customer for the car we are considering is single male, aged 40, working in IT as a systems administrator, earning $55,000, living in Brighton. He values the car's styling, its performance (particularly acceleration), 'badge cachet' which is how he sees the car manufacturers 'brand', engineering innovations and build quality. To generate the equivalent of these five dimensions, we suggest each member of the team works individually at first. The task is to put yourself 'in the customer's shoes' and think about what is important to this customer. Limit this to five dimensions. Do not include price as it is not a dimension of PUV. Price may be very important to the customer, but it is not a dimension of PUV. It's a good idea to have each team member working on their own for this step.

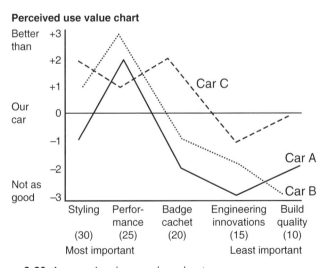

Figure 2.20 A perceived use value chart

Step 4: *Share your dimensions of PUV.* When we share the lists of PUV dimensions, this can reveal a lack of consensus around what is seen to be important to this customer. This is vital intelligence about our value processes. If we do not share the same understanding of the most critical person in the value process, the customer, then it is likely that in our priorities, decisions and actions we are working at cross purposes. If there is a lack of consensus, this usually triggers an urgent need to get better information through some kind of formalised or informal market research. For the purposes of this initial exercise, form some agreement about the most important five dimensions.

Step 5: *Weight the PUV Dimensions.* In Figure 2.20, the dimensions have been organised from the most important to the left (styling) and the least to the right (build quality). Attached weightings to these, for example, styling: 30 percent, performance: 25 percent. Figure 2.21 can be used as a template.

Step 6: *Rate three competing products across the five PUV dimensions.* Choose three credible competitors. If you face a large number of different competitors, then choose a representative for each different group of competitors. But always choose a real firm, not some made up 'typical' competitor. Then for each competitor, rate their product compared to our product: are they as good as us? better? or

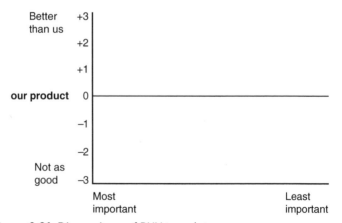

Figure 2.21 Dimensions of PUV template

		Car A		Car B		Car C	
	Weighing	Rating	Rating x weight	Rating	Rating x weight	Rating	Rating x weight
Styling	30	−1	−30	−1	+30	+2	+50
Performance	25	+2	+50	+2	+75	+1	+25
Badge Cachet	20	−2	−40	−1	−20	+2	−40
Engineering innovations	15	−3	−45	−2	−22	−1	−15
Build quality	10	−2	−20	−2	−22	0	+10
Total	100		−55		+25		+110
Price		$20,000		$21,000		$25,000	

Figure 2.22 Table for calculating PUV scores: Car example

worse? from this customer's point of view. Thus, we are constructing the lines for Cars A, B and C in Figure 2.21 compared to our car which is the horizontal benchmark running across the chart.

Step 7: *Calculate PUV scores.* The PUV score for our car will be zero, as it is the benchmark. The score for Car A is derived by multiplying the weighting by the rating and summing these. For example, for Car A this is (30 × −1) = −30, added to (25 × +2) = +50, etc. Figure 2.22 offers a worked example, and below it is a blank template for these calculations.

And above is a blank template for these calculations:

Step 8: *Plot products on the PUV/Price matrix.* The PUV score for 'our car' is zero. The scores for Car A = −85, B = +25, C = +110. Their prices are $20,000, $21,000 and $26,500 respectively. These PUV scores and prices enable us to locate the products in the matrix in Figure 2.24.

Step 9: *What are the implications of this analysis?* This is the pay-off for this work. From inspecting the PUV/Price matrix, which we refer to as the **Customer Matrix,** we can see an interesting (and quite common) plot, which reveals how the products are perceived by this target customer. What does this plot reveal? This customer will not buy our car. The reason is

	Weighing	Competitor A		Competitor B		Competitor C	
Dimensions	100	Rating	Rating x weight	Rating	Rating x weight	Rating	Rating x weight
Perceived use value							
Perceived price							

Figure 2.23 Template for calculating PUV scores

that Car B offers more consumer surplus than ours: Car B offers both more PUV and it is at a lower price. Now, we can't know from this plot whether this customer will buy A, B or C. The reason for this is we do not know-how *price sensitive* he is. If he is very price sensitive, then he may choose Car A as although the PUV is lower than ours or Car B, the price is much lower which could be attractive to him. If he is price insensitive over this range of prices, he may choose Car C.

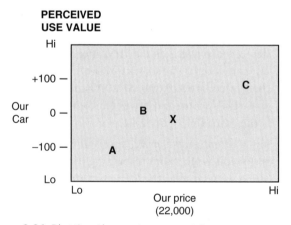

Figure 2.24 Plotting the customer matrix

If we are positioned at point X, and if this customer represents a wider *segment of demand* we are in trouble. What could we do? If we choose the *excellence strategy* and aim to continually improve PUV, we know the PUV dimensions we need to work on: Styling and Performance. Or we could choose to pursue a *low-cost strategy* which might enable us to shift to a lower price position to the left of Car B.

If we think that more customers are becoming price sensitive, we could opt for a *no-frills strategy*. This would require us to reposition where Car A is by really identifying the elements of 'styling' and 'performance' that are critical to this customer, and stripping out the less critical elements, thereby producing a no-frills version of the car.

Chapter

3

The firm as a value system

In this chapter we explain our approach to value creation and value capture.[19] We consider the firm as an open system which is made up of three core activities: *sourcing, operations* and *selling*. This system acquires inputs like know-how, raw materials, components and power, transforms these into products, and then sells the products. The purpose of the system is to generate a flow of *cash*. This is a simplified representation of the firm, but one that focuses on the *essential* processes of value creation and value capture. Most firms will have many different functions, departments and a hierarchy of managerial positions. We are arguing that it is necessary to clarify what role any positions and functions have in these three core activities: *sourcing* valuable inputs, *operations* activity which transforms inputs into saleable products and services, and *selling* them, that is, realising the value created by the system.

We summarise the value system and the key value flows in Figure 3.1. Suppliers provide use value *inputs* which are combined with the assets and capabilities within the firm to produce products and

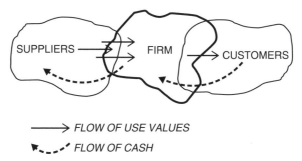

——→ *FLOW OF USE VALUES*

◄- - -◄ *FLOW OF CASH*

Figure 3.1 The firm's value system

service *outputs*. The reciprocal flows of cash are also indicated: revenue flows from sales and cost flows out of the system to suppliers.

Three core value activities

Firms can create a flow of cash where the value system **delivers customer-perceived use value efficiently**. In Figure 3.2 at the heart of the value system are the *operations* activities involved in converting inputs into product outputs. To the right we have the activities involved in *selling* products and services. Here the outputs from the system are converted into a flow of cash (revenues).

Customers determine whether products become use values. Customers *confer* use value on products. Price distributes the value realised in the exchange between the firm and the customer. As we explained in Chapter 2 the firm captures value in the form of price; the customer captures value in the form of consumer surplus. Relevant activities involved in *selling* are marketing, advertising, sales negotiation and after-sales support which enables the customer to gain the maximum use value from their purchase.

To the left we have *sourcing*, the activities involved in procuring materials, hiring staff, negotiating and assuring quality. Sourcing involves acquiring use value inputs, in exchange for cash. This way of looking at the firm as a system of three phases of activity, *sourcing, operations* and *selling* is based on the open-systems thinking developed by Katz and Kahn.[20]

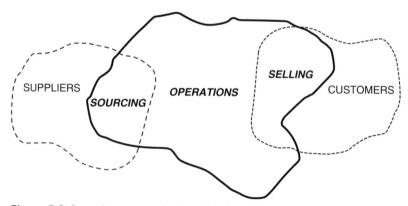

Figure 3.2 Sourcing, operations and selling

Note that the figure depicts both the *sourcing* and *selling* activities as extending beyond the 'boundary' of the firm. These activities are open to the external environment, whereas to a varying extent the operations activities involved in creating products are 'buffered' from the environment. There are advantages to buffering operations: this can provide a degree of predictability in the production process. The obvious downside is that buffering effectively insulates these activities from necessary feedback from the environment, leading to inefficient processes and/or less effective products being produced.

Coordination between all three core activities, *sourcing, operations* and *selling,* is vital for an effective value system. The larger the scope of the system, the more functional silos there are, the more difficult coordination across the three core activities becomes. Our competitive strategy approach promotes feedback from across the three core activities to help to ensure that the effects of a change in one part of the system are tracked across the whole system.

In Figure 3.3 we set out the three core activities and the critical flows of use values and cash. Across the top of the figure we have the different forms of use value. Firstly, we have the quality of the use value *inputs* procured by the firm. These include components and materials that are consumed during the transformation process, the quality of enduring procured assets, for example, computers, and the quality of the skills and capabilities that employees bring. *The prices and volumes of inputs determine the flow of cash out of the system.*

Inputs combine in the *operations* domain with enduring assets like equipment, brands, reputations, patents, client relationships,

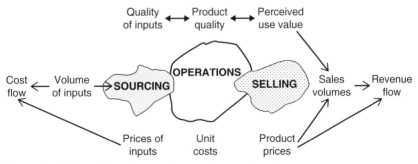

Figure 3.3 The critical flows of use value and cash

systems, etc., to create products and services. Here the internal measures and perceptions of what product 'quality' means will guide and drive behaviour and decisions. The third definition of use value, and the most significant for the firm is the customer's perception of use value (PUV). PUV and price determine consumer surplus, and this is what drives sales volumes. *Sales × average prices gives us the flow of revenues.*

It is vital for firm performance that these three forms of use value, the quality of inputs, what the firm perceives to be product 'quality' and customer perceptions of use value are *aligned.* If there is poor alignment, then we will not be procuring the right inputs, the quality of products will meet our 'internal' criteria, but these criteria may not align with what customers actually value. Thus, in the figure the double-headed arrows indicate the requirement for alignment and coordination across the three core activities.

Value is created by **know-how in action** with other nonhuman assets like equipment, brands, software, etc. (Figure 3.4). Know-how refers to the skills of individuals and teams, and when know-how **interacts** with other assets value is created.

A **capability** is a combination of know-how and assets interacting in *context,* that is, in a particular time and place (see Figure 3.5).

The strategy guides future changes to know-how, assets and how they interact as set out in Figure 3.6.

In each value process, there will be know-how that is similar to competitors, and they may have the same assets, for example, they use the same software package, bought from the same supplier. But we will also have superior know-how, or assets which we label *strategic assets,* which give our business an advantage over rivals. These strategic assets are explained at length in Chapter 13.[21] A successful strategy-guided change process should create strategic assets by

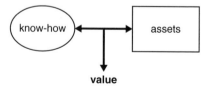

Figure 3.4 Value is created through interactions between know-how and assets

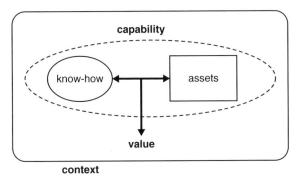

Figure 3.5 Capabilities comprise of know-how and assets interacting in context

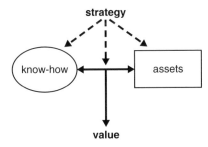

Figure 3.6 The strategy impacts know-how, assets and their interactions

building superior know-how, by developing and building non-human assets, or by changing the way know-how and assets interact.

As we explained in Chapter 1, the chosen strategy works *indirectly* through the structures, systems and culture of the business, which we term the *practices* of the organisation. Thus, changes to, for example, the way we group people can have the effect of building different capabilities.

Customer interactions

The value system is an *open system*: open to both suppliers and customers. The interactions the firm has with suppliers and customers can be purely *transactional* at one extreme where there is minimal interaction between the firm and suppliers/customers, or *relational* where there is a good deal of ongoing communication between the firm and suppliers/customers. An example of a transactional relationship would be where a customer visits our website and orders one product which is delivered by a parcel service. There is no direct communication between the customer and anyone in the firm, and the transaction is a 'one-off' purchase.

Relational interactions are quite different. Relational interactions typically extend over time, involve conversations and exchanges of information and ideas, and the outcome of a tailored service 'solution' is *co-created* by the firm and the customer. There is strong evidence that firms that engage extensively with customers, that listen carefully to what their needs are and how they may be changing, and that genuinely see that the customer is at the centre of all they do perform better than firms adopting a more transactional approach. Building relationships with customers tends to me more achievable in B2B situations but the principles of working alongside customers to develop solutions that genuinely meet their evolving needs seems to be a sound approach. Engagement with B2B customers can happen at many levels, for example, your sales manager meets regularly with their head of procurement, your lead engineers work with their development team, the installers discuss access issues as the project evolves, etc.

The transactional interactions between the firm and customers are depicted in Figure 3.7. In this pure form, the only interactions between the firm and customer involve the offer of the product at a set price, the customer purchase and the transfer of cash.

Figure 3.8 represents a very different approach to interacting with customers. Firstly, the interactions occur over an often extended time period and involve extensive exchanges of information about customer needs, possible solutions, etc. The outcomes of the successful engagement would be a satisfied customer; the process of

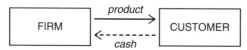

Figure 3.7 Transactional interactions between the firm and customer

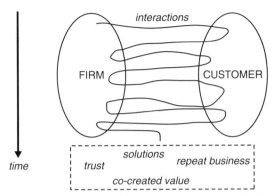

Figure 3.8 Value co-creation between customer and the firm

interaction *co-creates* a solution that meets the customer's needs. The firm's representatives need to listen attentively, to suggest possibilities and to work with the client to meet their evolving requirements. Often customers may be unaware of what might be possible solutions, and their expectations may be exceeded or modified through these interactions. But the co-created solution is not the only outcome from this engagement process: mutual trust is built, and that can lead to more business.

The ability to develop bespoke solutions will not be feasible or appropriate in many contexts. However, we would argue that all of the seven competitive strategies will be more successful if the **customer is seen as central to everything we do.** This must be right, as customers supply the cash that flows into the system. If you choose the *low-cost* strategy, understanding what customers truly value in your products enables you to strip out all costs that do not feed through to customer PUV. If we have a deep insight into customer PUV, this should guide our choice of initiatives whether we are pursuing *excellence, innovation* or *no frills.* So a deep-seated customer orientation will enhance the effectiveness of any of the seven competitive strategies.

Cash flow

We focus our attention on the flows of **cash** in and out of the system.[22] Where revenue flows exceed cost flows, we have a viable value system. More precisely, we focus on *changes* to these flows.

When we consider a competitive strategy, and any initiative associated with this strategy, the focus is on whether and how this initiative, project, change or experiment will positively affect *free cash flow*. For any change to create value, it has to ultimately have a net positive impact on the flow of cash.

The capital invested in the past, for example, in buying premises, acquiring equipment and training employees, is a 'sunk cost'. In some circumstances, some of these costs may be converted into liquid assets or working capital, for example, the sale and leaseback of premises, but for the most part, major past investments collectively form a relatively fixed set of assets.

What was once cash in the form of finance capital now exists as a set of interacting use values. The value of any one of these use values, for example, a machine, as part of the wider system is impossible to determine. In practice, these use values work in concert, with a myriad of subtle interactions which means that it is only possible to determine the value of the system as a whole. The *exchange* value of the machine is what someone would be prepared to pay for it today; this may bear no relationship to what we initially paid for it.

Any change to the system that doesn't increase cash flow doesn't create value. Actions that don't increase cash flow in the long term will not create value, regardless of their short-term impact on earnings or balance sheet. Hence, the model of the firm value system that we present in this chapter emphasises the *flow of cash* – from customer to the firm, and from the firm to suppliers – as the key measure of the system's performance.

Stakeholders

A popular way of viewing the firm is that it consists of a number of *stakeholders*.[23] Each stakeholder in the legal entity that is a firm has different interests, and their reasons for engaging with the firm are to pursue their own agendas. The firm, then, acts as a vehicle for different stakeholders to interact in pursuit of their own interests. Each stakeholder will have a different view about the value they gain from interacting with a firm and each stakeholder group trades use values and exchange value with the firm.

Shareholders can benefit from owning shares in two ways: dividends and/or increases in the share price. Dividends are typically paid out of profits. The share price is affected by the anticipation of *future* dividends. Thus, shareholders are rewarded when the value system generates a flow of profit. Profit flow is the outcome of two other flows: the flow of *costs* out of the system, and the flow of *revenues* into it.

In addition to shareholders, we have two broad stakeholder categories: *customers* and *suppliers.* We considered customers and consumer surplus in the last chapter and in Chapter 12 we explore customer-perceived use value in more depth. We now consider suppliers, what value means to them and their role in the process of value creation.

Suppliers provide inputs into the value creation process. *Suppliers* would include employees who contribute different types of labour, suppliers of capital and suppliers of materials, equipment, power, etc. We would also see society at large as a supplier of infrastructure, the rule of law, legitimacy, education services, etc., which benefit the firm.

Suppliers provide product or service inputs to the firm and they typically receive payments for the goods and services provided. Employees and managers not only receive wages or salaries from engaging with the firm, they can also get additional benefits, for example, job satisfaction, or a sense of belonging to a social group. Value to suppliers of labour would be some assessment of the benefits received (pay and intrinsic rewards) compared to the effort expended.

In certain circumstances, suppliers can provide additional use value to the firm in the form of some guarantees of continuity in supply. We would view this as an additional use value over and above the actual products or services being provided, which allows those running the firm more predictability in managing their operations.

Advocates of the stakeholder view would suggest that when executives make decisions, that the interests of all stakeholder groups should be taken into account. However, this is a monumentally difficult task. It is highly unlikely that any decision will add value to one stakeholder group without necessarily impacting others. It is also unlikely that a decision will add value to all stakeholder groups simultaneously. There will inevitably be trade-offs. For example, lower prices would increase customers' consumer surplus but may well reduce the profits received by shareholders. Alternatively, profits may be increased if the firm is able to reduce wage costs or the costs of supplied goods and services. And given the complexity of the real world, it is not possible to calculate the impact of a change on any stakeholder group.

The fact is that all these stakeholder groups are not equal in their relationship to the legal entity that we call a firm. Legally, the firm must be managed in the interests of one stakeholder group, the *owners* or *shareholders* in the firm. Therefore, when executives evaluate alternative courses of action, they should be privileging the profit impact of these actions above all other stakeholder concerns. This is not to say that the interests of other stakeholders can or should be disregarded. Clearly, it is important to meet customers' needs and expectations, as it is important to have a group of employees who are motivated and committed to the firm, but the point is that the satisfaction of these stakeholders' interests should be viewed as a *means to an end* rather than ends in themselves.

This is not only a legal argument; it is a practical one too. If a firm doesn't make a profit for any significant period of time, then the chances are that the firm will disappear. In contrast, a firm may well survive and prosper in circumstances where customers may not feel they get a good deal, for example, in the case of a monopoly provider, or where employees do not feel sufficiently rewarded, that is, in a situation where there may be very few alternative local employment opportunities. Firms may well continue to prosper even where they are able to avoid paying any taxes or where they are able to continue to pollute their local environments, as long as they make profits.

The scope of the value system

We have choices about the *scope* of the firm: whether to extend or reduce it horizontally or vertically. Extending the *horizontal scope* of the business means moving from one product being sold into one market to many products serving many markets. This process kicks in as soon as you offer the same product to a new market, or offer new products into the same markets. Once we move from the single-product/one-market circumstance to many products/many markets, the complexity of the system inevitably increases.

If we decide to make rather than buy a component, this would be an example of extending the *vertical scope* of the system. If you extend or reduce the vertical scope of the system, you *redefine the set of customers and suppliers*. If we extend the vertical scope 'upstream', what was formerly bought in from the market is produced 'in house'. We explore vertical scope further in Chapter 14.

In Figure 3.9 we set out some of the choices we face with respect to horizontal scope. The least complex system would be the one-product/one-market system in the top left of the figure, the most complex being the multiple-products/multiple-markets situation in the bottom right.

Increasing the horizontal scope can be a major engine of growth. This can occur proactively where we make choices to extend into new products and markets, but it can happen as a result of customer pressures. Customers may wish to source several components from a single supplier, and if we can't respond to this requirement we may lose the business. As a value system grows, it changes. We often see increasing task specialisation accompanying growth which presents new coordination challenges.

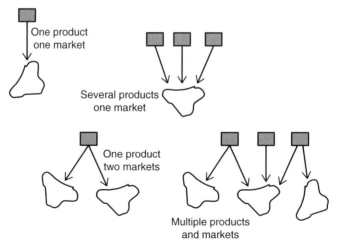

Figure 3.9 Horizontal scope choices

Horizontal scope and choice of strategies

Few businesses sell just one product into one market; typically, even small firms will have a range of products that they sell, often into different markets. We have argued that a competitive strategy should guide change across the three value activities of *sourcing*, *operations* and *selling*. If the firm offers a range of products, it might be appropriate for each product group to pursue a different competitive strategy.

In Figure 3.10 we depict a firm that manufactures adhesive tapes and produces three types of products (A, B and C). Product Group A are sold to volume car assemblers; Group B are sold to tradespeople, for example, carpenters, plumbers; and Group C are tapes specially developed for manufacturers of mobile phones located primarily in Asia.

We have set out the value activities associated with each product group, as well as a collection of more generic activities, like finance, legal, accounts and IT, which support all of the three product groups. As depicted in Figure 3.10, each product group has its own dedicated value activities (sourcing, operations and selling).

We decide that the appropriate strategy for product Groups A and B to pursue is *low cost*, but the best one for product Group C is

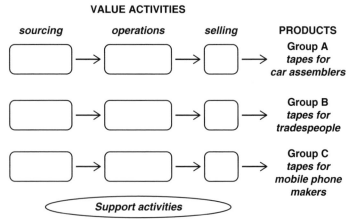

Figure 3.10 Three product groups with dedicated value activities

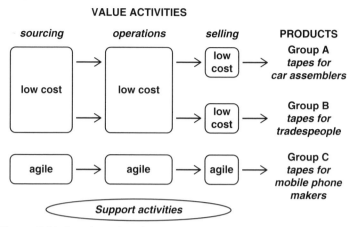

Figure 3.11 Combined and separated value activities

adaptive, to enable the firm to respond to the changing needs of the mobile phone manufacturers. In Figure 3.11 we set out one structural solution that the firm could adopt, which should preserve the integrity of the two strategies.

We decide that there are benefits from combining the sourcing activities for product groups A and B. By so doing, we can benefit from better bargaining relationships with our key suppliers, and by integrating these sourcing activities, we can also save on staffing costs by reducing some duplication. Also there are significant cost savings to be had by combining the production activities of A and B. In particular, we can get much higher levels of capacity utilisation. In both these cases, integrating the value activities does not have any negative impacts on $PUV or costs, only positive cost savings.

In Figure 3.12 we pose three questions which can inform choices about whether to combine value activities across different product groups, or whether they should be kept separated so they can develop product-specific capabilities. For products A and B, the same *know-how* and *assets* are required in the sourcing and operations processes; hence, there is no 'downside' in combining these value processes for A and B. Moreover, the same *strategy*, low cost, is being introduced to guide the development of the capabilities in A and B.

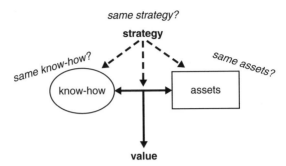

Figure 3.12 Three questions in deciding whether to combine activities

However, whilst products A and B can be manufactured using the same systems, equipment and capabilities, each product group is sold into quite different markets: group A products sell to industrial customers, and group B to tradesmen, so we decide that we need to preserve different sales teams who can develop their relationships and skills by focusing on their respective target markets.

Whilst there are some common processes in making tape for car makers and phone makers, the mobile phone makers have far more exacting requirements, which require the development of special sizes and adhesive qualities of the tapes for each customer. The appropriate strategy for phone tapes is *adaptive,* and it makes sense to keep all three value activities, sourcing, operations and selling separate from the product A and B activities. In this way, the choice of the adaptive strategy can help to guide initiatives and priorities that are in line with the demands and requirements of the phone makers.

Value is *realised* through exchange

Some have argued that value is *co-created* by the producer and consumer.[24] The point they make is that the consumer *confers* value on the product and creates use value for themselves when they consume or use the product. We take a slightly different approach. A firm creates a product or service which is offered to the market. A customer assesses the usefulness of this offering, and thus confers use value on it. If products are produced that no one wants, then no use value has been created, and as no one will pay for them, no exchange value is captured. No exchange takes place unless a customer perceives there to be use value in the product or service.

A deal between a customer and seller is made at a point in time. For the deal to go ahead *at that time,* the customer perceives there to be more consumer surplus to be had in this deal than any other deal. This judgement is made *in advance* of the customer consuming and using the product, or receiving the service. The customer may be very experienced in buying this product, and as a consequence, they know exactly what use value they will get from this transaction. In other circumstances, deals are made in relative ignorance and what the customer experiences after making the deal can lead to disappointment, or indeed the customer may be surprised and delighted that the product or service exceeded her expectations. But value is not *created* through the exchange, it is *realised in exchange.*

Price determines how much of the value created is captured by the buyer and by the seller. Where a high price is paid, then the seller captures the 'lion's share' of the value, and conversely, a low price means that the buyer may be capturing most of the value in the form of consumer surplus. We explained that price distributes the value created between the buyer and the seller in Chapter 2. We now look at how the perceived dependence of both buyer and seller influences the 'carving up' of value.

Dependence and bargaining power

The firm acts as both a buyer of use value *inputs* and a seller of use value *outputs.* The firm's ability to bargain when making deals with customers and suppliers determines to a significant extent how much profit is captured by the firm.

As Michael Porter explains, if the firm has power over its *customers,* it can command higher prices, but if it has a weak bargaining position with key *suppliers,* a large proportion of these revenues will be passed on to suppliers in the form of high input costs, leading to average profit performance. Thus, bargaining power is central to Porter's argument.[25]

As we explained in Chapter 2 what the buyer is willing to pay factors in their evaluation of the product's use value, and its scarcity. You may value a cool soda on a hot day. What you are willing to pay for a specific can of soda depends on whether you perceive that there are readily available cans from other soft drink providers. We explained that the difference between what the buyer is willing to pay and the actual price paid is *consumer surplus*. The difference between the lowest price the **seller will accept** and the price actually paid we will refer to as the **seller's surplus.** The actual *price struck in the deal determines how value is shared out between buyer and seller*: A lower price means that the *buyer* captures most of the value in the form of *consumer surplus;* a higher price means that the *seller* captures most of the value as *seller surplus.* So the question then is 'what determines the price?'

If the buyer or seller has many alternatives to making this deal, at this time they would perceive themselves to have *low dependence* on this particular transaction. Alternatively, where buyer or seller feel that they have no alternative to this deal, then they perceive *high dependence.* The *relative dependence* of both buyer and seller strongly influences the behaviour of each party in approaching this transaction. These behaviours in turn influence the resulting price, and hence the distribution of value between buyer and seller. Central to dependence is the availability of feasible alternatives; hence, the more scarce the item being traded, the more dependence the buyer has on the deal. Alternatively, if the seller perceives there to be few potential customers, the more dependence they perceive they have on doing a deal with a particular buyer.[26]

Dependence can be symmetric or asymmetric between buyer and seller. The matrix in Figure 3.13 juxtaposes buyer and seller perceptions. Note that the buyer could be an agent acting on behalf of the firm, for example, a procurement manager. It is important to recognise that firms don't negotiate, *people* do, and they do this on behalf of the firm. The firm's agent would be someone working within the *sourcing* process. They may be hiring new staff, ordering components or negotiating with a bank for a loan. Or the firm could be the seller, trying to cut a deal with a customer. The 'seller' again would be an agent of the firm, for example, a salesman.

In Cell 1, *Commoditised* deals the seller perceives low dependence, as does the buyer. Both parties perceive that they could walk away from this deal with no loss as they perceive that there are multiple

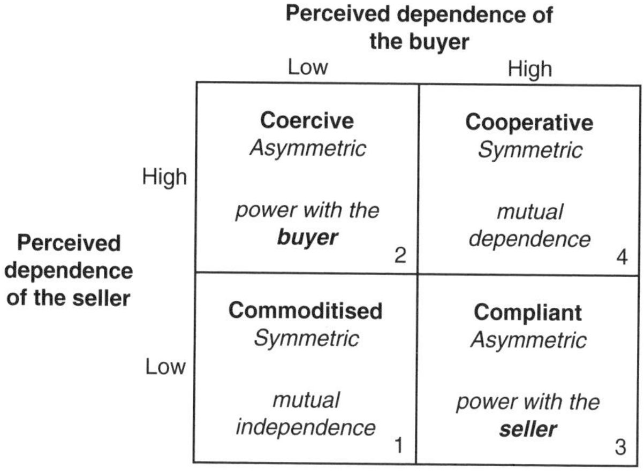

**Perceived dependence of
the buyer**

Figure 3.13 Buyer and seller dependence

other opportunities to trade. They are likely to bargain from a position of more or less equal perceived power, but no great energy is likely to be expended in this bargaining process. Perceived power, based on mutual perceptions of their *independence* with regard to this deal, then would be *symmetrical*. The price may well reflect a functioning market for the product or service where there are many buyers and many sellers. The market approximates to the economist's 'perfect competition'.

In Cell 2, *Coercive* deals the seller sees himself to be highly dependent on doing this deal at this time. But because the buyer perceives there to be many alternative potential suppliers to transact with, there is an *asymmetric* power relationship. Here the power lies with the *buyer* and we would assume that if the costs involved were significant for the buyer, they would look to bargain hard and drive price down. In these circumstances, the seller has to take whatever the buyer is prepared to pay for their product.

Cell 3 is the reverse of Cell 2: *Compliant deals*. Here we have the case of an asymmetric power relationship where the power lies with the *seller*, not the buyer. The buyer perceives the seller to be offering something special, something that could not be easily acquired elsewhere. However, the seller perceives that they can easily (rightly or wrongly) take their product or services to another buyer, who would be happy to deal with them. The seller could then negotiate from this position of perceived strength and hold out for a high price. Note, however, that for any deal to be done, the buyer must nevertheless perceive there to be value in the deal, there must still be some *consumer surplus*. The danger in Cell 3 negotiations is overpaying at time T1 for value that does not materialise at time T2. Thus, some poor recruitment decisions would be Cell 3 problems.

Finally, in Cell 4, *Cooperative* deals both parties perceive themselves to be dependent on doing this particular deal. What is being traded is perceived by both parties to be valuable and neither party perceives that they have viable alternatives at this time to the current opportunity. But both parties also understand the dependence of the *other* party to this deal. There is likely to be a 'sharing of the spoils' where the terms of the deal are attractive to both parties, with value distributed equitably between them. Cooperation is likely to be high because both parties depend on the deal.

The firm as seller

The firm does not want to be in a weak bargaining position with respect to its customers. A Cell 2 *Coercive* and dependent relationship gives all the power to the customer. The effects of the firm being in this weak bargaining position are manifested in low prices and low sales volumes. How can the firm move towards a more attractive cell? The ideal position might be Cell 3 *compliant* relationship where the power is clearly with the firm. Here the customer is heavily dependent on the firm, and it should enable the firm to capture the lion's share of the value realised in the deal: price is high, but customers still get enough consumer surplus to make the deal worthwhile.

To get to a Cell 3 relationship, the firm must be offering something special that customers believe they can't get anywhere else, that is, superior levels of $PUV. So even though they pay a high price, they still get more consumer surplus than they would from a competing product. To get to this relationship with the customer, the firm needs to understand what customers really value and deliver this level of $PUV in ways that rivals can't match. But to make profits on these deals, the firm must have control over its costs. There is no advantage in delighting customers and losing money on each deal you make. Our competitive strategies are intended to enable the business to improve its bargaining relationships vis-à-vis customers, that is, to shift towards this *compliant* relationship.

A Cell 1 *commoditised* relationship with customers may be preferable to the Cell 2 *coercive* relationship. A properly functioning competitive market is a good place to be especially if you are able to meet the customers' $PUV requirements at lower costs than rivals. Any sustained cost advantage your firm may have could be used to ultimately drive out higher cost competitors, and maybe the 'end game' moves the firm into Cell 3 as a more or less monopolistic supplier of a commoditised product.

The Cell 4 *cooperative* relationship has both parties seeing that they are mutually dependent on this deal. These relationships come about especially where there are significant investments by both parties in the transaction. For example, we may be a supplier of car seats, and the customer is setting up a new car plant. For the deal to work, we will have to build a seat-making facility close to the new assembly plant. But the car maker is also heavily reliant on the continual flow of seats direct to the assembly line in order to achieve cost efficiencies. There is a *mutual dependence* and we would expect price would be set to allow both parties to think they have made an acceptable deal.

Segments of demand

Customers can be grouped according to their *needs*, and what they perceive as use value. They can also be grouped according to their price *sensitivity*. How much a customer is 'willing to pay' for a product factors in their current needs, their perceptions of the use value dimensions will meet those needs, the PUV of the products they are aware of, and their financial situation. Jeff might think that a Range Rover is 'worth' $70,000 even if he has no intention of buying one. Although he values the Range Rover, and appreciates its performance and styling, he is only able to borrow $30,000 to fund the purchase of a new car. Jeff may well represent 20,000 people who have similar needs and PUV dimensions in relation to cars. Thus, Jeff represents a segment of demand.

Thus, 'willingness to pay' includes how much the customer is *able* to pay. Whilst these 20,000 car buyers have similar needs and PUV dimensions (e.g. performance, styling, brand values), they don't all have the same financial resources. Those with limited funds will be very price sensitive, and at the other extreme there will be some who are relatively insensitive to price.

The firm as buyer

The firm needs to avoid being in Cell 3 *compliant* relationships with any *supplier*, be they suppliers of raw materials, special kinds of know-how or funding. Any change that reduces the firm's *relative dependence* with respect to suppliers would be advantageous. If the firm is able to reduce its relative dependence on suppliers, it should be able to capture more consumer surplus. Here the value captured by the firm takes the form of *use values* that are deployed in the creation of products and services, for example, components, equipment, know-how.

Where the firm is the buyer, any initiatives that increase supplier dependence or reduce the firm's dependence will enable the firm to capture more value from suppliers. For example, multiple sourcing reduces the firm's reliance on a single source of supply. This idea extends to the suppliers of skills. Where the firm is able to *de-skill* work, it has less dependence on a limited supply of skilled people and is able to draw on a wider pool of potential employees.

Firms can increase supplier dependence through long-term contracts which lock in a favourable price. Where suppliers make investments that only have value in relation to a single customer's business, they are subject to 'hold up', where the firm (as customer) captures the lion's share of the value, that is, the supplier has very high dependence due to these relationship-specific investments. In our car seat supplier example, once the seat-maker has invested in a dedicated facility, there is a risk of 'hold-up', so contracts in these circumstances have to be very carefully negotiated.

Economies of scale in sourcing would flow from the firm being in a strong bargaining relationship with the supplier (Cell 2 *coercive* relationships). Where corporations with several business units consolidate their procurement activities, they are able to exert more bargaining power over suppliers, and hence get better prices. We explore this source of synergy advantage in Chapter 14.

But procurement advantages can be developed other than through this blunt display of buying power. Initiatives that reduce dependence on high-priced inputs should lead to lower costs. Where procurement specialists build their negotiating skills, there will be enduring advantages. These *sourcing* skills would include the gathering of intelligence about suppliers, developing negotiating, bluffing and signalling skills, and reducing dependence by multiple sourcing.

Linking PUV with 'quality'

Whether a product is perceived as valuable is purely in the gift of the customer. The customer determines willingness to pay ($PUV), and whilst the firm can charge what it likes, the customer will decide what price can be *realised*. For example, a strategy consultant could charge $10,000 per day for his service; however, he could end up getting no work. So *realised* prices are in the gift of the customer.

The firm has the ability to directly affect both product *quality* and *unit cost*. If the firm really understands what customers value, that is, what $PUV is, if they are able to create products that deliver $PUV, and if they can signal this value to the target customer, then an increase in product quality would be mirrored by an increase in customer $PUV. But these are difficult and complex processes and therefore we cannot expect that it is straightforward to translate internal activities that affect product quality to be easily translated into product changes that the customer both values and perceives.

The linkage between what customers perceive as use value and internal measures of quality is critical. If 'quality' means one thing to those 'inside' the firm and different things to customers, efforts to improve quality may not lead through to changes in customer perceptions. We can understand customer perceptions through formal processes like focus groups, or through informal interactions and conversations with them. Those who constantly interact with clients and customers will likely build up a deep intuitive understanding of what customers' value. Therefore, staff that have regular client interactions are a vital source of market intelligence.

The firm has more ability to impact quality and unit costs, and improvements in these can enable product improvements that customers perceive. Thus, we focus attention on options that the firm has to affect *quality* and *unit cost,* and changes in these gives the firm options to reposition products in the eyes of the customer. For example, a reduction in unit costs could allow us to compete more aggressively on price. Or if we substantially improve quality, this could enable us to not only translate this into $PUV improvements but also reap these rewards through premium pricing.

High-quality feedback from customers is one way to ensure alignment between internal quality measures and customer $PUV. Feedback from customers informs our understanding of $PUV and this feedback should enable us to derive appropriate ways of assessing quality. If we are able to communicate effectively with customers, then the levels of product quality we have achieved will be reflected in customer perceptions. We can communicate value through the product itself, through advertising, through the skills of our sales people and through signifiers, which can include price.

Thus, aligning internal 'quality' criteria with what customers actually value is critical if the system is to create consumer surplus. In Figure 3.14 we indicate how this alignment can be achieved: feedback from customers and potential customers enables us to adapt the quality measures and criteria we deploy, and we can communicate value to customers through marketing, advertising, packaging and through the skills of the sales team. Sales staff are critical links in achieving alignment. They are able to discern what customers really value in this purchase situation, and they can pass this intelligence on to those in the *operations* and *sourcing* processes. On the other hand, they can also communicate product attributes that meet customer requirements, and their demeanour also sends

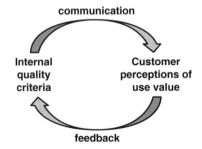

Figure 3.14 Aligning 'quality' with PUV

'signals' to the customer about the products or services the sales person is trying to sell. In Figure 3.14 sales people are critical in both the *feedback* and *communications* processes.

To summarise, our competitive strategies are intended to guide the development of the value system. A strategy should have the effect of shifting the system advantageously in terms of $PUV, realised prices or reduced costs. Managers have more influence over the variables 'inside' the system than they have over customer $PUV and realised prices. But feedback from customers and our ability to communicate effectively with them is critical in helping to ensure that changes in internal product 'quality' feed through to changes in customer $PUV.

Competitive advantage

The term *competitive advantage* is often used in the strategy literature. There are two connected aspects of competitive advantage: *who wins the business? and who makes the profit?* As we have explained, you only win the business if you offer more *consumer surplus* than all your rivals. You can achieve this by offering more $PUV but charging similar prices, or by offering equivalent $PUV at a lower price (or of course you can do both of these simultaneously). This wins you the business, you get the sale.

Whether you make a profit on this sale is determined by the relationship between your costs and the price you charge, that is, your *margin*. By dropping your prices, you could win lots of business but make no profits. Thus, you only have competitive advantage where you can deliver $PUV at a cost that enables you to make a profit. As Michael Porter points out, if you choose to compete on price, then your costs must be *lower* than your rivals if you are to have an advantage over them. If you compete by offering superior $PUV, then you must be able to do this at costs which are *similar* to rivals.

Not-for-profit organisations

As we explained earlier, our focus is on profit-seeking firms, but it is worth noting that similar reasoning can apply to not-for-profit organisations (NFPs) like charities, public sector organisations, the armed forces and voluntary organisations. The key difference is the relationship between stakeholders. Firms are established to make profits for their owners; other stakeholders' needs must be met along the way, but the primary purpose of the firm is to create value for shareholders. In most not-for-profit organisations, there are multiple stakeholders and they may all have some claim to decide what the organisation should do. However, it is very difficult to decide any course of action where some of these stakeholders will feel a benefit, whereas others may feel disadvantaged by the proposed change. The best solution we have encountered was put forward by John Argenti.[27] He suggests that the NFP should identify the primary *beneficiaries* of the organisation, and their needs or interests should be paramount.

For example, in a charity we may agree that the primary beneficiaries are older homeless people who are sleeping rough. Then value creation would be delivering value, from the perspective of these homeless people. What would they value? What would PUV mean to them? Maybe somewhere to sleep, where they can wash and eat in safety and where they aren't judged, or preached at. Then the charity can focus on how efficiently they deliver PUV to these beneficiaries, and initiatives can be explored that would either add to beneficiary PUV or lower the costs of delivering PUV. Note that in the case of NFP organisations, we refer to the perceived use value (PUV) of the beneficiaries. In many instances, for example, a charity, the beneficiaries don't pay or can't pay for the service provided so 'willingness to pay' ($PUV) does not apply.

Or take the case of a state secondary school. The stakeholders would include the current students, teachers, support staff, parents, local government, central government, local employers, teaching unions, etc. Trying to balance the often conflicting interests and priorities of all these groups is an impossible task. Life becomes much clearer when we identify the primary beneficiaries of the school, the *current students,* and manage the system in their interests. This could, of course, lead to decisions to remove ineffective teachers, who would otherwise, as a 'stakeholder', see themselves as having a right to remain employed.

Having identified the core beneficiaries of the organisation, the seven competitive strategies can be applied. Take our example of the charity set up for homeless people sleeping rough. A *targeting* strategy could have us focusing purely on the needs of alcoholics. We could develop capabilities that address the particular problems and issues faced by homeless alcoholics, for example, providing them with alcohol in a controlled environment, as they are dependent on it. Or a *no-frills* strategy might enable us to serve hundreds more homeless people with a basic level of care.

Excellence could involve providing better care for all our existing beneficiaries, and the *low-cost* strategy option would have us providing the existing levels of care more cost efficiently. We could explore an *innovation* strategy, whereby we find novel (and legal) ways of accessing and utilising unoccupied properties in the major cities. A *specialisation* strategy may emerge from our success with targeting alcoholics. Having focused on these beneficiaries, we have built a set of unique capabilities which we can now deploy in other cities. An *adaptive* strategy could shift us into a different space where we address the complex needs of older people with multiple health problems, for example, dementia, arthritis, type 2 diabetes, etc. Each individual would require a personalised care service.

Mutual organisations, for example, savings and loan organisations, or retail cooperatives, are owned by their customers. The need to deliver consumer surplus cost efficiently applies to mutuals as it does to firms. The difference is that customers reap the benefits of cost efficiencies through lower prices, thus increasing their consumer surplus.

Not-for-profit organisations: The role of values

In a profit-seeking firm, the overriding objective is making profits, and in our terms this translates into free cash flow. The competitive strategies are different ways to generate free cash flow. In a not-for-profit context, the leadership team might be able to agree to focus on the primary beneficiaries of the organisation, as Argenti suggests. If this is not feasible, then our advice is that potential leaders should be clear on *their core values* in relation to the organisation. If these are clear and consistent, then those charged with deciding who should lead the NFP should select the leader(s) who embody the values that are most aligned with the purpose of the organisation. For example, when choosing a head teacher, select the person who has the right values for the school. Because, whoever leads the complex system of a school cannot be selected on the basis of any strategy they articulate. Unanticipated events are more than likely to de-rail any strategy, whereas the core values of the leader will persist and be manifested in their behaviour, the decisions they take and what they prioritise. Strategies are transient, values endure. In pressure situations, the leader will decide a course of action based on their values.

Part

2

The change process

Chapter

Strategy-guided change

The competitive strategy approach considers both the direction the system needs to head and the *change processes* involved in moving the system. The literature on organisational change is extensive. Given the complex nature of firms and their contexts, we focus on prior theory that acknowledges emergence and incremental approaches to change. In particular, we build on two important contributions: Henry Mintzberg's notion of *emergent strategy* as a 'pattern in a stream of decisions' and James Brian Quinn's 'logical incrementalism'.[28]

Mintzberg's 'patterning' corresponds to our idea of strategy-guided change: the strategy shapes the emerging pattern of decisions and actions. Quinn's *logical incrementalism* recognises the challenges of managing strategic change but he argues that change need not be chaotic or 'disjointed incrementalism', instead change can be *steered*. He explains that strategic management involves guiding actions and events towards a conscious strategy in a step-by-step process.

Our strategy approach aligns with these contributions from Quinn and Mintzberg, and although these researchers do not explicitly relate their ideas to complexity thinking, their work nevertheless implicitly aligns with a complexity 'worldview' and we incorporate these ideas in our approach.

The strategy as a change process

Every firm is unique; it has its own unique history. So we cannot predict the impact or effect of a particular strategy or initiative on your firm, because we know nothing about the specific situation, and no one knows exactly what will be the ultimate impact of any change on the wider system. Your firm has evolved over time to look like it does today. Its value system can be viewed as a set of interconnecting routines.[29] Routines are patterns of action and interaction that are involved in the three value activities of *sourcing, operations* and *selling*.

These routines change and evolve. They adjust and flex as new people join the firm, as staff learn and as performance information is fed back. Routines are the lifeblood of the firm, they create the value and they provide needed stability. Some of these routines will inevitably have aspects that may add unnecessary costs or that don't enable the firm to respond quickly enough to a customer. But in even the smallest firm, you will find that these routines combine in complex ways to deliver value. Therefore, we need to be very careful before we go blundering in trying to change this complex system of interconnected routines.

The firm's value system is in a continual state of becoming. The firm is not a set of buildings and computers, or an organisation chart or a collection of processes and procedures. As we have explained, a firm is an open complex system where people act and interact. The system creates value through the application of *know-how*, which is embedded in people.[30] We can recognise that in some firms, particular individuals, teams or departments are critical in the value processes. And we also know that what enables a firm to survive are capabilities and assets that are difficult to copy like reputation, image and relationships (we explore the nature of inimitable assets and capabilities in Chapter 13).

Given the complex nature of the firm, its current configuration of assets and capabilities will be the outcome of management actions, emergent processes, surprises and luck.[31] They are more likely to have emerged through combinations of deliberate managerial interventions and emergent reactions, not by 'design' or intention alone.[32]

Almost by definition, sources of sustained advantage must be complex and difficult to understand and to replicate; otherwise, they would soon be imitated and become sources of competitive parity. Competitive advantage, therefore, rarely derives from easily observable discrete assets. Our starting point should be a recognition of the complexity of the system we are in, an understanding of how it came to be like it is and an acknowledgement that we cannot predict exactly what will be the effects of any change we introduce.

In Figure 4.1 we depict how the chosen strategy guides the change process over time. The strategy indicates what *capabilities* we need to develop and what *structures, systems* and *culture* would enable these capabilities to thrive. These in turn inform the choice of *initiatives*, projects and experiments. Initiatives that are in line with the strategy are introduced. These get translated into *actions*. Over time momentum builds as these initiatives get embedded and as synergies emerge between them.

We suggest any change or initiative should be introduced with caution. Thus, as far as it is possible to do this, we advocate introducing any initiative in an *incremental, low-cost* and *experimental* way. In this way you will be able to generate *feedback* from the system which can enable you to adjust your approach to the change. It could be that some unpredicted effect of the initiative means that you should abandon it, or less dramatically, that you might need to involve more people in effecting the change than you anticipated. So proceeding in an incremental and experimental way, generating feedback and acting on it as you go should help to reduce the risks of change.

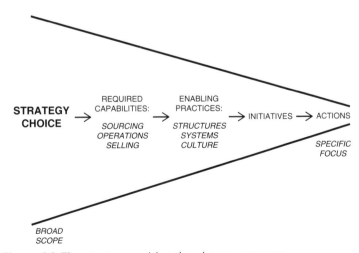

Figure 4.1 The strategy guides the change process

This cautious, incremental approach to change is respectful of the complex reality. However, it is clearly at odds with a managerial *command and control* mindset. This mindset is pervasive and it puts pressures on managers to be *decisive*, to *act* and to *lead*. We know that the most significant organisational changes occur in crisis, or with a change of leadership. The crisis situation in some way liberates managers, who feel less personal accountability when making significant changes to the system. The thinking is 'Hey, we're going under anyway, we might as well give this a go!' The only thing the manager would be criticised for in a crisis is *inaction*. As long as they are seen to be doing something, anything, they are probably OK.

But why weren't these changes made *before* the crisis? The reason for this is that if you choose to make a radical change to the system and it all goes horribly wrong, we all know who to blame. We believe the pressures on individual managers to be authoritative or to be commanding run counter to the natural change processes of a complex organisation. If we can't predict the future, if we cannot anticipate the ultimate effect of any action, it makes sense to approach change in a cautious and incremental way. And, if we continually seek to adapt and adjust the system as the future unfolds, maybe we will avoid crises and the need for the dramatic lurches in the direction they precipitate.

Three phases in introducing a strategy

In Figure 4.2 we set out the phases of the strategy change process. The *cognition phase* involves more thinking than doing. The team debates and discusses strategies as a concept, and alternative strategies are explored. The conclusion of this phase is a chosen strategy. This cognition phase is followed by a *development phase* where initiatives are trialled and evaluated. The development phase involves action and reflection where we use feedback from the emerging system to track the effects of an initiative. The third phase is where the changes to the system developed through the sequence of initiatives become the 'new normal'. This *embedded phase* is where the effects of the strategy in shaping the development of the system emerge, and assuming a sound choice of strategy and the selection of appropriate initiatives, in the embedded phase we would expect to see performance improvements.

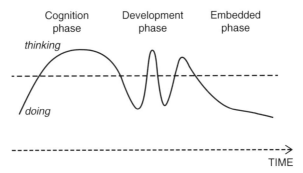

Figure 4.2 The three phases of development

The duration of each phase is obviously an empirical question. Some strategy-guided initiatives could realise performance benefits within weeks; other changes might take a year or longer before they show any impact on the system.

Regardless of the nature of the chosen strategy, that is, *low cost, innovation, adaptive,* the development phase will always involve creativity and there will be some uncertainty and turbulence in the system. Strategy-guided change is an *emergent creative process.*

Realised strategies

A competitive strategy is no more than an idea. This idea should shape the selection of initiatives (Figure 4.3). The system develops through the selection of practices and the introduction of specific initiatives that are congruent with the chosen strategy. Our sets of

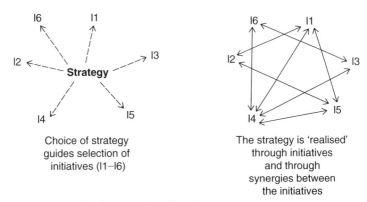

Figure 4.3 Initiatives and 'realised strategy'

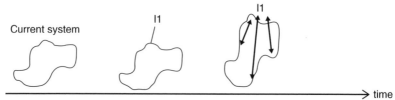

The initiative (I1) 'takes' and develops synergies

Figure 4.4 Strategy-guided change – 1

congruent practices and the case examples we present in Chapters 6–11 should help you generate specific initiatives that 'fit' both the chosen strategy and the unique context and history of your business.

Because the strategy informs the selection of initiatives, there are more likely to be *synergies* between the initiatives. Through the enactment of initiatives and through the generation of synergies, the centre of gravity of the system starts to shift in the direction of the chosen strategy.

In Figure 4.4 the selected initiative (I1) is introduced. Synergies then emerge between the initiative and some parts of the current system. Over time the centre of gravity of the system shifts in the direction of the strategy.

The speed with which the system shifts in the required direction is enhanced where additional complementary initiatives (I2, I3) are introduced (Figure 4.5).

Over time, as synergies build between the initiatives the centre of gravity of the whole system shifts as depicted in Figure 4.6.

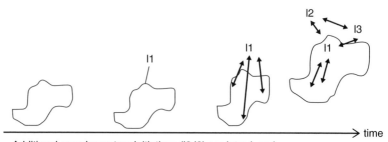

Additional complementary initiatives (I2,I3) are introduced...

Figure 4.5 Strategy-guided change – 2

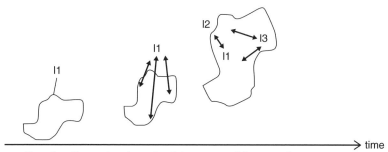

Over time the centre of gravity of the system shifts towards strategy...

Figure 4.6 Strategy-guided change – 3

However, it may be that a chosen initiative is introduced, but for whatever reason it doesn't 'take'. This could be because it was not a good place to start the change process, or it could be that insufficient resources were put behind the initiative. The ultimate effects of the initiative I1 on the system are negligible (Figure 4.7).

Strategy traction

If the chosen strategy is well explained to members of the organisation, and if there is 'buy-in' to the direction of travel indicated, then in addition to *deliberate* initiatives to shift the system, there will be a continual flow of *emergent* effects which will be influenced by the strategy. These effects will be manifested in a stream of big and small decisions about resource allocations, who we hire, how we organise people and what we emphasise in our marketing messages. Over time, the strategy becomes *embedded* in the system through a combination of higher profile initiatives, experiments, trials, etc., and a continuing stream of more emergent processes.

An initiative fails to 'take'...

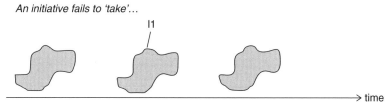

Figure 4.7 An initiative fails to shift the system

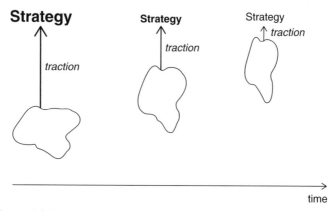

Figure 4.8 Traction decays over time

The strategy then inheres in the system, it becomes 'the way we do things around here', and as such its traction on the system withers away. The strategy in this sense has done its job.

We illustrate this process in Figure 4.8. The direction indicated by the chosen strategy implies a significant systemic shift. The tension between the strategy and the system creates a form of *traction*, which introduces energy into the system. Over time, the degree of traction dampens as the system shifts in the direction of the strategy. Ultimately, traction reduces to a point where it generates very low levels of change-energy into the system. At this stage, there may be sufficient momentum in the system to enable it to thrive or it may be that a shift to another strategy would be beneficial.

When stonemasons build an archway, they first construct a wooden scaffold. Stones, cut to fit the archway are laid from either side of the arch until the final 'keystone' is put in place. The keystone holds the arch together. Then the wooden scaffold can be safely removed. The strategy acts as a scaffold, a device that enables a shift in the system, one that 'withers away' as the required practices become embedded.

The selection of a strategy should shape the choice of initiatives and it should guide decision making. In Figure 4.9 at Time 1, there is a choice of doing A or B. A would be in line with the chosen *low-cost* strategy, whereas B would not be. Similarly at Time 2 the choice of D would not be in line with the chosen direction of travel.

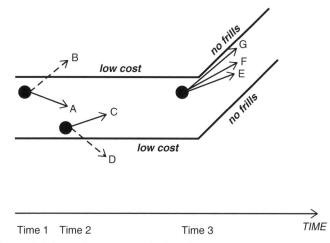

Figure 4.9 How the strategy helps decision making

An initiative may also be a catalyst which changes the strategy. At Time 3 a chosen initiative E reveals an unexpected opportunity. This provokes a debate about whether the firm should pursue this opportunity, which would involve a shift from one strategy to another, for example, from *low cost* to *no frills*. Having chosen to shift to *no frills*, two further initiatives are introduced (F and G) which start to shift the system in a different direction. Thus, there can be a *recursive* relationship between the strategy and selected initiatives.

Choosing a strategy

It may be that there is a strong consensus that a particular strategy is the right one for the business. But because the choice of strategy is potentially critical to the development of the organisation, we suggest that *all strategy options should be explicitly explored.* If as a result of this process the same strategy emerges as the right choice, then there should be a higher level of *belief* in this choice, and *commitment* to making it work.[33]

Here are some guidelines that should improve the selection process and build belief and commitment:

- *Use all the experience, intuition and knowledge available.* We cannot assume that those at the top of the organisation know enough to make the right strategy choice. In all but the simplest of businesses, insights and knowledge will be distributed throughout the structure. This distributed resource needs to be fully exploited in making the choice, so the strategy selection process should involve staff from across the business. There are two benefits from wider involvement: a) you should end up with a better quality decision and b) the process of involvement should help to build commitment to the chosen outcome.

- *Structure a proper debate.* To ensure that all strategy options are thoroughly explored, the debate should be structured. One way of doing this is to allocate people to teams; each team argues the case for one particular strategy. It can be useful to randomly allocate individuals to teams, which avoids some sources of bias and reduces preconceptions. It might be useful to have another team argue the case against each strategy, that is, a *thesis* is put forward that *low cost* is the right option, and the *antithesis* is presented, thus ensuring a fuller consideration of this strategy.

- *Listen carefully to all voices.* It is impossible to ignore the presence of a hierarchy. Some staff will feel intimidated or anxious about expressing their opinions. The 'safe' way of tapping into these ideas and views is to anonymise their contribution. Some ways of doing this: have group discussions which don't involve senior staff where a 'group view' is reported; use anonymous forums, the simplest is post-it notes on whiteboards, but online notice boards could work just as well.

- *Get follow-up information to inform the debate.* This is an iterative process. The first 'pass' through it may indicate where more information might be useful, for example, about customer needs, competitors, changing government regulations, the costs of new technologies.

- *Go where the energy is.* The choice of strategy cannot be a purely 'cognitive' process; emotions are critical. Maybe three strategy options are judged to be feasible, but one of them seems to generate more interest and enthusiasm. Go where the energy in the system is.

The choice of strategy should drive the future evolution of the business. In Figure 4.10 the strategy choice orients the system towards the needs of specific customers. These needs then drive the required

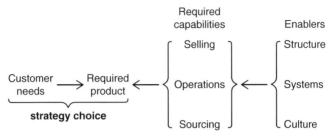

Figure 4.10 Strategy choice informs capability development

products that best meet those needs. On the right of the figure, we have the three value processes of *sourcing, operations* and *selling*. The capabilities *required* across these value processes are driven by the products we need to meet the needs of the target customers. The three value processes are enabled (or sometimes constrained) by the *structures, systems* and *culture* of the business. Capabilities have value only insofar as they are able to deliver customer-perceived use value (PUV) efficiently. And, in turn, the existing structure, systems and culture are only of any value where they *enable* the three core processes to deliver customer PUV.

From strategy choice into action

Figure 4.1 at the start of this chapter sets out the *process* of competitive strategy: once a *strategy* has been selected, this indicates the *capabilities* that are required. We can then identify the *practices* that would enable the development of these capabilities. Then *specific initiatives* are generated which are intended to introduce changes to the value system that are in line with the strategy. Nothing changes, however, until there is some *action* that 'invades' the system to effect changes. Thus, the strategy process moves from a broad intention through to more specific initiatives and then to actions that start to shift the system. The outcomes of the process would be manifested in changes to key variables like quality and unit costs.

Practices

Particular *practices* are associated with each strategy, and we set these out in Chapters 6–11. We have derived these practices from prior work in the fields of organisation design, competitive strategy, operations, marketing and supply chain and logistics.

These practices have also been augmented through the case studies we draw on to illustrate each strategy.

Initiatives

An initiative is a specific *project, experiment* or *pilot test* designed to introduce an appropriate practice into the system. Critical here is the *process of strategy initiatives*. We strongly advocate an incremental approach to introducing an initiative, which builds in 'real-time' feedback. Specifically, we need feedback on how the initiative is impacting unit costs and product quality.

Selecting an initiative is a two-stage process:

Stage 1: The choice of which initiative to trial

Stage 2: The initiative is trialled against the emerging system

Stage 1 is a creative process which generates potential initiatives. Ideas can emerge from many sources: conversations with clients, feedback from procurement staff, suggestions from production staff or ideas borrowed from other industries. In the early stages of the strategy approach, it might be beneficial to pick an initiative that can be trialled and evaluated in a relatively short time frame, and also, hopefully, one that has a good chance of success (we explore the process of strategy initiatives in more depth in Chapter 12).

The feedback generated during Stage 2 should be used to decide whether to **escalate** the initiative, **adjust** it or **abandon** it (see Figure 4.11).

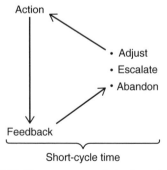

Figure 4.11 The process of strategy initiatives

Strategy initiatives are ways in which we can probe into the system, learn and adapt it, and if this sequence can be accomplished in a short time frame, we can learn faster and also avoid the damaging effects of poor choices. We need to generate a portfolio of initiatives that are informed and guided by a competitive strategy. Some will show immediate and clear benefits, others may not be successful. But feedback is vital in helping ensure that failing initiatives are abandoned before there is a negative impact on the system as a whole. Without the guidance of a competitive strategy, change initiatives may well not produce any synergistic effects as they lack coherence. Indeed, there is a risk with unguided initiatives that they may destroy value, or that whilst they may bring about an improvement in one part of the system, these benefits are more than offset by negative effects elsewhere.

For example, we may decide to reduce our dependence on skilled employees, who might be difficult to hire and retain, by simplifying and de-skilling the work they do. One unintended consequence might be that the new hires are less motivated and require more control and supervision, which increases costs, and they are less capable of adapting and adjusting what they do if customer needs change; thus, the system cannot adapt effectively.

Choices about strategies, practices and initiatives only take effect if there is some associated action which 'invades' the system. Managers have 'agency'; they are able to affect what happens in the system, but they cannot determine the *outcome* of their actions. That is why in Figure 4.11 we identify the role of both action and feedback in this ongoing change process.

The choices that are made are informed by experience of the context and feedback from it. Managers' experiences also inform how they interpret feedback; their cognitions are shaped by their experiences. Managers and their cognitions and choices are just as much a part of the value system as products, equipment, customer loyalty, etc. In Figure 4.12 we tease out these choices to focus attention on the way choices, action and feedback combine to change the value system, whilst recognising that these three processes are necessarily integrated into the system itself.

The choice of strategy, practices and initiatives are *cognitions*. These lead to *action*, and it is action that impacts the value system.

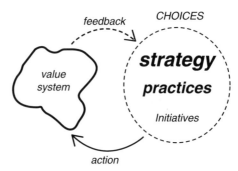

Figure 4.12 Choices, action and feedback in the change process

Managers may decide to pursue a particular strategy, for example, *innovation,* but unless this drives a change in action, there will be no impact on the system.

Can we choose any strategy?

As we illustrate in the next chapter with our Omega Business School case, it is feasible for any business to pursue any strategy. The degree of system change may, though, be more a change of *emphasis* from the current way the business operates, rather than a large-scale or 'transformational' change. Thus, we may aim to become *more adaptive* than competing firms in our market, or *more innovative* than them. If most competitors rarely engage in product innovation, we only need to be a bit better at it than them to gain some advantage. Recall the Usain Bolt principle we set out in Chapter 1.

Similarly, if most rivals compete on the basis of continuous product improvements, as in our *excellence* strategy, we may be able to gain advantage by augmenting this capability by becoming more adaptive and responsive to *changing* customer requirements. Our business will already have an embedded capability to continually improve products or services, which we can now overlay with an additional *adaptive* capability.

Strategy choice and the extent of change

Some strategy choices may be ruled out because we are not able to develop or acquire the resources and capabilities to successfully pursue the strategy. Therefore, in selecting a strategy we need to have some idea what capabilities would be necessary to embark on this trajectory.

In Figure 4.13 we place each strategy somewhere between two groupings of high-level organisational practices. We have focused on *structure* (stable or flexible), *knowledge* (systems or know-how), *centralisation* vs *decentralisation* and a *cost* or a *customer focus*.[34] As depicted in the figure, each strategy tends to orientate the organisation towards one or other clustering of these dimensions. The location of the current value system between these poles is represented by the solid oval. This suggests that there is no clear sense of direction in the organisation; the business is 'muddling through'.[35]

The point of the figure is to demonstrate the extent of change required once a particular strategy has been chosen. For example, were the organisation currently to be orientated towards a *low-cost* strategy, selecting *innovation* would involve considerable change over a range of organisation dimensions. In contrast, were a no-frills strategy to be selected, the extent of required change from *low-cost* to *no-frills* would be relatively small in scale and scope.

Thus, in choosing a strategy it helps to diagnose where the current system might be located. If there is no particular current orientation, as depicted in the Figure 4.13, then any strategy choice would probably involve a similar degree of change.

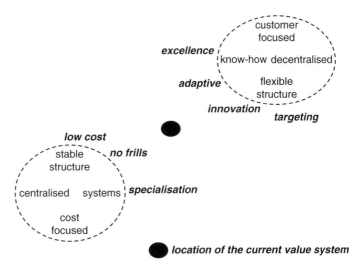

Figure 4.13 Strategies and organisational practices

Pursuing more than one strategy

This figure also indicates why pursuing more than one strategy at the same time is unlikely to be successful. If being *low cost* requires a stable and centralised structure whilst *innovation* calls for a flexible and decentralised structure, trying to pursue both strategies will lead to compromise and confusion.

Most of us perform better if we focus on one task at a time. Similarly, any organisation will likely perform more effectively if it has a clear focus. Thus, as a general principle we would advocate that a firm should pursue one strategy at a time. However, this does not rule out the pursuit of two strategies simultaneously. As we illustrate with the Omega Business School case, it could be that different *units* within a larger organisation could pursue different strategies. The key here is the extent to which the actions of one unit impinge on another and the degree to which they are required to *interact*.

In Figure 4.14 we have two organisational units. Within each unit, there is strong and continuous interaction between the unit members. But there is limited and infrequent interaction *between the units*: occasionally, C from Unit 1 has to liaise with H from Unit 2. In this structure, it is conceivable that each unit could pursue a different competitive strategy. However, this then raises questions about whether both units need to be in the same hierarchical structure, and also would those charged with supervising both of these units have the necessary skills to adapt their approach to the different requirements involved with different strategies? This raises the question of corporate or multi-business structures which we address in Chapter 14.

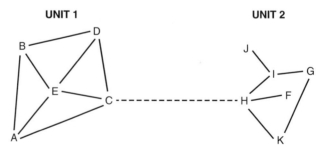

Figure 4.14 Organisational units and their interactions

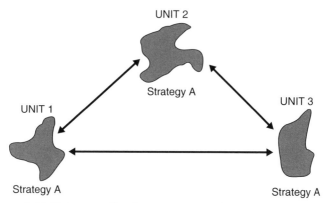

Figure 4.15 Tight coupling between organisational units

Deciding the boundaries that delineate an organisational 'unit' and distinguish it from other units is not straightforward. A strategic business unit (SBU) could consist of the *sourcing, operations* and *selling* activities associated with selling one product into one geographic market. This SBU could pursue a single strategy with probable success. However, it might not be successful if the sales activities are pursuing one strategy, for example, *excellence,* whilst the operations activities are guided by a *low-cost* strategy and sourcing activities are pursuing *innovation.* The likely outcomes would be conflicts across the system leading to poor performance. Thus, where the units are *tightly coupled,* they should pursue the same strategy (see Figure 4.15).[36]

If the business produces a range of similar products and sells them into different markets, it might be feasible to drive change across this spread of activities with the same competitive strategy. Thus, where the *same* strategy is perceived to be able to successfully drive change, then whatever the scope and size of the resulting unit, it is made coherent by the pursuit of a single strategy.

Where the units are loosely coupled, as in Figure 4.16, it is feasible for each unit to pursue a different strategy.

One of the challenges that firms face is the need to deliver a flow of innovations whilst at the same time they are efficiently producing the current portfolio of products. A start-up firm may well discover that over time the capability to innovate has reduced at the

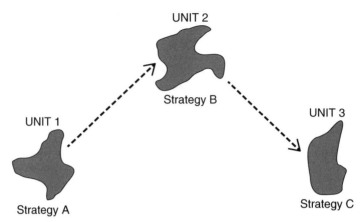

Figure 4.16 Loosely coupled units

same time as the capabilities to deliver existing products efficiently have been building. Our strategies are designed to operate on the *value system as whole,* and they span across the three core processes of *sourcing, operations* and *selling.*

Where we have multi-product organisations, it makes sense to group products and processes into SBUs. The advantage of a single strategy for each SBU is it reduces any confusion about where we are trying to take the system. Pursuing more than one strategy introduces ambiguity and inevitably increases system complexity. In the case of a start-up firm, the need to be innovative and efficient can be dealt with through shifting the strategy over *time.* At no point would the system be *simultaneously* innovative and cost-efficient and this clarity of direction may well contribute to its success. But trying to be efficient and innovative *simultaneously* creates challenges and conflicts in the system. The ability to efficiently *exploit* existing knowledge whilst simultaneously innovating, by *exploring* new knowledge, is referred to as *ambidexterity.*[37]

Ambidexterity

Using our strategy approach we would advocate that if ambidexterity is critical to firm success, then it can be achieved by either:

- *creating separate units,* one that focuses on *innovation* and the other that focuses on *low cost* or *excellence.* In this way, each unit has a clear unambiguous focus for change and development;

- *layering capabilities over time* such that the ability of the system to innovate becomes embedded in the culture and routines and the subsequent reorientation to cost-efficiency does not reduce the capability to innovate.

Neither of these options is easy to deliver. Whilst separation allows each unit to focus on one strategy, it creates the additional challenge of how we *integrate* the outputs from the innovative unit back into the production unit: this is a *coordination* problem. With layering, the challenge to be simultaneously innovative and efficient places significant demands on the capabilities of individuals in the system.

But either of these solutions can work, and as we have argued with the Usain Bolt principle, they only have to work better than rival firms. It is not necessary to deliver outstanding performance in innovation and efficiency; you just need to be a bit better at doing these simultaneously than competing firms.

An alternative solution to the challenge of ambidexterity is to change the *vertical scope* of the business. Vertical scope is all about the 'make or buy' decision, and in the case of ambidexterity, the problem could be resolved by reducing the vertical scope. We could choose to focus the business on innovation and outsource production, as Nike and Apple have chosen to do. Or, as in the case of Bavaria yachts (which we have as one of our cases in the *low-cost* chapter) we could choose to focus on efficient production and partner with specialist boat designers for our product innovations. Chapter 14 explores these vertical scope choices.

Strategy sequencing

We would expect a 'natural' sequencing of strategies as a firm grows. In the start-up phase when the firm is trying to get established, it is likely that different product or service ideas would be trialled. These ideas could flow from the entrepreneur, or they could be strongly indicated by the market. Where the product idea matches a market need, the firm will likely grow. Thus, a combination of *innovation* coupled with responsiveness to market feedback kick-starts the enterprise.

Our own experience of setting up a consulting business suggests to us that an alternative to product innovation in the start-up phase is being *adaptive*. Although we set out to offer a strategy consulting service, many of our initial engagements required us to augment this service with requests for research, or assistance with strategy implementation. The ability and willingness to respond to these customer requests helped establish the business.

As the business responds to growing demand, the emphasis can shift to delivering products more effectively and efficiently. The business settles on a particular combination of products and markets served. We would expect that the *excellence* and *low-cost* strategies may supplant *innovation* and *adaptive* strategies.

A possible pitfall that we have encountered can occur where a strong emphasis on efficiency drives out the firm's ability to innovate. Once competitors start to challenge the firm's market position with product innovations, the firm no longer has the resources to respond through further innovation. It may be that the best option is to re-double efficiency efforts or look to serve a price-sensitive segment with a *no-frills* offer. In crisis, we would expect the immediate adoption of an extreme form of the *low-cost* strategy, directed at short-term cost reductions. Then for the firm to build a way on from the crisis, one of the other strategies might be suitable, with the possible exception of *innovation*, particularly if considerable financial resources are required for R&D.[38]

In the next chapter, we set out the case of a fictional business school *Omega*. We show how it is feasible for Omega to pursue any one of the seven strategies. Thus, choosing a strategy on the basis that it's the one that generates interest and genuine enthusiasm may be the right thing to do. Given that embedding a strategy into the business takes effort and resources and will cause some disruption and present unanticipated challenges, it is essential that there is energy to sustain staff commitment through these episodes.

Application 2: Exploring contrasting strategies

In the process of selecting a strategy, we believe it is important to consider more than one option. Whilst there may be some assumed consensus that one of the seven strategies is the obvious way to go, the process of considering contrasting strategies should at the very least:

- build commitment to the initial choice as being the right one and

- generate ideas which may usefully be incorporated in the strategy change process.

This application could be used as a 'trial run' to familiarise your-selves with the strategies and the strategy process. If possible, split into two teams and work independently. As this is a 'thought exper-iment', to familiarise yourselves with strategy ideas, we would sug-gest setting aside about 90 minutes to work in teams, then share and discuss the ideas you have generated. Allow a maximum of 60 minutes for this stage. It is important to maintain energy through the application, so try to work at a pace. The important thing is familiarisation with the strategies and the process, not the quality or 'accuracy' of the ideas that emerge.

Step 1 Choose two contrasting strategies, for example, *low cost* and *innovation*; *excellence* and *no frills*.

Step 2 Organise into two teams, each team works on one strategy.

Step 3 For each strategy, identify the **target customer** segment(s), the **products and services** you will be offering to the segment, and the sources of **competitive advantage** that you will be build-ing through the strategy change process. The chart in Figure 4.17 can be used to summarise the thoughts of the team.

Step 4 Reconvene as a group and share your ideas.

Chosen play: {*e.g. no frills*}

Target customers	Products/ services	Sources of competitive advantage

Figure 4.17 Strategy choice template

Chapter

5

Omega Business School

We maintain that firms are able to pursue any strategy, as long as the strategy confers some kind of advantage, relative to rival firms. To support this idea, we explore the case of Omega Business School.

We know something about business schools, having both worked in them for many years, so based on this experience, we offer up Omega Business School as a hypothetical case study. Omega is an amalgam of schools we have worked in. The point of the case is to 1) illustrate that any firm can pursue any strategy, 2) work through the changes to practices that will likely transpire from the pursuit of each strategy and 3) indicate some of the challenges involved in delivering the required changes. The choice of strategy has significant and enduring impacts on the business school's value system, as we explain.

Omega: Low cost

A new Dean is appointed at Omega. In recent years, the school has barely broken even. In the past, the school's finances benefited from the enrolment of a large number of full-time MBA students. But the market for MBAs is now very crowded with new business schools setting up across the globe, who are attracting students who might previously have attended Omega. Given that there was no obvious way of growing their way out of the financial difficulties, the Dean decides that a focus on cost-efficiency, the *low-cost* strategy, is the best option.

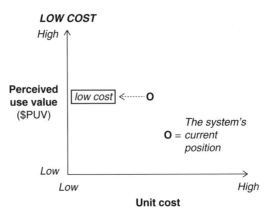

Figure 5.1 Omega's low-cost strategy

A small working group is set up to explore ways of reducing the costs of the core MBA and MSc programmes, which account for 80 percent of the student intake. The group identifies a long list of small changes to the programme curriculum, the enrolment processes and the student support and careers services, which are phased in over a three-month period. The Dean was very aware of the need to make sure that the quality of the student experience was not inadvertently reduced through these changes, and to this end, student focus groups were set up and regularly consulted. Indeed, the students themselves began to suggest changes that could save money.

The early success of these accumulating incremental changes did two things: it made all staff think about unnecessary costs across the whole of the school's operations, and it provoked ideas about more radical changes which could be explored once the 'low-hanging fruit' of relatively quick and painless cost reductions had been achieved.

The next phase involved initiatives to consolidate classes across the suite of MSc programmes. Negotiations with the Vice Chancellor enabled the school to lease a newly built 200-seat auditorium that was part of the University's library complex. The curriculum redesigns to enable large consolidated class sizes met with resistance from some faculty, and the school had to get approval from Senate. The lectures in the large auditorium were delivered by the most experienced professors, and to support the students, a large number of seminar sessions were timetabled. These were run by doctoral students who were trained to facilitate the seminars, and a standard set of resources were developed to support each seminar.

Again, in order to assess the impact of these changes, focus groups were regularly held with faculty and students. One surprising outcome was that many students felt the quality of their programme had improved as a result of being able to interact with many different students who were studying related management specialisms and because everyone got taught by the 'best' professors. Student satisfaction surveys still rate Omega as delivering a good quality experience, despite these cost-reducing initiatives.

Typically, the pursuit of cost-efficiency involves a degree of product standardisation, de-skilling some tasks and reducing expenditure on 'non-core' activities, for example, like research. By really understanding what customers value, it is possible to cut costs without reducing perceived use value (PUV). By pursuing the low-cost strategy Omega is repositioning the school as essentially a teaching school, delivering excellence in teaching, but without having a complementary research capability.

Omega: Adaptive

Omega has already established a reputation for running successful one-week courses for executives. One of the faculty who delivers these short courses is approached by two delegates on a director's development programme who work for the same professional services firm. They want to know whether Omega can deliver a tailored version of the one-week course just for their senior managers.

This request prompts a debate amongst the school's executive about whether to pursue this kind of business. Other colleagues recounted similar requests from Executive MBA students and delegates attending other short courses. The Dean decides that this is an idea worth pursuing and asks Jane, the Head of Executive Courses, to do some exploratory work to test whether this is a viable opportunity for Omega.

Jane gets some assistance from the central marketing team in the University and presents a brief report to the next meeting of the School Executive. The essence of the report is that, yes, there is an

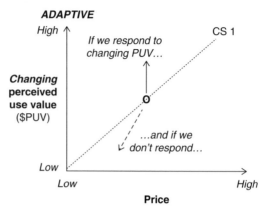

Figure 5.2 Omega's adaptive strategy

opportunity for Omega, but to pursue, it will require the establishment of a dedicated team.

The team is set up, and over time this unit grows to become the largest revenue generator in the school, eclipsing the full time MBA and all MSc programmes combined. The growth and success of the unit is in no small part attributable to the Dean's decision to establish it as a separate unit within the school, and to support its early growth by allowing it to recruit dedicated and specialised faculty. The unit is housed in its own block, near the main school buildings. Whilst initially the customised courses were staffed by existing faculty, over time the unit has drawn on a widening pool of specialist associate faculty. As the needs of their corporate customers have evolved over time, the unit has moved away from 'assembling' a tailored programme from pre-existing half-day modules, for example, on marketing, finance, strategy, to a more bespoke design and development service. This service is adapting to the specific needs of the client, who is typically an HR Director, Head of Talent or Head of Organisational Development.

One-off programmes have morphed into developmental interventions which can span years. Clients have become 'partners' and the unit's reputation is arguably stronger in the corporate executive development market than Omega's. Now, the Unit is typically invited to tender for most large-scale corporate customised development programmes and they have established a research centre, which exclusively investigates the effectiveness of these interventions. So when they tender for a customised intervention, they are able to support their design through past evidence generated through their research programme.

There are some general conclusions we can draw from the *adaptive* strategy pursued by Omega. The strategy was initiated on the back of a perceived opportunity. Key to its success was the provision of adequate resources in its early stages and the establishment of a separate and distinct unit. This enabled the unit to develop the dedicated capabilities to respond flexibly to changing and emerging client needs. The growing pool of associates enabled the unit to allocate the right specialists to meet the specific needs of the client. The fact that they were associates meant that the fixed costs of the unit were kept low and thus any significant fluctuations in the volume of business could be coped with without laying people off, or hiring full-time faculty. Teams are assembled to deliver a specific programme; when it's over the team disperses.

The unit was allowed to develop its own systems, capabilities, brand and logo and was given the freedom to staff the programmes using any mix of full-time or associate faculty. It essentially became a 'business unit' in its own right. Given that the degree of interaction between this unit and the rest of the school became less and less over time, as the unit become virtually autonomous, this example also illustrates that two different strategies could be pursued within the same larger business, but they need to be 'loosely coupled'.

Omega: Excellence

A group of alumni from the MBA class of 1993 ask to meet with the Dean. They have had very successful careers and they wish to 'put something back' and help the school. They are concerned that over the past decade, the school has slid down the *Financial Times* MBA Rankings (*FT* Rankings), and they want to know, if they donated, how the Dean would use the cash to arrest this decline. The *FT* Rankings are the critical signifier of the status of any school.

The Dean convenes a working group to explore some options. One initiative they undertook was to analyse in detail the criteria that the *FT* uses to compile the rankings. They already knew how important getting published in the *FT* list of approved journals was, as were the starting salaries of newly graduated MBAs. But there were other criteria with lower weightings in the index that the school had previously ignored. Were there changes that the school could make that might improve the school's relative performance on these other criteria? Taken together, they may enable Omega to climb the rankings.

But the high weightings on starting salaries and publications were the real challenge, and there seemed to be no low-hanging fruit or quick fixes. A team was established to scrutinise the recently revised list of 45 journals recognised by the *FT*. Three journals presented some opportunities for the school, which already had strength in the more 'applied' management subjects. These were the *Journal of Management Information Systems, Manufacturing and Service Operations Management* and *Production and Operations Management*. In all cases, the school had faculty who had recently published in the journal, and an Omega professor was the current editor of one of them. Three more journals, one focusing on international HRM, were also identified as 'targets' for publication.

The FT index recognises the importance of 'value added' in the MBA. One measure is the student's salary prior to doing the MBA compared to the salary after graduating. The team explored whether it was possible to use the extensive alumni network to target the brightest and best students in developing economies. A

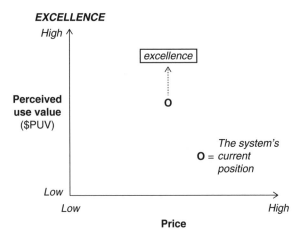

Figure 5.3 Omega's excellence strategy

pilot test of the idea was undertaken using active alumni associations in Indonesia and Malaysia.

The Dean met with the alumni and explained the way forward: targeting five journals on the FT list and promoting the MBA to the brightest and best students in developing economies, not those with wealthy parents. The cash would be used in the following ways: 1) to hire faculty to create teams in three very focused subject areas: logistics, information systems and international HRM, and in that way build 'critical mass'; 2) bursaries would be offered to excellent students from five targeted developing economies, so they effectively get a 'free' MBA; 3) a fund would be established to help build the school's contacts and networks in the five targeted developing countries to build the capability to find the right students; 4) hire the best careers and placement experts to help ensure graduates get the best jobs, and the visas and permits they require.

By focusing on the less recognised *FT* journals and by building a critical mass of expertise in those subject areas, over time the school should be able to increase the volume of *FT* journal publications. The MBA curriculum would be reorientated to leverage the specialist faculty expertise. Very bright and highly motivated students will challenge other students and faculty, creating a culture which should drive up the quality of the MBA programme. Better students getting better jobs combining with an increasing volume of *FT* journal outputs should start to move the school up the rankings. Higher rankings attract more students which enables the school to shift from being a 'recruiting' school to a 'selecting' school. A higher ranking also enables the school to attract and retain better faculty, leading to a virtuous circle.

Thus, whilst the excellence strategy focuses initially on improving the *signifier* of PUV, the *FT* ranking, the initiatives undertaken work through to deliver a better quality experience for the MBA students: livelier class discussions drawing on multinational perspectives, excellent faculty who are leading in their specialisms and an emerging culture of high attainment.

Omega: No frills

A chance conversation between the Director of Graduate Programs and a student on the part time Executive MBA programme set off a train of events. The student explained how difficult and expensive it was for her to attend the three-day modules held every month. She was funding herself and ran a small business in the Scottish Highlands. Whilst she recognised the value in 'face-to-face' interactions, the time commitment and travel costs seemed to her to outweigh the benefits. The Director met with the MBA course leader and asked him if he could explore whether it was possible to deliver a version of the MBA without the need for the student to attend. The obvious solution was a form of 'distance learning', which was not a new idea.

The leader of the MBA, an expert in information systems, also contributed to a programme the school ran for a global IT corporation (XYZ). He had made connections with executives who had attended the programme and arranged a meeting to discuss the challenge of delivering an MBA learning experience remotely.

The outcome is a distance learning MBA. The global IT corporation see this as an opportunity to learn and to trial some of their emerging technologies. In return for branding it the "XYZ" MBA, they have committed their staff and resources. In return, the school has set up several teams to figure out how to deliver the bulk of the curriculum remotely.

The school now offers the Exec MBA across the globe, they have 12,000 students accessing the dedicated course materials, attending webinars scheduled for all time zones and completing online

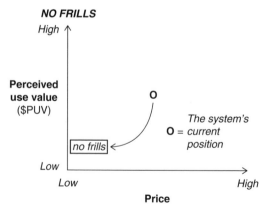

Figure 5.4 Omega's no-frills strategy

assessments which are marked automatically. It's not the same as the 'normal' MBA, but it's 75 percent of the value delivered for a fraction of the costs.

Omega: Targeting

Helen was previously the Executive Director responsible for Talent Management in BAE Systems and was a surprise choice to head up Omega. Helen takes stock of the current position of the school and concludes that they seem to be trying to compete on too many fronts with a limited resource base. Her recent experience at BAE Systems tells her that there are no business schools who are really meeting the needs of large corporations, particularly in the development of future leaders. Whilst most schools offer some short courses aimed at developing leadership capabilities, Helen believes that no school is able to effectively operate as a long-term partner in developing talent. Helen's experience is that schools have a standard course that they run routinely and they are unwilling or unable to adapt what they do to meet the specific needs of a large corporate client.

Through her extensive network, Helen is able to put together a steering group comprising talent directors from seven European corporations. This group holds frequent meetings with a development team within Omega that Helen sets up and leads. Over time, Omega develops a specific set of capabilities that enable them to

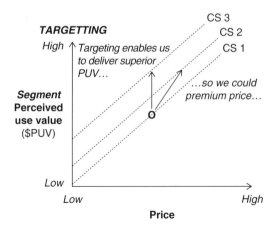

Figure 5.5 Omega's targeting strategy

diagnose, design and deliver long-term partnership relationships with over twenty large corporations. Whilst each contract is unique, they all share the same mix of 'blended learning' and 'live' in-company projects that have proven to deliver the skills required of senior leaders. This focus on the needs of the corporate clients has led to a thriving research centre that explores the impact of different learning designs.

One unanticipated outcome of these developments is a loss of energy and resources devoted to other programmes that the school offers. Eventually, Helen and the University accept that the school is no longer a 'full-service' school, and the declining numbers on the masters programmes leads to a decision to discontinue them. The good news is that the talent development partnerships now deliver more income than the masters programmes ever did, the school has built a reputation for this form of management learning and they have launched a new practitioner-orientated journal.

Omega: Specialisation

Following on from the decision to discontinue post-graduate master's degrees, Helen was searching for new ways of growing the school. Omega's Centre for Enterprise has been at the forefront of research into start-up firms and family-owned and family-run businesses. The centre runs an annual survey of entrepreneurial attitudes which is often quoted in the news media. Whilst the centre has primarily focused on research, it has also developed two short courses aimed at start-ups. These courses are well regarded but they have lacked investment in the past. Helen sets up a small team with researchers from the enterprise centre and

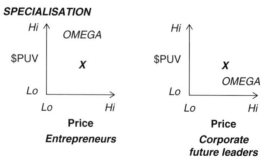

Figure 5.6 Omega's specialisation strategy

two experienced course design and development professionals seconded from the Corporate Future Leaders team. The aim was to create appropriate training and development interventions that can support entrepreneurs.

The outcome is a thriving suite of programmes, supported by coaching and counselling services that complement the Corporate Future Leaders offering. Omega has come to be seen as the specialist provider of development programmes for those assuming enterprise-wide responsibilities. The programmes serve those moving into strategic leadership positions within corporations and entrepreneurs dealing with the challenges of growing small businesses.

Omega: Innovation

The school decides to compete through innovation. The aim is to reorientate the research focus towards a 'practice-based' research agenda. Traditional research in business schools (often referred to as *Mode 1*) is designed to add to an accumulating stock of knowledge about business.[39] The research is conducted using tried and tested methods derived from the social sciences (sociology, economics and psychology), mostly using quantitative techniques, for example, surveys, or secondary data from annual reports, government statistics, etc. This Mode 1 research, when done well, produces contributions to knowledge which are evaluated by other business school academics, who edit the A-rated journals.

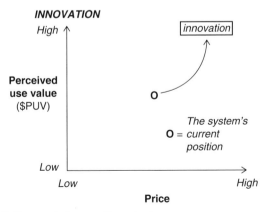

Figure 5.7 Omega's innovation strategy

One of the problems with Mode 1 research is that its journal outputs are not necessarily of any immediate use to managers. The Omega Dean, supported by some faculty but not all, sees there is an opportunity to adopt a 'Mode 2' research agenda. Mode 2 research is about 'knowledge creation in the context of application'. It involves academics working with practitioners to co-create novel solutions to real issues facing a business. On the back of these practice-orientated research initiatives, Omega intends to develop a suite of short courses that communicate these findings to managers, and the managers who attend these courses could be the source of new opportunities to conduct Mode 2 research.

Having made the choice to pursue *innovation*, the first strategy initiative was undertaken by the Research Director, who had contacts with a large civil engineering firm. This research project looked into improving the reliability of health and safety processes across multiple construction sites. The research was conducted by a team of people with complementary know-how: social psychology, operations management, management accounting, organisational development and the team included two managers from the construction company. An additional person was hired from a consultancy, and for the second phase, the team included two researchers from another business school. The findings suggested a certain set of practices which can deliver high reliability, especially when conducting projects using many sub-contractors. These findings formed the basis of a two-day development programme, aimed at construction industry executives and managers with H&S responsibilities. This led to other versions of the basic programme being run for different sectors, including government organisations and NGOs.

The demonstrable success of this project led to the launch of two more Mode 2 research projects. However, some faculty were not convinced that Mode 2 research was necessarily going to enable them to publish in the top ranked journals, which they saw as critical to their career ambitions. Some of them left to join other schools. The reputation of the school as being 'about practice' encouraged more people to join the school's Executive Doctoral programme, new faculty were recruited from consultancies, who were then trained in Mode 2 research techniques. The innovation strategy has enabled the school to carve out a reputation as a distinct school, serving the needs of practitioners.

More generally, introducing an innovation strategy into a traditional school requires a shift to cross-disciplinary team working,
loosening up departmental and job demarcations, forming and
reforming teams of specialists and increasing horizontal communication through the extensive use of liaison devices. The aim is to
generate new knowledge, to explore new course offerings, new
ways of operating, etc. If the early strategy initiatives are successful,
momentum is generated which facilitates the introduction of subsequent initiatives.

Three more case examples

We have used the strategy process with a variety of businesses. Here
we summarise three businesses that each explored the set of seven
competitive strategies. We have selected B2C organisations as it is
easier to understand the different strategy options in these contexts. The process of generating seven options may seem a waste of
time, as probably when embarking on the process only two or three
strategies might be seen to be feasible. However, our experience is
that forcing the exploration of all seven strategies can generate new
insights and possibilities, and in any event the extended consideration results in more confidence in the strategy that is finally
selected.

In Figure 5.8 we set out the seven strategy options generated by
managers working for a pizza delivery company, and in Figure 5.9
we have the options produced by a supermarket chain.

Pizza Home Delivery Co

Specialisation ——→ Focus on drive-through outlets

Adaptive ——→ Extend offer to serve non-pizza eaters

Low cost ——→ Systematic examination of costs across the entire process

Innovation ——→ 'Pizza without the pounds': low calorie pizza recipes

Excellence ——→ Ramp up quality of ingredients

No frills ——→ 'Pizza Pack': limited range of toppings, one size, plus drink for $5

Targeting ——→ Explore lunchtime/office worker market with 'single slice' offer

Figure 5.8 Possible strategy choices: Pizza delivery company

Supermarket Co

Specialisation ⟶ Reduce offer to groceries and fresh food only

Adaptive ⟶ Locally sourced produce wherever possible

Low cost ⟶ Explore franchise model for smaller stores

Innovation ⟶ Develop 'no check-out' technologies

Excellence ⟶ Improve ready meals, delicatessen and fresh meat/fish offer

No frills ⟶ Exploit buying power and beat discounters at their own game

Targeting ⟶ Develop offer to appeal to health- and environment-conscious customers

Figure 5.9 Possible strategy choices: Supermarket

Lastly, in Figure 5.10 we have a retailer of toys who targets the early years (0–8 years).

The process of generating these options is a creative one, where people are using their experience of the company and knowledge of the markets they operate in to generate alternative possible futures for the business. Whilst some were considered to be radical, and too 'left-field', they nevertheless provoked debate. In all three cases, the chosen strategy option incorporated some of the ideas generated from the other options.

Early Years Toy Co

Specialisation ⟶ Only offer 'educational' toys aimed at 0–4 years

Adaptive ⟶ Extend range through alliances

Low cost ⟶ Shift from 35% to 90% sourcing from Far East suppliers

Innovation ⟶ Explore product 'tie-ins' to movies, TV series

Excellence ⟶ Develop learning and child development capabilities of product range/back up with academic research

No frills ⟶ Close stores and shift to online only

Targeting ⟶ Focus on children with special needs/target professionals who support them

Figure 5.10 Possible strategy choices: Toy company

In the next six chapters, we illustrate the competitive strategies with case studies culled from a wide range of industries.

Application 3: Brainstorming all seven strategies

The strategy process is creative, and it is very useful to 'loosen up' our thinking and to challenge assumptions we take for granted about the business. By exploring all *seven* strategies this will generate new insights into what we have as a business and provoke thoughts about what we could be in the future. To sustain energy allow a maximum 120 minutes for this application.

Step 1 The team to read Chapter 5 prior to this session

Step 2 Allocate each *strategy* to a sub-group

Step 3 Decide the *target customers* and the nature of the *products/services* we would offer

Step 4 What changes would be required to the *sourcing, operations* and *selling* processes?

Step 5 Judge the *feasibility* of the strategy

Step 1 Ask all team members to familiarise themselves with Chapter 5 prior to the group work.

Step 2 Either collectively as a group, or if the group is big enough allocate each strategy to sub-groups of at least two people. To reduce the effects of any in-built biases, allocating sub-groups to each strategy should be done by drawing the strategies out of a hat.

Step 3 Each group works independently to generate a feasible future for the business based on the selected strategy. Figure 5.11 provides some structure for the exercise. Having clarified the chosen strategy, for example, *targeting*, the team figures out what this would mean in terms of target customers served and the kinds of products we would be offering (which may be the same as we currently offer, or a subset, or variations to the current product offering may be necessary).

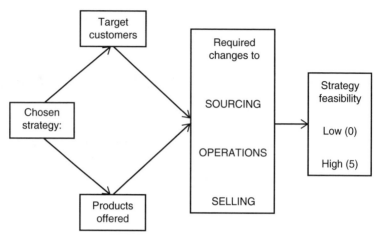

Figure 5.11 Strategy feasibility exercise

Step 4 Having indicated the required products and the target customers, what changes to the *sourcing, operations* and *selling* processes would be necessary to embed the strategy?

Step 5 Then, stepping back from this analysis, how feasible does the team think it would be to pursue this particular strategy? A simple scoring system will capture this judgement: *0 = not really a feasible option, 5 = this is the way forward!*

Part

3

Case studies

Chapter

Excellence

To recap, a competitive strategy indicates a broad *direction of travel*. The choice of strategy indicates what *capabilities* we need to develop and what *structures, systems* and *culture* would enable these capabilities to thrive. These in turn inform the choice of initiatives, projects and experiments. The effectiveness of any particular initiative should be enhanced through *synergies* that develop across a set of initiatives. These synergies are more likely to be realised where the selection of initiatives is guided by a clear strategy.

In this and the following five chapters we illustrate each strategy through a series of brief case studies. These examples can help in identifying some *generic practices* that might be adapted to the circumstances of a particular business. To be clear, these case examples illustrate the success of a particular strategy. Success is driven by the combination of the strategy and the context, as illustrated in Figure 6.1.

The *strategy* interacts with the *context* of the organisation to produce *outcomes*. The cases we have selected are where the interactions between strategy and context have produced positive performance

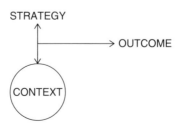

Figure 6.1 Strategy, context and outcome

outcomes. As the context changes, the interactions between strategy and context will necessarily change, as will the outcomes. Therefore, we should expect that changes in context that are not matched by appropriate changes to the organisation and possibly to the selection of a different strategy are likely to result in inferior outcomes. Thus, these cases are examples of successful matches of strategy, choice and context. Whilst we present examples of past successes there is no guarantee that any of the companies we use as illustrations will continue to be successful into the future; if the context changes significantly, but their strategy choice remains fixed, they may experience a decline in performance.

We begin with the *excellence* strategy. The intention behind *excellence* is to embed practices that improve customer perceived use value ($PUV) whilst keeping costs under control. This gives the firm the ability to offer superior levels of $PUV which may enable premium pricing. Superior $PUV is delivered through a continuous flow of incremental product or service improvements.

As we have emphasised, no matter what we choose to do 'inside' our organisation, what materialises in the market place is ultimately in the gift of customers. The prices we can command and the volumes we can sell depend on how customers *perceive* our products and services.

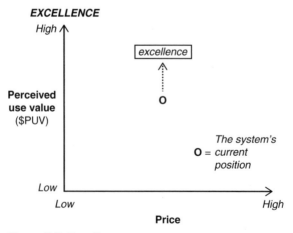

Figure 6.2 Excellence

Case study
John Lewis

Our first case is the retailer John Lewis. We chose this case as it illustrates how an excellence strategy doesn't just apply to 'professional services' organisations in sectors like law, medicine, accountancy, etc. A culture of excellence can be embedded in most organisations. But it takes time to build and many different aspects of the value system need to align to ensure that the excellence culture persists.

John Lewis is one of the best known and admired department stores operating in the United Kingdom. The story of John Lewis is unique in terms of its evolution and its partnership structure. The origins of John Lewis begin with John Lewis (senior) who made his way to London in 1856 and worked as a salesman and then as a silk buyer for an Oxford Street draper. John Lewis' early retailing philosophy was to buy good quality merchandise and sell it at a modest mark-up. His store carried a wide range of products with little effort invested in displaying it and no advertising. A large part of the initial success of his store lay in his skills in sourcing quality goods at competitive prices. Rather than offering frequent price cutting 'sales', he was intent on building a stable and permanently in-demand business.

Some of the early principles which John Lewis embodied, that is, a wide range of merchandise, modest mark-ups, pricing to reflect good 'value for money' for customers, persist through to this day. But the individual who had the greatest impact on the John Lewis business was his first-born son, John Spedan Lewis.

Given an opportunity to manage one of the largest retail properties in the group, known as Peter Jones, situated in Chelsea, J. Spedan Lewis could make changes as he saw fit. He determined that the underlying problem was that staff had no incentive to do a good day's work because their pay and conditions were not aligned with that of the business. He implemented a number of changes to address this including shortening the working day, creating a commission-based reward system for each department, paying sales staff based on sales levels achieved and establishing regular meetings at which staff could raise grievances.

J. Spedan Lewis went on to make further changes to improve the conditions for staff. These included granting a third week's paid holiday per year; installing hot and cold running water in staff bathrooms; publishing a fortnightly newspaper to share information with staff on the performance of the business; instituting a staff council; and endorsing the first decision of the staff council to pay staff weekly instead of monthly.

What was the rationale behind J. Spedan Lewis's changes? His radical idea was that the profits of the business should not be paid solely through to shareholders. Instead, shareholders should receive a reasonable return for their provision of capital. His view was that employees should receive a 'fairer share' of the profits that they generated. His idea of 'fair' extended to include sharing knowledge and power with his staff. He backed his ideas with direct action. One of the most significant acts, initiated in 1920, was to start distributing Peter Jones preference shares to staff, who were now called 'Partners'.

In 1925, J. Spedan Lewis devised the slogan 'Never knowingly undersold' which remains in force to this day. This slogan gave customers assurance that they were not paying any more for identical goods available at any other store. In 1950, he executed a deed of settlement which passed ownership of the John Lewis partnership to trustees to hold for the benefit of those who worked in the business.

One of the lasting legacies of John Spedan Lewis is the unique organisational structure and governance practices that apply through the business to this day. Each employee is a Partner in the John Lewis Partnership and has the opportunity to influence the business through branch forums and divisional councils. Sitting above the branch forums is the Partnership Council, to which Partners elect over 80 percent of the representatives. The councils have the power to discuss 'any matter whatsoever' and are responsible for the noncommercial aspects of the business.

The Partnership Board is responsible for the commercial activities. Five of the board's directors are elected by the Partnership Council, five are appointed by the Chairman and the other two board positions are assumed by the Chairman and Deputy Chairman. Every non-management Partner also has an open channel for expressing his or her views to management and the Chairman. In weekly in-house magazines, partners can write anonymous letters holding management to account.

As part of looking after its own, the John Lewis partnership has a very extensive programme of social activities for its Partners, including two large country estates with parkland, playing fields and tennis courts; a golf club; a sailing club with five cruising yachts; and three country hotels offering holiday accommodation for the Partners and families.

Partners also are participants in a favourable pension scheme; they receive generous holiday allowances and are eligible to receive an annual bonus which is a share of the profits. The bonus is calculated as a percentage of salary, with the same percentage applying to all partners, from top management to the shop floor staff. The percentage varies each year depending on results, but in recent years has varied from between 9 percent and 20 percent of an individual's annual salary.

The amalgam of the core retailing principles of John Lewis senior and the philosophical principles of John Spedan Lewis combine to form a unique organisation which delivers superior value to its customers. The retailing principles that persist include offering a wide range of merchandise, pricing goods to represent value for money (generating modest profits) and putting more emphasis on merchandise sourcing, selection and availability, than store presentation alone.

John Lewis continues to effectively communicate its value-for-money proposition. It is able deliver on its competitive price promise through a combination of factors including smart sourcing, leveraging buying power and economies of scale in logistics and distribution. These factors reflect many of the original ideas developed in the early stages of the John Lewis business. The partnership structure aligns well with delivering both high service levels to customers, whilst keeping costs under control.

The Partnership philosophy, focused on partner well-being, results in greater staff retention and this in turn produces more knowledgeable staff. Happy and knowledgeable staff, who collectively benefit from the success of the store chain, translates to delivering better customer service.

Some of the merits of the John Lewis employee-owned business model were confirmed in a study undertaken by Lampel, Bhalla and Jha from the Cass Business School, London. They concluded that employee-owned firms have a lower risk of business failure, and during a recessionary period actually outperform in their markets. They also concluded that employee ownership confers particular advantage in knowledge and skill-intensive industries through building and sustaining in-depth knowledge competencies.

The collective synergistic benefits created from all of the practices that John Spedan Lewis put in place are significant and have proved durable too. The partnership structure delivers an alignment of incentives and motivation. This structure is relatively democratic in that any issue or suggestion can be raised by any partner through the various forums. But a significant benefit results from the partners being the eyes and ears of the business. The whole business is continuously striving to deliver excellent service. In the John Lewis business, providing excellent service to customers is valued above all else.

So how do these practices translate to superior $PUV for customers? Key PUV dimensions, for the purposes of illustration, include the following: quality and attractiveness of merchandise; comfort of store environment; ease of shopping experience; wide range of merchandise on offer; knowledgeable staff; customer service and attentiveness; and low price. These PUV dimensions and illustrative ratings for John Lewis are set out in Figure 6.3.

When it comes to price, John Lewis markets itself as very price-competitive reflected in its pledge of *never knowingly undersold*. In the below figure, the price sensitivity of customers is reflected in the high weighting – 40 percent – afforded to the "Low Price" dimension. The combination of creating superior use value (PUV) and delivering at a relatively low price reflects a compelling value for money proposition for its customers.

We would argue that John Lewis has managed to instil a *culture of professionalism* in a sector where typically front-line staff are treated quite differently, for example, low pay and little training, 'zero-hours' contracts and high staff turnover. The John Lewis culture has emerged over decades and is a valuable asset for the company, reflected in delivering relative higher levels of $PUV, which other retailers find difficult to replicate.

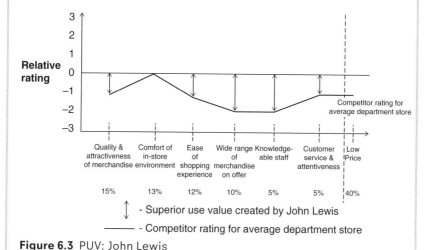

Figure 6.3 PUV: John Lewis

Case study
Lexus

The excellence strategy involves a relentless focus on delivering superior customer-perceived value. A good example of how this can deliver sustained success is Lexus. Most people are familiar with the Lexus brand and the high-quality reputation of its cars. However, when Lexus was launched, many were unaware that Lexus was a division of Japanese automaker Toyota Motor Corporation. How Toyota established Lexus as a high-quality luxury automotive brand is an extraordinary illustration of the *excellence* strategy in action.

Lexus originated from a project, code named "Flagship One" (F1), which began in 1983. Toyota chairman Eiji Toyoda issued a challenge to build the world's best car, which became the mission for the F1 project. The steer provided to the F1 designers was to target their new sedan at international markets. In response, the F1 designers focused their sights on US luxury consumers as the ideal target customers.

To better understand their target customers, Toyota F1 researchers visited the United States in May 1985 to observe and study the lifestyle and tastes of wealthy American consumers. This effort included the use of focus groups, conducting market research and even embedding a research team in Los Angeles to directly observe the lifestyles of luxury consumers.

After a period of observation and research, the F1 designers drafted their designs and specified exceptionally high-quality criteria to apply in the manufacturing process. These high-quality specifications resulted in significant changes to manufacturing facilities, production lines, plant roles and responsibilities, and performance management and measurement systems.

Whilst the first Lexus vehicles were manufactured in Toyota's main Tahara plant, additional investments in the plant were made exclusively for the Lexus. Entirely new assembly lines were developed for the Lexus models that incorporated specialised manufacturing equipment. New manufacturing techniques, such as welding processes, were developed. Furthermore, the level of quality control applied to the Lexus, covering body panel fit tolerances and paint quality standards and other aspects, were more stringent than those applied to other Toyota models.

To ensure the highest standards of quality, only the best technicians, identified through performance evaluations and ranked by skill grade, were accepted to work on the Lexus assembly line. Toyota also assigned its highest level engineers to be responsible for maintaining production standards at key points in the assembly process, such as testing engine performance. Upon final assembly, further quality tests were conducted including visually inspecting for flaws, test drives at high speeds and vibration tests.

So effective was the F1 design team and the technicians that built Lexus, the minimal barely detectable vibrations became a feature in the debut TV advertisement for the Lexus LS400. In this ad, 15 champagne glasses were stacked on the hood of a revving LS400 with no detectable movement. In keeping with the champagne hood test, the advertising team developed an apt marketing slogan following a visit and observation of Lexus designers in Japan – 'The Relentless Pursuit of Perfection'.

Consistent with developing separate assembly lines and new manufacturing techniques, an entirely separate sales, marketing and dealer network was created for the Lexus brand. Lexus' early marketing success is largely attributed to higher levels of perceived quality and lower price than competitors, bolstered by a reputation for dependability and reliability. This enabled Lexus to attract customers and gain share in the luxury mass-market car sector. Whereas European rivals leveraged their decades of heritage and pedigree, Lexus' reputation rests primary on its perceived quality, a reputation that has helped to establish Lexus as a luxury brand.

During the six-year F1 project period, 1983–89, Lexus was also competing with local Japanese automakers who were seeking to break into the luxury car sector. The opportunity for Japanese manufacturers to export more expensive car models had grown in accordance with terms negotiated by Japanese government and US trade representatives. For example, in 1986, Honda launched its *Acura* marque in the United States; in 1987 Nissan unveiled its plans for a premium brand, *Infiniti*; and in 1988 Mazda began selling the Mazda 929 in North America. However, none of these rivals were ultimately as successful as Lexus.

An objective measure of the success of Lexus is reflected in industry ratings of build quality, owner satisfaction and reliability. Lexus has consistently outperformed other manufacturers in successive years since 1995. J. D. Power and Associates, a Global Market Research Firm, has named Lexus the most reliable brand in the United States fourteen times since 1995, based on its Vehicle Dependability Survey of over 53,000 vehicle owners in the first three years of ownership. In a survey of over 16,000 vehicle owners in the UK, Lexus was the highest scoring manufacturer for 10 years in a row.

Through pursuing an *excellence* strategy, Lexus has effectively achieved quality parity with European luxury vehicle manufacturers on key quality dimensions. This impressive result is the outcome of a deliberate and sophisticated engineering project and considerable investment. The extended development process for the Lexus LS400 involved 60 designers, 24 engineering teams, 1,400 engineers, 2,300 technicians, 220 support workers, approximately 450 prototypes and over $1 billion in costs.

Case study
Birmingham Children's Hospital[40]

Our final illustrative case of the *excellence* strategy is perhaps a surprising choice: it is Birmingham Children's Hospital, part of the UK's National Health Service. We think that the transformation effected at the hospital captures the essence of the *excellence* strategy.

Birmingham Children's Hospital, has become the first of its kind to receive a rating of 'outstanding' from healthcare inspectors in England. Birmingham Children's Hospital was criticised eight years ago for having insufficient numbers of beds, operating theatres and trained staff, but now the Care Quality Commission has praised the hospital for working effectively to provide the best care.

Supporting the whole family and helping young patients feel relaxed in a busy and daunting environment are amongst the extra challenges for specialist children's hospitals, beyond providing good medical and nursing care.

Sarah Jane Marsh is the Chief Executive who oversaw the turnaround. She explains how they did it: 'The main thing we have done to make a difference is to put children, young people and families at the heart of everything we do and continually do the right thing for them. Previously staff had got the ideas for how we needed to do that. They knew what needed to happen in the hospital, but we as the leadership team weren't listening properly. Over the last eight years we've continually invested, listened and developed and supported our staff into a fantastic team that now deliver outstanding care.'

She adds that 'staff are the people who have got the answers to all the problems in the NHS, from the little things on the wards to the big strategic changes. If we listened to the clinical staff on the front line and those that support them we can make the changes that are right for families and in our case, obviously, listening to the children as well.'

But there was not instance success: 'It took a long time. The first two or three years after the report we focused on getting everything right, so getting the right equipment, the right number of theatres, beds, etc. The last five years we have focused on the culture. I was very hit by the statement that organisations don't have two cultures: the way you treat the staff is the way the staff will treat the patients and families, and so compassion is at the heart of how we lead and develop our teams at the hospital, and in return for that they give compassion and care to every single one of our patients. Transformation requires that listening and continuous improvement approach, so I am confident that we can continue with using the same methods in a resource constrained environment. Of course, if more money was available we could do even more and even better things.'

Excellence practices

An embedded *excellence* strategy delivers a continual flow of incremental improvements to product/service quality. To sustain advantage, these processes of product enhancement must be difficult for competitors to replicate.

The excellence strategy requires a dynamic and continuous focus on understanding what customers value, converting these understandings into quality criteria and developing the system to deliver quality as efficiently as possible. Excellence works best where there is some stability in customer needs and in the product solutions to meet those needs. These stable conditions enable the development of *deep know-how* which is directly connected to improving customer-perceived use value ($PUV). The stability in customer needs enables the closer alignment of $PUV with the 'internal' measures of product quality.

We chose our cases to illustrate that *excellence* can be embedded across many different industry contexts; here we have a diverse selection of organisations: a retailer, a car manufacture and a hospital. What they have in common is a *culture* which drives the relentless pursuit of customer value.

Those that succeed and persist in their industries deliver excellence through integrating practices into a coherent system. These practices reinforce each other to deliver high levels of performance. In addition, the complex relationships between these practices make it much more difficult for rival firms to imitate this web of synergies. In Figure 6.4 we illustrate how some of these practices interact to deliver superior outcomes for a professional services firm. At the heart of the firm is the individual and collective **know-how** embedded in the system. This is what clients are paying premium prices to gain access to.

One of the benefits of a strong brand and reputation is that it *lowers* selling and sourcing costs. A well-known and respected brand reduces the need to spend on marketing and selling, and the best graduates will want to work for the best firms, so sourcing costs are lower.

Practices associated with the excellence strategy are summarised in Figure 6.5. We group them into those associated with the *culture, structure* and *systems* of the business. We use this categorisation for

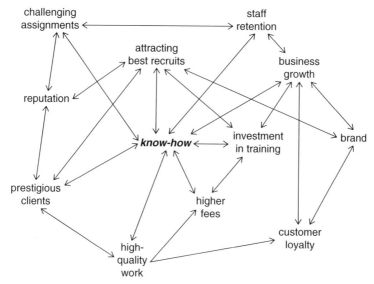

Figure 6.4 Synergistic linkages in professional services

all of the seven strategies, and we put culture first in the list as it reflects the most enduring and significant features of the strategy, and these practices are typically the most challenging to change and to embed in the system.

EXCELLENCE: Practices

Culture

- *values knowledge creation, sharing and retention and where insights into customers' needs are widely shared and valued*
- *trust-based relationships which value professional expertise*

Structure

- *specialisation of tasks to facilitate the building of deep expertise*
- *decentralised structures that encourage decision making by those with the greatest expertise and who are closer to the problems and issues*
- *strong coordination mechanisms to ensure specialised activities are integrated to deliver customer value*

Systems

- *reward systems that recognise and encourage excellence*
- *building strong brand and reputation which improves bargaining relationships with customers and suppliers*

Figure 6.5 Excellence practices

The practices we have selected are informed by prior contributions to our understanding of the 'fit' between particular strategies and organisation structures, systems and cultures that support them. In deriving appropriate *enabling practices*, we draw extensively on the theory of organisational configurations, notably the work of Miles and Snow, Mintzberg, and Miller and Friesen.[41]

This set of practices is not exhaustive and will differ from firm to firm. But for firms pursing the excellence strategy, the above set of generic practices drawn from the case studies and prior research should stimulate some useful thinking about how to translate the excellence strategy into action.

Application 4: Envisioning the future culture of the business

This application should be used for all of the seven strategy options. The purpose of the application is to try to think about what the business would *look like* and *feel like* if we successfully embedded a chosen strategy. This is a powerful way of generating insights into what might need to change and what 'success' would be like, and it can help to generate some energy to drive through the necessary changes.

As we have stressed from the start of the book, all businesses are complex open systems. There is a danger that we focus only on those aspects of the organisation that are easy to identify, discuss and change like the formal organisation structure (who reports to whom, which activities get grouped together), the physical location, equipment, systems, etc. But although these are more amenable to analysis, they only account for a fraction of the range of variables that go to make up any business.

Gerry Johnson derived a very valuable tool, the 'culture web', from his research into strategy processes, which we have used over many years to surface issues around organisational culture. Here we offer an application of the technique that can help us envision what the future might look like, following the pursuit of a particular strategy.

Johnson's Culture Web

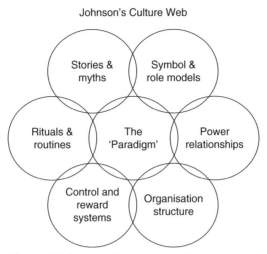

Figure 6.6 Johnson's culture web

The components of the culture web are explained in what follows.

Routines: 'The way we do things around here' on a day-to-day basis. What does a routine day look like for someone working in sourcing, operations or selling?

Rituals: Activities or events that reinforce what is currently important in the business, for example, what we do when someone leaves or joins the business, formal events like the annual sales conference.

Stories: What we choose to remember and recount to ourselves and new hires who tell us something about how we see the business. They are often stories about heroes, mavericks, past disasters and successes.

Symbols: These convey meanings over and above their functional purpose, for example, office locations, sizes, who has a desk, who hot-desks, job titles and the informal language used to describe customers.

Power structures: Who has formal power? And who has *informal* power, where they seem to exert influence over decisions and resource allocations?

Organisation structure: The roles, and reporting relationships and how we coordinate across different activities and departments.

Control and reward systems: How do we monitor and measure activity, and what people get rewarded for doing.

Paradigm: The beliefs and assumptions held in common but often taken for granted. These shape how people think about the business and are usually reinforced by the other elements of the culture.

We have long experience of using the culture web diagnostically. Typically, having explained the elements of the web, the group are tasked with constructing the web for their **current** business. This invariably is used as an opportunity to dump critical and negative feelings and attitudes about the business. This happens despite us briefing the activity in a 'neutral' way. We can only conclude that for most managers, they are using this as an opportunity to raise a host of issues and frustrations they experience with the way things currently are in the business. This may be a necessary cathartic process, we don't know as we haven't done the research to prove it!

But this application of the web we see as enabling the team to explore a more holistic *impression* (because that's all it can be, given complexity) of what the future state of the business might be if we opted for this particular strategy.

Step 1 The team to familiarise themselves with the *culture web*.

Step 2 Divide into two sub-groups. Each group selects *one* strategy to work on.

Step 3 Assuming the strategy has been successfully introduced, each sub-group envisions what the culture **might be like,** using the seven categories in the culture web. Capture these agreed ideas on a flip chart.

Step 4 Sub-groups re-convene and share their ideas.

Whether this snapshot of the future is enticing or dystopian rather depends on the mood and inclination of the team at the time of creating the future culture web. Clearly, this envisioning of the future is entirely subjective and will be the outcome of a collective process. Nothing produced is 'true' in any sense, but what it can do is paint in many of the 'blanks' that a focus on purely 'objective' changes will inevitably create.

Chapter

7

Low cost

The aim of the *low-cost* strategy is to deliver acceptable levels of customer PUV but with a continuous and relentless focus on cost reduction. Critical to successfully executing the low-cost strategy is a detailed knowledge of customer needs and what they really value in our products. With this understanding, it is possible to identify and strip out unnecessary expenditures which don't deliver $PUV. When pursuing a low-cost strategy, obtaining continuous customer feedback is vital to ensure that cost reductions do not damage PUV.

This strategy is designed to deliver equivalent PUV at lower *costs.* The products remain the same, the customers served remain the same, but the unit cost of producing the products is continually reducing.

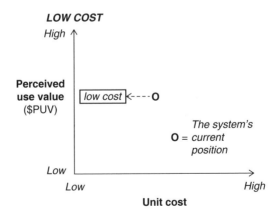

Figure 7.1 Low cost

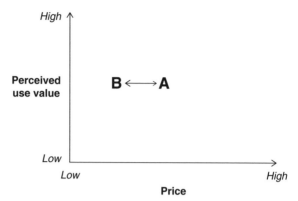

Figure 7.2 Low cost: Pricing options

This is achievable if the low-cost strategy initiatives are able to deliver cost savings that *are independent of sales volumes.* For example, improved quality assurance processes could reduce scrap and rework costs and warranty claims. These benefits are not dependent on increasing sales volumes.

In Figure 7.2 we set out the pricing options that a low-cost strategy might allow. At A we keep prices the same and reap the benefits of lower unit costs in the form of higher margins (Price *less* Unit cost). If there are significant cost advantages that can result from larger sales volumes, then a shift to point B might be beneficial. Volume-sensitive cost savings would be economies of scale and the advantages of accumulating experience at a faster rate than rivals. One obvious scale advantage would be leverage over suppliers. If you buy larger volumes of components, raw materials or power, this should enable you to negotiate lower prices from your suppliers.

The low-cost strategy is particularly suited to contexts where customer needs and product solutions remain relatively *stable.* A stable environment permits a continuous focus on cost reduction. If the basic features of the product or service remain stable, we can focus attention on reducing costs whilst maintaining product quality. This stability means we can expect that the outcomes of various trials and initiatives will be valuable in the future, leading to sustainable process improvements.

Failure demand

There are many ways of reducing costs in the process of creating products. One critical start point in any efficiency strategy is to really understand what customers' value in the product. There is no point in incurring costs which don't feed through to customer PUV. Clearly, if we can get the product 'right first time', then this helps keep costs down. The same issues occur in service industries, and there may be some 'low-hanging fruit' to be picked where the service operations fail to deliver what the client or customers wants 'first time'. The term *failure demand* has been coined to capture this idea of costs incurred by failing to deliver satisfaction to the customer during the first interaction between the firm and the customer.

In Figure 7.3 we depict the results of *failure demand*. The value system incurs increased costs due to often repeated demands on the system caused by our inability to solve the customer or service user's problem first time. For example, an insurance company's claims department routinely fields multiple calls from a single claimant due to an inability of the first call made to resolve the claim. The effect on the system is to not only increase costs but also drag down the customers' perception of the organisation. These demands on the system caused by failure can be

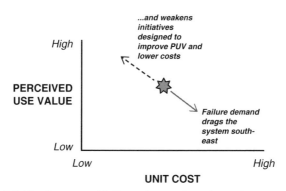

Figure 7.3 The impact of failure demand on the value system

substantial, and relatively simple changes can help to eliminate them. One would be to empower call centre staff in the insurance company to make more decisions. This would involve an initial investment in training which could reduce follow-up calls to a minimum.

Case study 1
Bavaria Yachts

Traditional images of Bavaria are likely to involve lederhosen, veal sausage, snow-covered mountains and beer-drinking festivals. Yet amongst this agricultural heartland of Germany has emerged one of the world's leading yacht manufacturers. Located miles away from the nearest body of water, Bavaria Yachts is one of the largest and most successful boatbuilding companies in the world. In their manufacturing facility, Bavaria Yachts combines German engineering principles and European craftsmanship to produce a fleet of sturdy, high-quality yachts ranging in size from 28 feet to 57 feet.

Yacht building is a sector that has traditionally been a craft industry where yachts are built as one-offs or in small batches. Bavaria Yachts' success is largely due to its philosophy of importing advanced manufacturing techniques and equipment into the boatbuilding process. In 1979, Winfried Hermann, the founder, created this philosophy and successfully built his company to be unique amongst all other boat manufacturers. Given his focus on manufacturing efficiency and automating many aspects of the boatbuilding process, industry commentators describe Hermann as 'the Henry Ford of the Yacht Production world'.

Bavaria Yachts lead its sector in utilising advanced manufacturing techniques, computer applications and robotics that combine to form the world's most modern boatbuilding plant. All of the yachts are created in a single production facility, located in Giebelstadt. Siting production in a single location helps to ensure consistently excellent construction standards and the maximisation of economies of scale. The Bavarian shipyard has state-of-the-art production facilities, with high-precision robots and CAD/CAM programmes working seamlessly together with skilled craftspeople over a six-kilometre assembly line.

Examples of production innovations include: lamination halls with permanent humidity and temperature controls, laser-assisted accuracy for CNC milling machines, automated varnishing lines and beam-to-beam assembly, rather than traditional bow to stern assembly. The result of these innovations is to maximise through-put, minimise man-hours and achieve consistency of outputs. The outcome is a significantly lower cost per yacht compared to competitors.

Although Bavaria Yachts are produced using large batch and mass production techniques, the yachts themselves are pro-duced upon receipt of an order from the dealer. This enables each customer to configure an individual yacht to their tastes from a range of options. The speed of Bavaria's production line permits production 'on demand' and at the same time incorporat-ing a degree of customisation.

Bavaria Yachts has produced over 30,000 yachts since 1979. Its current production mix is split approximately 60 percent sailing yachts and 40 percent motor boats, with an output of 3,000+ yachts every year.

From Bavaria's perspective, it is important to achieve low-cost design and manufacture to deliver Bavaria's pricing strategy, to undercut its major competitors. The combination of achieving near parity in terms of manufacturing quality against its competi-tors, and doing so at a significantly lower cost through utilising efficient manufacturing techniques, is at the heart of how Bavaria Yachts creates and captures value.

Bavaria combines its in-house manufacturing capability with *out-sourced* yacht design expertise. They draw on prominent naval architects Bruce Farr Yacht Design for hull designs, and Design Unlimited, a British firm, for its interior designs on its award-winning Vision series of yachts.

In summary, Bavaria Yacht's processes have been developed from ideas and equipment used in other manufacturing sectors. The transfer of knowledge into Bavaria Yachts provides it with an innovative edge that enables it to deliver equivalent $PUV at lower costs than rival boat builders. By outsourcing yacht design, it can focus energy and attention on reducing manufacturing costs.

Case study 2
McDonald's

McDonald's needs no introduction. As the world's largest chain of hamburger fast-food restaurants, it is hard to argue with McDonald's phenomenal success. This success is largely attributed to Ray Kroc who joined the company as a franchise agent in 1954. He subsequently purchased the chain in 1961 from the McDonald brothers, Richard and Maurice, for $2.7 million and directed its worldwide growth through to his retirement in 1974.

Ray Kroc's approach centred on the relentless standardisation of the tasks involved in making and selling hamburgers. This drive was rolled out across the whole chain of franchises. In 2016 revenues were $25 billion, and $14 billion was returned to shareholders through dividends and share buyback. McDonald's serve around 65 million customers daily in 119 countries across 35,000 outlets.

Relative to its traditional competitors, McDonald's has consistently achieved a competitive advantage, resulting in it being a clear market leader with the largest share of the fast-food sector.

A large part of McDonald's success has come about from its continuous and relentless focus on refining its processes to eliminate inefficiencies and make them as low cost as possible. The focus that McDonald's places on process improvement and execution has allowed it to achieve unparalleled levels of consistency in food service provision.

To achieve this consistency, McDonald's built its own Hamburger University, a 130,000 square foot training facility located in Oak Brook, Illinois. This facility is designed to instruct personnel employed by McDonald's in the various aspects of restaurant management. Restaurant employees receive approximately 32 hours of training in their first month with McDonald's and more than 5,000 students attend annually. No rival fast-food providers have yet matched this level of training and detailed work process design. The stability that is inherent in the McDonald's business allows it to make significant investments in continuous learning and education of its managers and workforce.

McDonald's has shown itself to be the leader in the fast-food sector in terms of standardising its core processes. This system has been perfected by McDonald's over many years of reengineering and refining processes and procedures.

Other practices that are evident at McDonald's include work simplification and deskilling. This involves breaking down tasks to their most basic level and then allocating them to specific roles and individuals to perform. This helps achieve specified levels of product and service quality at low costs; it also allows for relatively unskilled staff to be able execute the required tasks. It's not necessary to be a chef or even a cook to be able to help produce a Big Mac. But other basic skills, such as being alert, for example, to a timer, the ability to focus and the ability to work at pace are all needed.

Through the codification and measurement of key metrics, McDonald's is able to identify superior work practices which can then be transferred across other franchises and outlets. The result is the enterprise-wide adoption of best practices all geared towards running low-cost and efficient operations.

McDonald's is also very effective at exploiting its leverage with suppliers, which enables the company to acquire quality foodstuffs and other materials, for example, packaging, at lower costs than rivals.

All of the practices seen in this case analysis are consistent with a *low-cost* competitive strategy. There is no disputing that the superior returns that McDonald's consistently generates are largely due to its ability to control costs. Low-cost practices, if coherent and well executed, can provide a cost advantage that is reinforced as firms scale up, contributing to a significant and enduring competitive advantage.

However, when customer needs and competitors change, firms need to respond. Here is an excerpt from an article in *The Guardian* on Monday 25 January 2016.

McDonald's is to introduce table service and cooked-to-order gourmet burgers at hundreds of restaurants across Britain as it tries to head off competition from upmarket rivals.

The fast food chain will roll out table service at 400 revamped restaurants before the end of 2016 after a successful trial last year. It will also double the number of locations selling a new range of premium burgers, called the Signature Collection.

The initiatives are designed to modernise McDonald's restaurants and attract more families. The company is facing growing competition from gourmet burger brands such as Five Guys and Shake Shack, Mexican chains such as Chipotle and established rivals Burger King and KFC.

McDonald's had been trialling table service in 14 restaurants. The number of locations selling the Signature Collection will double from 30 to 60 within six weeks. These burgers come in classic, BBQ and spicy versions and are served in brioche-style buns. They cost $4.69.

The company is taking advantage of the table service system to launch the burgers. The extra thickness of the meat means customers have to wait for their burger to be served, in contrast to hamburgers and Big Macs.

McDonald's successful *low-cost* strategy eliminates the need for table service and delivers *fast* food through the precooking of burgers and fries. The Signature Collection violates these core principles as the burgers are cooked to order and delivered to the customer's table. It is too early to judge whether the systems and culture that have been honed over decades to deliver low-priced fast food can successfully deliver the Signature Collection. Some early indications suggest that restaurants that have the normal take-out operation, a drive-thru and the Signature Collection are struggling to cope. To avoid long queues of cars, there is a tendency to prioritise the drive thru customers which leads to delays in delivering the Signature burgers. It could be that McDonald's is trying to compete for two different types of customers from the same outlets and using essentially the same systems.

As we explained in the introduction to the previous chapter, if the context changes, then the strategy may also need to change.

Case study 3
H&R Block

H&R Block was founded in 1955 by brothers Henry W. Bloch and Richard Bloch in Kansas City, USA. The Bloch brothers had learnt that the market for providing services to small businesses was set for dramatic growth. To ride this wave of growth, they established the United Business Company that focused on providing book-keeping services and also some tax advice work. As an aside, the Bloch brothers chose to spell their business name "Block" with a K to avoid the name being mispronounced as "blotch".

In the early days, the Bloch brothers found that doing taxes was time-consuming and decided to end that service. However, one of their clients, John White, an ad salesman for The Kansas City Star, had an alternative suggestion. This was to make tax preparation a separate business and he designed an advertisement announcing tax services for $5. The brothers, somewhat unsure, agreed to run the ad. The following day the brothers had an office full of new clients and H&R Block, the tax advisory and return business, was born.

H&R Block developed a franchise model which proved to be very successful, leading to rapid growth and an IPO in 1962. Soon thereafter, H&R Block opened its own tax training school to meet the demands for skilled tax professionals at its franchise offices.

H&R Block went on to achieve great success. H&R Block lay claim to be the world's largest tax services provider having prepared more than 650 million tax returns since 1955. In 2016 alone, H&R Block prepared 23.2 million tax returns and generated revenues in excess of $3 billion. The firm prepared one in every seven US tax returns. Tax preparation services were provided through approximately 12,000 company-owned franchise retail tax offices staffed by professional tax preparers and using H&R Block Tax Software products.

This success is all the more remarkable as the market for tax services is extremely price competitive. A recent H&R Block promotion offered federal returns for free and state returns for $9.99 using their do-it-yourself tax preparation software. How are H&R Block able to deliver their services at such low prices? There are a number of factors, but one of particular interest is keeping down the costs of the tax personnel who provide advice and assist customers with their tax preparation.

H&R Block's hiring criteria require candidates to be able to provide outstanding customer service, be effective communicators and be able to adapt to different situations. Many of the tax personnel positions are available only on a seasonal basis – tax season – which runs from January to April in the United States. To meet their hiring requirements, H&R Block will train thousands of people to prepare tax returns in their storefront offices throughout the tax season. To a large extent, these seasonal associates are the face of H&R Block.

H&R Block are able to keep their tax personnel costs low by hiring non-professionals and training them to be tax preparers. As featured in some of H&R Block's advertising campaigns, their tax preparers could be anyone from an air-traffic controller to a Zumba instructor. They are able to pull this off through the development of a set of procedures, supported with its tax preparation and submission software products that contain much of the knowledge required to deliver a tax return. Because they have routinised and standardised the service, it is possible to train up candidates from a wide variety of backgrounds to successfully execute its processes in a reliable way. The quality of the service they deliver is fine for the typical personal or small-business tax return.

A simple tax return for a single individual with no complicating circumstances may be appropriately completed by an H&R Block employee working with their systems and processes. The customer gets the PUV they desire, without paying for skills and knowledge that they don't require. H&R Block pays below the industry average for its staff, and that translates into a significant cost saving for their business.

By focusing on customers who require a standard tax service, H&R Block are able to take out costs that other broader scoped tax advisory competitors cannot avoid. The service that their customers receive is not seen by the customers to be inferior or lower quality. H&R Block has perfected a process of delivering critical perceived use value dimensions at low cost, enabling it to compete for customers who want a standard-grade service and who can avoid paying for unused or unwanted capabilities.

We now explore some generic practices associated with the *low-cost* strategy.

Low-cost practices

The aim of the *low-cost* strategy is to deliver equivalent product quality with a relentless focus on cost reduction. This strategy is not seeking to fundamentally alter the product, unlike the *no-frills* strategy (see Chapter 10), but instead to alter the *sourcing, operations* and *selling* activities to strip out as many unnecessary costs as possible.

There are a number of generic practices consistent with pursuing the low-cost strategy which are summarised in Figure 7.4.

LOW-COST Practices

Culture

- *A culture that abhors waste and rewards efficiency*
- *Valuing the team rather than the individual*
- *No fancy offices, promotion from within*
- *Building stability to allow for continuous learning*

Structure

- *Low overheads*
- *A focus on supply chain and logistics to strip out unnecessary processes*
- *Outsourcing more complex and expensive processes, for example, product R&D*
- *Eliminate stages in logistics, for example, stockholding, handling, inspection, paperwork*

Systems

- *Work simplification and de-skilling, and automating wherever feasible*
- *Limited range of products, no variations*
- *Cost information widely shared and visible*
- *Stripping out unnecessary costs that don't deliver PUV*
- *Codifying and transferring 'best practice'*
- *Refining processes and procedures*
- *Reducing variation in processes*
- *Use of franchising to motivate people*
- *Enhanced procurement expertise which may exploit bargaining power*

Figure 7.4 Low-cost practices

Chapter

Innovation

The intention behind the innovation strategy is to 'jump' the system to a higher perceived use value ($PUV)/price position through the creation of novel *product* solutions. Product innovations can have a dramatic effect on the market in a relatively short time period, although producing innovations usually requires a long period of research and development activity, change to production systems, productising scientific breakthroughs, acquiring patents, etc.

For the innovation strategy to be successful, the firm would typically need to be able to charge premium prices, to recoup the additional R&D costs. This would work where there is a segment of demand that is willing to pay to get the unique benefits conferred by the innovation. Innovation can be guided where we have clear insights into underlying customer needs that may not be met by the existing products on the market. Thus, the *innovation* strategy

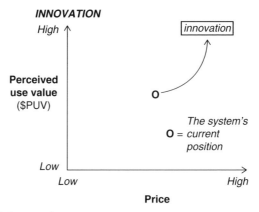

Figure 8.1 Innovation

shifts the system to serving customers who are prepared to pay premium prices to acquire new and superior products.

Case study 1
NetJets

NetJets is a world leader in private aviation. NetJets offers part ownership and rental of private business jets. It sells 'fractional ownership' in aircraft which gives the owner a share in the use of the aircraft.

NetJets history goes back to 1964 (then called Executive Jet Aviation) when it became the first private business jet charter and aircraft management company in the world. However, the real innovation came about much later. In 1984, an entrepreneur, Richard Santulli, purchased Executive Jet Aviation and introduced a 'time share' concept of fractional ownership previously applied to resort properties. NetJets sells a fraction of specific aircraft, chosen from several available types at the time of purchase. The fractional owners are then entitled to access to that aircraft – ranging from 50 hours to 400 hours, depending on the level of ownership – with as little as four hours' notice.

If the owners' aircraft is unavailable, another aircraft of the same type, or larger, will be provided. For this service, fractional owners pay a monthly maintenance fee and an 'occupied' hourly operating fee. Alternatively, companies or individuals that required less than the minimum 50 flight hours and five-year commitment of fractional ownership can buy flight hours in 25-hour increments.

NetJets are not alone in providing this type of service. Competition includes CitationAir, Flight Options, Bombardier Flexjet and Delta Private Jets. However, NetJets has established a market leading service with a substantial global presence and fleet size. At the time of writing this book, NetJets flies to 170 countries and operates more than 650 planes co-owned with their clients, managing 300,000 flights annually at 2,200 airports. It has also been extending its offering to provide a variety of travel-related services including additional catering options and emergency medical treatment.

Its innovative product is delivered at a higher cost than alternative executive travel options because of the nature of the product and service – that is, tailored jet usage – which involves high-cost inputs, such as leasing expensive private jets. But there is a segment of air travel customers that are prepared to pay a premium price for this exclusive service.

NetJets came to the attention of Warren Buffett when he became a customer in 1995. Impressed by the business, his investment vehicle, Berkshire Hathaway Inc., purchased NetJets three years later in 1998 for $725 million in stock and cash.

A representation of how NetJets' product is higher quality than some competing travel options is set out in Figure 8.2. In this figure, key product dimensions are identified: flight schedule flexibility, reduced check-in and check-out time, destination airport options, reduced flight time, in-flight interior comfort, and

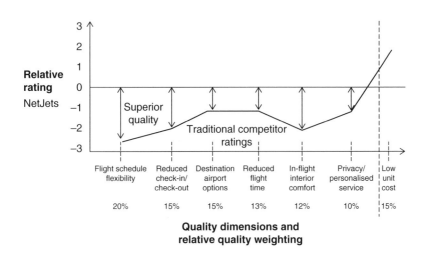

Figure 8.2 PUV: NetJets

privacy and personalised service. These are weighted in terms of importance to the client at 20 percent for flight flexibility through to 10 percent for personalised service. We have compared NetJets offering with a first-class seat on a scheduled service. It is evident that NetJets has a significantly superior product offering from a client's perspective.

As you can see in Figure 8.2, this analysis also pays regard to 'Low unit cost'. This is weighted by the customer at 15 percent, which indicates that they are not price sensitive. According to the relative rating, the customer perceives NetJets product offering to be more expensive than a first-class ticket and hence a potential disadvantage. However, this is more than compensated for by relative superiority in all of the other important product dimensions.

A comparison of NetJets to its direct competitors, such as CitationAir, Flight Options, Bombardier Flexjet and Delta Private Jets, reveals some differences in the service offering. For example, guarantees concerning jet availability, terms of ownership, cost predictability and options to upgrade the aircraft. Additional differences exist depending on the focus of operators on business customers versus the friends and family customer segment.

Thus, there are degrees of product innovation. The big disruptive innovation was the idea of time sharing a jet. This has been followed by further incremental innovations which have refined the product offering and enabled NetJets to tailor their service to the specific needs of different clients.

We can see how critical Richard Santulli's original insight was, but moving from this basic idea of a 'time share' for executive jets to a fully functioning and profitable business involved intense interaction and knowledge sharing across a diverse range of experts, including pilots, IT specialists, ground handlers, aircraft suppliers and providers of finance. They didn't solve all the problems first time. Mistakes were made but they learned from these and crafted different solutions to the problems and challenges that emerged along the way. It is one thing to come up with the great product idea, but turning an idea into a profitable business is a much bigger challenge.

Case study 2
Google: DeepMind

Product innovations can emerge from many sources. In the NetJets case, the trigger was an insight from a former customer of executive jets Robert Santulli. In this Google case, we see how a broad view about possible product innovations led to a deliberate strategy to recruit the necessary know-how to bring these ideas to fruition. This case illustrates the importance of recruiting people with outstanding talent and enabling them to interact with others who have different but related expertise. These interactions can produce ground-breaking innovation.

The case in point here is Google's recent programme to secure experts in the field of Artificial Intelligence (AI). For some time, Google has been intent on developing an AI capability. As early as 2006, an internal company memo stated that Google should build the world's top AI research laboratory. Google founders, Larry Page and Sergey Brin, consider that AI would be the ultimate version of Google; a search capability that is so intelligent that it understands exactly what information you are seeking.

Some of the possibilities of applying AI to Google's core search service are to create a more effective and efficient search facility tailored to an individual. One aspect of Google's initiatives in this area is to build software that can learn from the information stored in its data centres. This is no mean feat given the quantity of data that Google has housed in its centres. The fact that Google now has some of the largest and most interesting data sets on the planet is leading academics and scientists to embrace Google and Silicon Valley.

One of the highest profile mergers of academic scientists and Google in the development of AI came about with Google's acquisition of DeepMind, a UK-based AI research company. DeepMind was acquired by Google in January 2014 for a reported $400 million. Founded by Demis Hassabis, his firm DeepMind specialised in machine learning, advanced algorithms and systems neuroscience.

Demis Hassabis himself is an example of a deep mind if ever there was one. He is a British AI researcher, neuroscientist, computer games designer and world-class gamer. Early signs of his unique talents were revealed when Demis reached master standard in chess at 13 with an Elo rating of 2300. However, unlike most other young chess prodigies, his gaming expertise extended well beyond chess. He has won the world games championships at the Mind Sports Olympiad a record five times, securing a reputation as the best all-round games player in the world. Following a successful career as a computer games designer and programmer, he completed a BA in Computer Science from the University of Cambridge, followed by a PhD in Cognitive Neuroscience from University College London and became a visiting scientist jointly at MIT and Harvard.

So why did Google pay a reported $400m for Demis' company and what were they buying? According to an AI researcher at the University of Montreal, Yoshua Bengio, Google were buying AI brainpower. According to Yoshua, there were only about 50 experts worldwide in deep learning and DeepMind employed about a dozen of them. In other words, what Google bought was the capability and the skills of the individuals at DeepMind.

Since the acquisition, Google's DeepMind has been working on developing a computer system that works like a human brain, using information from its environment to make decisions free of human interaction. In November 2014, DeepMind unveiled a computer prototype capable of mimicking properties of the human brain's short-term memory, called the Neural Turing Machine. This machine learns and stores algorithms and data as 'memories' which it is then able to retrieve later to perform tasks it has not been previously programmed to do. This builds on the work of American cognitive scientist George Miller who first began research into the capacity and function of short-term memory in the 1950s.

According to Demis Hassabis, this is an exciting time for AI research with progress being made on many fronts including speech and image recognition. Perhaps not surprisingly, Google has also recently made acquisitions reflecting its interests in these areas as part of its overall AI programme. In October 2014, Google expanded its AI team by acquiring two Oxford University spin-off companies, Dark Blue Labs and Vision Factory.

Dark Blue Labs specialises in deep learning for understanding natural language. This is something that Google's search products have been pioneering on a large scale with both typed and spoken natural language queries. For Google, this technology is eminently scalable. An example is Google's voice search which is built into every Android-supported smartphone and tablet. The key principals and researchers within Dark Blue focus on research to enable machines, whether they be computers or robots, to better understand what users say and are asking of them.

Vision Factory specialises in visual recognition systems and deep learning, applying AI techniques to enhance the accuracy and speed of object recognition and other vision-based computer systems. The key individuals and founders behind Vision Factory now work to help Google improve its vision systems, which include object recognition in camera-based search applications and no doubt the data-processing systems for the Google developed self-driving cars.

It seems clear that machine learning is a technology whose time has come. Other companies in the information technology space have also been quick to recognise this. According to analysis firm Quid, AI has attracted more than $17 billion of investment between 2009 and 2014. Like Google, Facebook has recruited is own dedicated AI team. Other prominent technology firms – Amazon, Microsoft, Yahoo, Intel, Dropbox, LinkedIn, Pinterest and Twitter – have also invested in AI capabilities or companies since 2013. Reportedly, private investment in the AI sector has been expanding at 62 percent per year since 2010.

In its drive to become the leader in the field of AI, Google has embarked on a strategy to hire the leading experts. The Google team now includes Geoff Hinton who is sometimes referred to as the godfather of computer neural networks. A further prominent Google AI team member and recent hire is Ray Kurzweil, a proponent of 'hard AI' who argues it is possible to create consciousness in an artificial being.

Google appears to be ahead of the game in cornering the market on deep learning. It is spending hundreds of millions to build software that can learn from the information in its data centres to help create new types of products that can understand and learn from images, text and videos. To further its goals to innovate in the AI field, Google continues to pay premium prices to attract the best minds to its AI programme.

Case study 3
Space X

Space X is an example of product innovation that is aimed to deliver the quality that customers demand at lower unit costs. However, whilst the rockets that SpaceX has designed can be launched and recovered at low cost, getting to this position has required considerable capital investment.

SpaceX designs, manufactures and launches advanced rockets and spacecraft. It was founded by Elon Musk in 2002 with the aim to "revolutionize space technology with the ultimate goal of enabling people to live on other planets". Many followers of successful business mavericks will already know of Elon Musk and his prior industry-redefining ventures – most notably PayPal, the online money transfer service, and Tesla Motors, the electric car manufacturer.

The impetus for SpaceX came about through a project that Elon Musk conceived of in 2001, titled 'Mars Oasis'. The aim of the project was to land an experimental greenhouse on Mars and so grow plants on Martian soil. To realise this project, Musk attempted to generate public interest in space exploration and increase the budget of NASA. However, he soon came to realise that the NASA budget required would be prohibitively expensive. He then sought out an alternative option by approaching some Russian aerospace companies to purchase refurbished ballistic missiles. However, this route also proved too expensive. Musk ultimately concluded that to realise his goal he would need to start a company that could build affordable rockets. Musk aimed to cut the SpaceX launch price by a factor of ten relative to competitor offerings. Consistent with reducing the cost per launch, Musk set out to build a simple and relatively inexpensive *reusable* rocket. His idea was that a single rocket would go into space multiple times and could be promptly turned around ready for the next launch, similar to the turnaround process that applies to commercial aircraft.

SpaceX began modestly by developing a small orbital rocket, the Falcon 1. Since then it has gone on to achieve a number of first milestones for a privately funded company, including the successful launch into orbit and recovery of a spacecraft (Dragon) in 2010; sending a spacecraft (Dragon) to the International Space Station in 2013; and the landing of a first stage orbital capable rocket (Falcon 9). The last milestone was especially significant as it was the world's first successful landing of a rocket that was used for an orbital launch. This paves the way for rocket reuse, significantly reducing the cost per pound placed into orbit.

Because Musk sought to develop an entirely new type of rocket – a truly reusable rocket – he concluded that they needed to vertically integrate manufacturing. In a clear departure from the industry norm, SpaceX builds its rocket engines, rocket stages, spacecraft, avionics and all software at its in-house facility in Hawthorne, California. The types of components that are needed to build a reusable rocket were simply not available from existing suppliers. For example, SpaceX designed a machine that could friction stir weld aluminum lithium alloy for the airframe of one of its rockets, the Falcon 9, because it did not exist elsewhere. In the same vein, it has also developed new engineering technologies, such as its own computational fluid dynamics (CFD) software to better evaluate rocket engine combustion design.

The resulting economies of vertical integration and the ability to re-use its rockets are quite staggering. In late 2013, SpaceX priced a launch to low Earth orbit using its Falcon 9 rockets at approximately $57 million. This price was the cheapest in the aerospace industry at the time. On the basis that SpaceX will successfully finalise the operation of re-usable rockets, it expects that price could drop by an order of magnitude, capitalising on the ensuing economies of scale, to as little as $5 to $7 million per launch.

SpaceX is an example of an integrated and coherent product innovation strategy: the aim was to develop a reliable and re-usable rocket that would transform the economics of space travel. Reliability is key in this sector for reasons of safety and the value of the payloads sent into orbit. In this case, the innovative creation and utilisation of new knowledge in design and manufacturing led to a quantum leap forward in space rocket design. Pursuing an innovation strategy resulted not only in a higher quality product, but also in lower unit costs.

Innovation – practices

At the heart of achieving product innovation is the creation of new knowledge. New knowledge and its application drives product breakthroughs. It therefore is no surprise that the practices most commonly associated with innovation are related to knowledge creation and knowledge management. Some of these practices are set out in Figure 8.3.

One critical determinant of a firm's ability to innovate is its 'absorptive capacity': the firm's ability to recognise the value of new information, assimilate it and apply it.[42] Absorptive capacity depends on prior related knowledge and some diversity in background and experience amongst the team. Absorptive capacity builds over time and investments in building it in one period will make it easier to accumulate it in the next one.

INNOVATION: Practices

Culture

- *A culture which values importing knowledge from 'outside' and which encourages and rewards the generation of new ideas and promotes constructive collegial rivalry*

- *Inspiring visions that motivate*

- *Management attitudes which encourage experiments, expects some 'failures' and recognises learning from them*

Structure

- *Forming of 'loose', fluid, temporary project teams which can generate new knowledge by enabling specialists with complementary knowledge to interact*

- *Create time and space for interaction*

- *Vertical integration to speed up coordination, change processes and the pace of innovation*

- *Joint ventures, alliances and cross-organisation collaborations*

Systems

- *Place many 'bets' but have timely appraisals so that failing projects can be 'killed' and resources can be readily redirected to more promising projects*

- *Frequent trialling of prototypes with high-quality feedback*

- *Recruitment and retention of talent is a strategic priority*

- *Capture the best brains, and 'lock out' competitors*

Figure 8.3 Innovation practices

Chapter

9

Adaptive

The *adaptive* strategy enables the business to adapt to changes in customer needs, which may be difficult to predict. This strategy fits circumstances where the environment is in a state of flux. Customer needs could be changing, products and technologies could be evolving. The adaptive strategy can also be deployed where the firm chooses to meet customers' needs with a bespoke service offering.

This strategy builds the system's capability to adapt and adjust to the unfolding changes in the environment. Key to the adaptive strategy is enhancing both the ability of the system to *sense* early signals of impending change and to have the flexibility to adapt to what unfolds. Whilst it is possible to create new knowledge inside the organisation, this process is enhanced by the ability to absorb knowledge from the external environment. The 'absorptive capacity' of the system is driven by the ability to *acquire* information, to *assimilate* it and *combine* it with existing knowledge and to *exploit* the resultant benefits. Managers have to see that there is value in acquiring knowledge externally, to prioritise its acquisition and to ensure that it gets to the staff who can use it best. An 'open' attitude to information from outside can be contrasted with a 'closed' view that does not value anything that was 'not invented here'.

As we suggest, the adaptive strategy can also be appropriate for markets where customers require 'bespoke' solutions. Flexibility in the value system can enable the firm to meet specific customer needs. This can be a source of sustained advantage which could command premium prices. In summary, the adaptive strategy enables the system to adapt to *changing* circumstances.

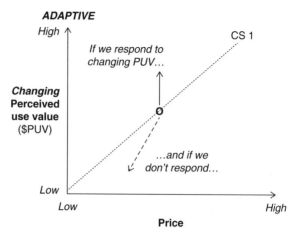

Figure 9.1 Adaptive

In Figure 9.1 the firm is seeking to serve existing customers whose needs are changing. The intention behind the adaptive strategy is to develop the system's capability to rapidly adapt and respond to these changing external circumstances. The figure also indicates what happens if we *fail to respond* to changes in customer requirements: PUV falls and we have to discount price.

Case study 1
Zara

Zara is a good example of a firm pursuing an *adaptive* strategy. Established in 1975 by Amancio Ortega and Rosalia Mera, the original store was opened in Galicia, Spain, and featured low-price lookalike versions of high-end fashion clothing.

Throughout the 1980s the business expanded and evolved to be able to quickly react to new fashion trends. Ortega identified that to prosper in the fickle fashion sector, Zara would need to be flexible to capitalise on trends as they arose, and limit losses when trend forecasts did not materialise. According to some reports, Zara requires just one week to develop a new product and get it into its stores. This compares to the months it typically takes its competitors.

To achieve the desired level of adaptability, Zara re-engineered its entire design, manufacturing and distribution processes to significantly reduce lead times. One example of how it achieves high levels of market responsiveness is the introduction of in-store radio frequency identification (RFID) technology in 2014. RFID chips are embedded in the security tags that allow for accurate real-time location and tracking of inventory and the identification of stock.

But the really distinctive feature of Zara's business is that its products are manufactured only where there is consumer demand for them. Its highly responsive and adaptive supply chain results in it shipping products to stores twice per week.

Once products are designed, they typically only take 10–15 days to reach the stores. A key component of the responsive and adaptive supply chain is its major distribution centre located in Spain. In this centre newly produced items are quality inspected, sorted, labelled and loaded into trucks.

Zara's supply chain operates a JIT system that successfully launches 12,000 designs per year and minimises the cycle time from assessing consumer trends through to procurement, manufacture, product completion and distribution. Another unique feature of Zara's operation is the location of its manufacturing facilities. Zara manufactures its fashionable items in company-owned factories in proximate countries such as Spain, Portugal and Turkey. Most of Zara's competitors outsource production to Asia.

By shortening the time to get new products to customers, Zara achieves greater success in meeting the changing fashion preferences. If a design does not immediately sell well, then it is withdrawn from shops and no further orders are placed. This adaptive approach is central to Zara's ability to successfully compete, and so far has proved exceptionally hard for others to replicate as it is embedded throughout Zara's value system.

Hannah Marriott (from The *Guardian, a UK newspaper*) says: *'In terms of style, there are subtle permutations and differences that Zara are able to respond to and deliver exactly what the customer wants. If shoppers are saying to store managers "do you have this with longer sleeves?" that message will be fed back to their HQ and very soon there will be a version with longer sleeves. So you often see 5, 6 or 7 very similar tops next to each other in Zara. They are responding to exactly what the customer wants.'*

Case study 2
BuzzFeed

Another example of a firm pursuing an adaptive strategy is Buzz-Feed, an internet media business that positions itself as 'The Media Company for the Social Age'. It describes itself as a social news and entertainment business and utilises digital technologies to share breaking news, original reporting and entertainment content.

This business was founded back in 2006 by Jonah Peretti and John Johnson as a lab that focused on tracking viral content. Since then, it has grown into a global media and technology company providing coverage on a variety of topics including politics, DIY and business.

A gauge of the success of this recent start-up is its ability to raise $50 million from the venture capital firm Andreessen Horowitz in August 2014. This reflected a valuation of the business at around $850 million. This was followed up a year later, August 2015, with a $200 million equity investment in BuzzFeed by NBCUniversal. The business is now actively hiring journalists worldwide to expand the site into 'serious journalism', long-form journalism and develop an 'investigative unit'.

So what does BuzzFeed offer? It presents daily content based on work done by its staff reporters, contributors, cartoonists and its 'community'. In the past, BuzzFeed focused exclusively on viral content, but recently it has added more traditional content with a reputation for delivering breaking news and widely reported articles. It also features formats showing popular lists, videos and quizzes.

Most of the traffic that BuzzFeed receives is based on content that is created and shared on social media websites. For example,

BuzzFeed regularly ranks near the top of 'Facebook Publisher Rankings'. Reportedly 75 percent of its views are from links on social media outlets such as Pinterest, Twitter and Facebook. BuzzFeed is able to do this by assessing its own content and determining how viral it will become. This is achieved through *continuous feedback* whereby all of its articles and videos are subject to sophisticated data analysis. Through an algorithm titled 'Viral Rank' the firm is able to try lots of different ideas to maximise distribution.

Whether BuzzFeed will continue to develop into a well-established global media firm is subject in part to its continued ability – algorithm assisted or otherwise – to generate content that leads to viral fuelled viewing that drives high traffic. Key to doing this is monitoring and being responsive and adaptive to content and news items that are garnering the greatest level of public interest.

Case study 3
Sir Ben Ainslie

Sailors have many variables to deal with and these variables interact in complex ways. The wind varies from minute to minute, the tides will be different each day and local currents will interact with changing wind speeds and directions in unpredictable ways.

The Olympic sailing course will be set differently for each race and competitors will approach the course in their own way. Successful sailors have to be physically fit, but they also have to be able to continually analyse the changing conditions, the competitors and their likely behaviours and positions on a second-by-second basis. This can only be done *intuitively*. Great sailors build their intuitive know-how through many years of competing, and some, like Sir Ben Ainslie, the most successful sailor in Olympic history, seem to operate on a different level to everyone else. It's difficult to create another Ben Ainslie; his know-how built through experience provides a fitting example of an adaptive capability.

Adaptive practices

There are some generic practices that are consistent with a firm pursing an adaptive strategy. The key theme across these practices is the need to build in flexibility to enable the system to respond to changing customer needs. Practices associated with this strategy are set out in Figure 9.2.

ADAPTIVE: Practices

Culture

- A customer-centric culture focused on delivering solutions to clients, not selling a product to them
- Encouraging initiatives and experimentation in response to market changes
- Recognise when staff go 'the extra mile' to solve a client's problem

Structure

- Developing adaptive and fluid organisational structures
- Localising decision making to speed up response rate and stay in sync with the market
- Moving to a tow-fixed/high-variable cost mix
- Building flexible operations to enable rapid adjustments
- Acting as project 'integrators' rather than doing everything 'in-house'
- Developing multi-skilled staff and empowering them to respond to changing circumstances

Systems

- Strong coordination to ensure clients' specific requirements are met
- Share learning from working with demanding clients
- Basing decisions more on intuitive insights than analysis of the past
- Seeking multiple sourcing options
- Improving market-sensing capabilities to detect impending change

---

Figure 9.2 Adaptive practices

Chapter

10

No frills

The no-frills strategy is intended to shift the system to a low-price, lower PUV position. The main aim behind pursuing a no-frills strategy is to serve price-sensitive customers with an acceptable but basic version of the product or service.

In Figure 10.1 we indicate the changes associated with the *no-frills* option. The focus of the system shifts to serve price-sensitive customers and the product or service will likely require significant modifications. To successfully pursue the *no-frills* strategy, it is critical to understand what price-sensitive customers perceive as 'essential' product features. With this understanding, we can strip out costs that don't deliver these essential features.

Whereas the innovation strategy shifts the system through *product* innovation, the no-frills strategy focuses mainly on innovation in

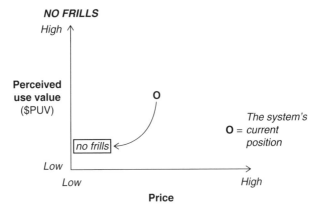

Figure 10.1 No frills

processes. Generally, the no-frills strategy shifts the system to a new position which creates and delivers a familiar and stable product or service in a novel way. Key to success here is the understanding of customer needs and preferences, coupled with a deep understanding of the costs associated with additional product features or quality levels. Put simply, *no frills focuses on the valued core dimensions of $PUV and strips out non-core product features and their associated costs.*

Case study 1
ALDI

A business that exemplifies the *no-frills* strategy is ALDI. ALDI was built up by brothers Karl and Theo Albrecht. They took over their mother's small store in a suburb of Essen, West Germany, in 1946, and soon expanded the number of stores in the Ruhr Valley.

The Albrecht brothers set out to provide the cheapest food through rigorously removing inventory that didn't sell, cutting costs by not advertising, refraining from selling fresh produce and keeping the size of their retail outlets small.

ALDI's current business practices still reflect much of the original emphasis on cost cutting, simplification of merchandise offering and selling at low prices. ALDI's business proposition and practices are distinct in many ways. Its ability to generate profits whilst competing on price can only be sustained through processes that are truly tailored to delivering the lowest costs compared to rivals.

Most of the discount supermarkets that compete in this price-sensitive segment, for example, Netto and Lidl, achieve low costs through a combination of *many practices that synergise* to deliver acceptable levels of PUV very efficiently. There are not just one or two sources of low costs; their value systems exploit *multiple sources of efficiency.*

For example, the checkout process in ALDI is far quicker than rival supermarkets. How is this achieved? Products are scanned at a higher speed than rivals, the length of the 'conveyor belts' is

---

longer, to allow customers to upload all their purchases, so there are no delays when customers are still uploading, and trying to 'bag' their items. And due to the speed of the scanning, it is not possible to 'bag' the items as they are scanned. Customers are only able to reload the items into their trolley. So bagging occurs 'off line', which again speeds up the process. This means the productivity of the checkout assistants is significantly higher than rivals, so they don't need as many assistants.

Until, 2004, ALDI stores only accepted cash. Since then, debit cards (and not all credit cards) are accepted. Another low-cost operational practice that ALDI adopts is requiring a coin, or a reusable token, to use a shopping trolley. This helps counter theft and reduces employee time that would otherwise be spent returning carts left in parking areas. ALDI's value proposition is to specialise in staple items that constitute the shopping basket of price-sensitive shoppers and not to stock slow-moving 'luxury' foods.

A major difference compared to other international supermarket chains is ALDI's management of brands. Many of the products that ALDI offers are own brands with the number of other brands usually limited to a maximum of two for a given item. ALDI's main sales are of its exclusively produced custom-branded products, which are often identical to products produced by major brand manufacturers. The impact of this tactic is to increase sales for each article and reduce the required retail square footage.

ALDI can more than compensate for the relatively lower level of PUV that it is delivering by offering very low prices. ALDI's offering is so distinct from traditional competitors that to survive it needs to appeal to a distinct customer segment that values its differentiated and simplified product offering, at a significantly reduced price point. The ALDI value system accumulates *multiple sources* of cost efficiencies that enable it to be both price-competitive and profitable. Provided that there is a customer segment that is attracted to a different value-for-money proposition, the *no-frills* strategy can prove very successful, as it has been for ALDI.

A final point, ALDI delivers exceptional customer value without paying rock-bottom wages to its staff. The rewards, terms and conditions for ALDI's staff compare favourably with the best employers in the retail sector.

Case study 2
Ryanair

Ryanair is a low-cost airline that has achieved staggering growth since it was established in 1985. Its rapid expansion is largely due to the success of its *no-frills* approach combined with opportunities provided through deregulation of the aviation industry in Europe in 1997.

When first established, Ryanair started operations with a 15-seat Embraer Bandeirante turboprop aircraft. This aircraft flew between Waterford, Ireland and Gatwick with the aim of breaking the duopoly on London to Ireland flights held by British Airways and Aer Lingus.

Determined to grow rapidly, Ryanair made its first significant investment in expansion in 1986 through taking an 85 percent stake in London European Airways. This investment enabled Ryanair to extend its flights beyond the UK and Ireland, into Amsterdam and Brussels. Ryanair Europe was up and flying. However, despite increasing passenger numbers the airline generally ran at a loss. The financial situation continued to deteriorate until Ryanair Europe was closed. A turnaround and restructuring was required and the task of making the airline profitable fell to Michael O'Leary.

O'Leary was deputy chief executive of Ryanair between 1991 and 1994 and was promoted to chief executive in January 1994. As part of the effort to turn it around, O'Leary reportedly went to the United States to study SouthWest Airlines and the low-cost model that it had developed.

SouthWest Airlines, founded in 1967, are the pioneers of the low-cost airline model that is now widely adopted. The on-board service experience they offer is 'no frills'. There is only one travel class, that is, no first class or business class. Boarding procedures at SouthWest Airlines are simplified and broadly based on grouping passengers into three groups – A, B or C – whereby each passenger lines up at their specified letter for boarding. Another feature of the SouthWest Airlines model was that it used only Boeing 737s, except for a few years in the 1970s and 1980s when it leased a few Boeing 727s. Each SouthWest 737 aircraft was heavily utilised, averaging six flights a day, with a scheduled '10-minute turnaround' which became the standard ground time for many years.

Clearly, the SouthWest Airline model was a significant influence on O'Leary's turnaround plan for Ryanair. O'Leary decided that the key to return Ryanair to profitability was low fares, quick turn-around times for aircraft, a "no-frills" offering, no business class and operating a single model of aircraft. As at early 2018, Ryanair operates over 330 Boeing 737-800 aircraft. Its commitment to con-tinue to operate 737s exclusively is evident in terms of past and projected future orders. In March 2013, Ryanair signed an order for 175 new Boeing 737-800s. Following this, in September 2014, Ryanair further committed its future to the Boeing aircraft with an order of 100 new Boeing 737 MAX 200s, plus options for an addi-tional 100 MAX 200 aircrafts.

Purchasing aircraft from a single manufacturer, and purchasing one type of aircraft, presents a number of cost-saving opportuni-ties for Ryanair. These include limiting the costs associated with personnel training, maintenance and the purchase and storage of spare parts, as well as affording greater flexibility in the sched-uling of crews and equipment. Furthermore, because Ryanair is the most significant purchaser of Boeing 737 aircraft in Europe, it secures contract terms that are very favourable.

Whilst Ryanair looked to SouthWest airline and adopted a low-cost model, it didn't stop with just adopting that model. Instead, Ryanair has been a pioneer within the low-cost carrier sector and continues to innovate and devise new methods to cut costs and increase profits.

Many of Ryanair's cost-cutting methods are evident to the pas-senger: window shutters have been removed, head rests are vel-croed on, polyester seats are locked in a stiff upright position, there are no seatback nets for storing items in flight and the seat pitch is tight due to the aim of maximising the number of permis-sible seats on-board.

Other methods that Ryanair has pioneered to drive profit concern additional services and generating ancillary revenue. Ryanair is known for putting great emphasis on selling the absolute lowest airfare, and then charging for each additional 'service'. For example, if a passenger forgets to print a boarding card, there's an additional (and hefty) charge. Likewise, additional charges apply for checking in luggage. If your carry-on bag is overweight, charges will follow. These charges mount up, which is good news for Ryanair. In 2012, Ryanair grossed more than $US1.2 billion in ancillary revenue due to these charges.

A further innovative method pioneered by Ryanair to reduce cost comes about through its use of secondary airports. By landing at smaller regional airports, Ryanair pays much lower airport fees and taxes, compared to those charged at the larger international airports. Ryanair extended this advantage further by negotiating with regional governments to receive non-taxable subsidies for the promise of delivering a certain number of passengers into their regions, thereby creating a local economic benefit.

Thus, Ryanair has adopted numerous practices all consistent with a *no-frills* strategy. It has integrated many sources of incremental cost savings and exploited its bargaining power with its aircraft supplier Boeing. In the customer's mind, Ryanair has clearly presented itself as the leading *no-frills* European airline and it has developed a company culture that is aligned with this positioning.

Competitive strategy no frills – practices

Practices that are typically associated with the *no-frills* strategy are set out in Figure 10.2.

NO FRILLS: Practices

Culture

- *Fostering a culture that is open to ideas from any source*

- *A ruthless focus on what are essential product features and stripping out non-essential features*

- *A culture that is driven to achieve a clear and defensible market position*

Structure

- *Exploring vertical scope choices: is it cheaper to make it 'in-house' or buy it in?*

- *Seeking opportunities for multi-tasking and flexibility within production and delivery processes*

Systems

- *Continuous search for innovative ways to cut costs*

- *Integrating many sources of incremental cost savings*

- *Exploring ways in which customers can perform activities themselves and thus eliminate associated costs*

- *Exploiting bargaining power over suppliers of major cost items*

- *Gaining deep insights into price sensitive customers and their needs*

Figure 10.2 No-frills practices

Chapter

11

Targeting and specialisation

There are two ways to specialise: firstly, by focusing on a specific segment of demand through *targeting* and delivering more customer PUV than less focused rivals; secondly, through **product specialisation** where you focus on a limited range of products and sell them as widely as possible. *Targeting* is dependent on there being different types of customers with different needs. The firm needs to be keenly aware of the requirements of the segment that it serves and sensitive to often subtle changes in those requirements. This is important to manage down the risk associated with serving a narrow slice of the market.

De-risking the pursuit of targeting and specialisation is brought about through securing the 'number one' position as favoured supplier and continuing to protect and defend that position. We first explore the *targeting* strategy.

Targeting

Where a market subdivides into segments of demand, each segment having different needs and preferences, there is an opportunity to pursue a *targeting* strategy. Customers could have the same needs and have the same dimensions of PUV, but they might weight these dimensions differently or their dimensions of PUV might be different.

These differences are sources of opportunity for a firm pursuing a *targeting* strategy. Choosing the targeting strategy could require a substantial degree of change to the system as both customers served and products supplied to meet their particular needs are likely to be different to the status quo.

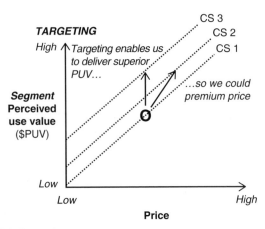

Figure 11.1 Targeting

If we get the targeting strategy right, we will be offering more $PUV to these targeted customers (Figure 11.1). We can reap the rewards of superior $PUV in two ways: if we keep prices the same, our market share will grow; or we could raise prices and thereby increase margins.

We can use a lock and key analogy to characterise the *targeting* strategy. In Figure 11.2 we have market-led segmentation where the role of the strategy is to steer the value system to more closely fit the specific needs of the customer segment: **to cut the key that 'fits' the customers' lock,** and thus unlock the potential value that is as yet unrealised. By more accurately meeting the segment's specific needs, there should be opportunities to premium price, and if there are similar customer segments in other geographic markets, there should be opportunities for growth.

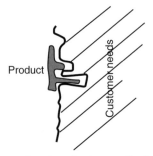

Figure 11.2 Targeting: Cutting the key to fit the lock

Case study 1
Long Tall Sally

Long Tall Sally is a retailer of clothing and shoes for women 5' 8" and over. It was established by Judy Rich, a UK domiciled American. At 5' 11" Judy struggled to find clothes that fit her well. Her experience was that clothes for taller women were simply made longer as opposed to being tailored for tall women. She opened the first store in the West End of London in 1976.

Like other firms that adopt a targeting strategy, Long Tall Sally is very clear and focused on one particular segment of consumers. This focus is reflected in its strap line – 'Global destination for tall fashion and footwear'.

Growth at Long Tall Sally has been achieved through a combination of acquisitions and international expansion. Recently, the chain has expanded with multiple stores in the United Kingdom, the United States, Canada and Germany. As well as physical stores, the business sells through its catalogue and website. Its website sets outs specific sizes and dimensions in its welcome message as follows:

'Welcome to Long Tall Sally where style starts at 5' 8" and shoe size 7. Our mission is to be the first choice for tall women. Clothing is designed in house for the ultimate fit in size 8–24 and shoe size 7–13. Discover the world's finest collection of clothes for tall women and fabulous footwear. Tall girls rejoice!'

The challenge in executing the targeting strategy is two-fold: firstly, the firm needs to figure out and specify the exact target customer segment; and secondly, the firm needs to work out how to market to them in just the right way. This is especially important in the B2C space.

When a target customer is exposed to a firm's marketing campaign, it should stop them in their tracks. They should be 'wowed' with a sense that the firm 'gets their audience'. This is by no means easy to achieve. But the rewards for matching target segments with on-point compelling market messages can be substantial.

In the 1980s, Long Tall Sally was an early adopter of the catalogue model which led to the development and growth of a successful mail order business. Post 2000, this meant that the business was perfectly positioned to utilise the internet as a platform to establish a leading e-commerce presence.

The path to success for Long Tall Sally has not been without its problems, however. A major challenge occurred when growth stalled due largely to the limitations of focusing solely on the UK market. This led to the company going into administration before being bought out by Amery Capital, backed by Michael and Maurice Bennett, the creative retail entrepreneurs behind Warehouse, Oasis, Coast and Phase Eight.

The turnaround engineered by Amery Capital came about through growing the online business not just in the United Kingdom but also internationally. This strategy of e-commerce internationalisation dramatically altered the business model and profile of Long Tall Sally. In its early years, more than 90 percent of the business was conducted in the United Kingdom, and more than 75 percent was done through physical stores. Now the profile is very different; less than 40 percent of business comes from the United Kingdom and more than 60 percent is done online.

Extending the targeting strategy to overseas jurisdictions meant identifying businesses with a similar focus – tall women – with similar or complementary product offerings. This acquisition activity resulted in Long Tall Sally establishing important footholds in new markets in the United States and Germany.

Going forward, making acquisitions of complementary brands is an inherent part of the growth strategy. As e-commerce is a key pillar of its strategy, this means focusing on countries with the most developed internet economies.

But the core of Long Tall Sally's success is staying focused on its very specific segment of tall women. This means investing in understanding what it means to be a tall woman and using that insight to be the first choice of fashion for tall women. In this context, the targeting strategy means keeping in tune with changing tastes across the world.

The challenge of tracking forward on this segmentation strategy has recently passed onto TriStyle, the German direct fashion retailer, who acquired Long Tall Sally in August 2016. If there's one thing that is likely to remain constant under this new ownership, it is a continuing focus on the target market.

Product specialisation

With product specialisation, the aim of the strategy is to *seek out* those segments of demand that value the specific and often unique qualities of the product or service. As indicated in Figure 11.3, and using WD40 as an example, specialisation involves incremental product improvements with the relentless search for new customers. The figure suggests three different types of customer, home owners, vehicle mechanics and aerospace engineers who all value the unique properties of WD40.

Case study 2
WD40

The specialisation strategy is built around a specific product offering. WD40 is a standout singular product that is now reportedly used in four out of every five American households. Its

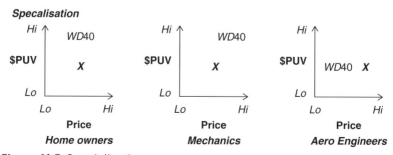

Figure 11.3 Specialisation

origins go back to 1953 when a small business, Rocket Chemical Company, and its staff of three aimed to develop a rust-prevention solvent and degreaser for the aerospace industry. After working up 40 attempts to get the water displacing formula worked out, they settled on Water Displacement 40 formula, now known as WD40.

The founder of the Rocket Chemical Company, Norm Larsen, reasoned that consumers might find a use for the product at home, leading to them offering WD40 for sale in San Diego in 1958. Interestingly, to avoid disclosing its composition the product was not patented but instead remains a trade secret.

Such was the success of this product, that the company was renamed after its single product in 1969 to become the WD40 Company Inc. Following its successful listing on NASDAQ in 1973, WD40 has grown by leaps and bounds and has applications in numerous markets including automotive, manufacturing, aviation, construction and home improvement.

Today WD40 is a global single-product success story, selling in more than 160 countries, with a market capitalisation of $1.43 billion as at April, 2017. It is an outstanding example of specialisation and market dominance built around a niche product.

The aim of the product specialisation strategy is to target an emerging or existing market and establish your products and

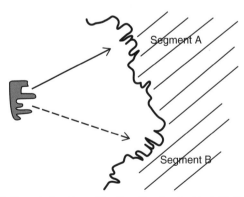

Figure 11.4 Specialisation: Finding the locks that fit the key

services so well that it isn't worth another firm attempting to enter that sector. In this sense, the successful specialisation strategy builds entry barriers that deter other firms from competing in the market.

In Figure 11.4 we are *finding the locks that fit the unique product 'key'*. Whilst segments A and B may have different needs, they both see the value in the product.

Case study 3
Carpigiani

Our second specialisation case is Carpigiani. Carpigiani is not a household name, yet you may well have tasted the output of their machines. Carpigiani is an Italian company that specialises in the manufacture of ice cream-making machines, and claims that every day 100 million people around the world eat ice cream produced by its equipment. According to some reports, Carpigiani controls over half of the world market for ice cream machines which produce both Italian-style gelato and soft ice cream.

The business was created back in 1944 by two Italian brothers, Bruto and Poerio Carpigiani. An early breakthrough resulted in Carpigiani producing and patenting a gelato machine, Autogelatiera. Applying their specialist knowledge of the ice cream-making process, the company developed machines that create fluffy ice cream due to the particular whipping action which mixes air and other ingredients during the process.

In more than 100 countries, Carpigiani has come to represent the very Italian art of making ice cream. The popularity of ice cream, and the successful international expansion of Carpigiani, means that exports account for over 80 percent of the business.

Carpigiani tuned in to its international client base and recognised something very significant: most of them have no idea how to make proper gelato. Based on this realisation, Carpigiani saw an opportunity to better serve their customers and further cement their reputation as the leading niche provider of ice cream-making machines. They decided to set up Gelato University.

Carpigiani teaches the art of gelato making near Bologna where its factory is based. Courses attract students from all over the world who get to share in the secrets of creating excellent ice cream. Due to its international growth, it also teaches overseas in countries including the United States, China and Australia.

Running ice cream-making courses provides Carpigiani with the opportunity to better understand its customers and showcase its expertise. The hands-on training is a way of passing on the specific know-how and the famous Italian passion for the craft to its current and future client base. The genius of setting up Gelato University and running these paid-for courses is that the costs are covered and a significant proportion of students will go on to buy ice cream-making equipment from Carpigiani.

Gaining a deep understanding of the requirements of your customers is necessary for both the segmentation and product specialisation strategies. This requires a firm to develop expertise in scanning and sensing changes and differences in customer needs.

A closer look at Carpigiani's customer base reveals different segments of demand. For example, Carpigiani has a set of artisan gelato products that cater to cafe owners and operators. These customers display their art by making gelatos in a cafe setting under the watchful eye of customers.

A second category of products is for caterers for whom it is important to be able to freeze batches of gelato for later serving. There is also a selection of products aimed at the quick-service restaurant sector. An example is the GK3 machine, the most advanced unit for combined production of shakes and soft-serve ice cream.

In this case study, the successful pursuit of the product specialisation strategy requires insights into each major customer segment. The needs of those customers who own and operate small cafes will differ from fast-food chains looking to efficiently serve soft ice cream. Caterers too will have a different set of needs and a scale of business that Carpigiani needs to accommodate.

Carpigiani clearly bring Italian passion to their business. Its vision is no less than to spread the gelato concept worldwide through daily encounters with other cultures. With an established programme to teach the art and science behind its trade and gain continuous market feedback, it is well positioned to truly understand and anticipate the requirements of the range of customers it serves.

Practices

Some practices that are consistent with *targeting* and product *specialisation* are listed in Figure 11.5.

TARGETING AND SPECIALISATION: Practices

Culture

- Relentless focus on narrow product range and/or the needs of a specific segment

- Shared aspiration to become the best in serving the chosen niche

- A culture that values being 'under the radar' in a low profile protected niche

Structure

- Flexibility required where customer needs are changing unpredictably, otherwise stability in roles to build specialist know-how

Systems

- Often established by a person who can't get what they need, or who are themselves the target customer, thus they intuitively understand the customer's needs

- Need continuous information on customer needs and competitors' products to ensure leadership position, and this information must be widely shared

- Opportunity to build capabilities that would be too difficult/expensive for new entrants to re-create

- Exploit growth opportunities if the segment exists in other geographies

---

Figure 11.5 Targeting and specialisation practices

Part

4

From strategy into action

12

Strategy initiatives and feedback

Having opted to pursue a particular competitive strategy, we can explore the broad 'menu' of congruent *practices* associated with the chosen strategy. We then need to identify specific *initiatives* that, once introduced, will start shifting the system in the required direction. Each initiative has to be translated into specific *actions*, which are achievable, and which are clearly 'owned' by someone.

Generating strategy initiatives

Ideas for initiatives can be generated at every level of the organisation. We take the view that the overwhelming majority of employees want to contribute to their organisation and they want to succeed. Too often, the control systems, culture and predominant managerial attitudes lead to demotivated staff. To invoke Douglas McGregor's assumptions about human nature in his *The Human Side of the Enterprise*, we are believers in *Theory Y*.[43] Here are McGregor's two contrasting sets of assumptions about human nature:

Theory X assumptions

- The average person dislikes work and will avoid it if they can.
- Therefore, most people must be forced with the threat of punishment to work towards organisational objectives.
- People prefer to be directed, to avoid responsibility and they are relatively unambitious and want security above all else.

Theory Y assumptions

- People will apply self-control and self-direction in the pursuit of organisational objectives, without external control or the threat of punishment.

- People usually accept and often seek responsibility.

- The capacity to use a high degree of imagination, ingenuity and creativity in solving organisational problems is widely, not narrowly, distributed in the population.

- In industry the intellectual potential of the average person is only partly utilised.

The real insight that McGregor had was the 'self-fulfilling prophecy' of Theory X assumptions. If a manager assumes people are like Theory X, they will behave accordingly: they won't trust their staff; instead they will try to control them, check up on them and they will not involve them in decisions that affect what they do. If you treat people this way, they will likely react in kind, that is, behave like a naughty child, and their behaviour will reinforce your Theory X assumptions.

We believe that not only is the potential and motivation to contribute distributed widely across the business, the knowledge and insights into value processes are not restricted to the top of the organisation. Indeed, those involved in the sourcing, operations and selling processes know the *detail* of what happens now and have insights into how things could be different. As in our Birmingham Children's Hospital case, staff are often a huge and untapped repository of knowledge and ideas. When translating a strategy into action, we need to tap into this reservoir of knowledge about processes, customers, problems, new product ideas and market opportunities.

The *practices* we set out associated with each strategy in Chapters 6–11 can act as a stimulus to generate ideas about initiatives, as can the case studies. But ideas can come from many outside sources: customers, suppliers, competitors, and they can be imported from other industries.

The strategy can shape the generation of ideas for change initiatives and can act as a selection mechanism. In this way, initiatives that align with the strategy should be selected for trial, and over time, congruent initiatives will generate additional synergies, which will boost the development of the system in the direction of the strategy.

It is essential that any changes introduced into the value system do not destroy current sources of competitive advantage. There are two ways of reducing these risks: 1) try to understand how the current system actually generates value, 2) get 'live' feedback from the system as initiatives are trialled.

'Forewarned is forearmed': if we have a deep understanding of the existing system, we can avoid introducing changes that could negatively impact it. The application at the end of the chapter explains a simple mapping process which can help in building a rich picture of the current system. Later in the chapter we explore the kind of information that can provide useful feedback as changes are introduced.

The strategy initiative process

We need to build in explicitly and upfront how we will generate and use the feedback to **adjust, escalate** or **abandon** any initiative. This sequence of action, feedback and response needs to cycle through continually and in 'real time'. We need feedback as far as possible instantly and in the moment to enable the processes of adjustment to take place. Thus, the cycle time between action, feedback and response needs to be as seamless and current as possible.

In Figure 12.1 we summarise the *process* of strategy initiatives. Actions generate feedback, this feedback enables us to *adjust*

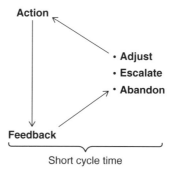

Figure 12.1

subsequent action, *escalate* our commitment to the changes or *abandon* the experiment. The faster we cycle through this loop, the better the chances of intervening successfully in the value system.

Realised strategies

As we explained in Chapter 1, given the complexity of the value system we cannot know the ultimate effects of any initiative we introduce. The sequence of initiatives interacts in unpredictable ways with the wider system, so what ultimately emerges may be different to what was expected. We can reduce the risk of any changes we introduce by using *pilot tests* where possible and gaining high-quality *feedback* from the system.

In Figure 12.2 the intended strategy is *excellence,* that is, to continually improve the quality of a product or product group. Initiatives are embarked on to produce continuous improvements in customer PUV. However, these intended outcomes may not be realised as there are many variables in the system that are not amenable to control.

The *realised strategy* (Figure 12.3) shows the effects of initiatives on $PUV and *unit costs* (not price) over time. An initial set of initiatives had the desired effect of improving product quality (the dotted arrows in the figure). Then an initiative was introduced that used a different technology (the solid arrow) which resulted in a marked

Figure 12.2

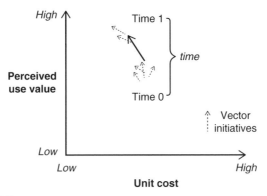

Figure 12.3

increase in quality coupled with a lowering of costs. Subsequent initiatives built on this breakthrough to enhance product quality whilst continuing to lower costs.

The technology-led breakthrough allowed the firm to increase prices, and subsequent product enhancements enabled these higher prices to be sustained. The intended outcome, in terms of $PUV and price was position A; the current realised position is C, where the customer receives more $PUV and we charge higher prices than at A (Figure 12.4). This happy outcome came about because competitors were unable to match the innovation, and the fact that unit costs were continuing to fall led to a marked increase in margins over the period.

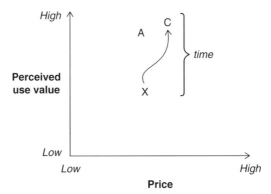

Figure 12.4

Thus, the initiatives that were introduced had an effect on customers' perceptions of the product's $PUV, but the ability of the firm to premium price and to sustain these prices is not something the firm can control. The firm cannot control what customers value, nor can it determine the actions and reactions of competitors. And whilst we maintain that the firm has some control over unit costs and product quality, again this is limited. Should a key supplier choose to raise its prices, it might be impossible for the firm to keep costs under control, certainly in the short term.

The example we have given here has the firm enjoying considerable profit improvements as a result of its choice of competitive strategy and the successful implementation of appropriate initiatives. But, of course, things might turn out differently. It could be that a competitor launches a product that instantly nullifies any relative $PUV advantage we may have. If it is judged that it is not possible to try to replicate what the competitor has done, this may force a rethink about the competitive strategy. It might then be necessary to shift to a *low-cost* strategy that tries to sustain quality but to significantly reduce costs. Or another option might be to adopt a *no-frills* strategy, strip out non-core product features and attract more price-sensitive customers.

Proceed with caution

Value creation takes place in an uncertain world. We cannot predict the future, and in order to survive, firms need to be able to respond to unfolding circumstances. As we have stressed, we need to *work with* the complexities of the real world, and not assume these away, or pretend to ignore them.

An initiative may have a positive impact in one part of the system, but result in negative impacts elsewhere. For example, you could move to a low-cost source of supply, which would reduce input costs, but the effect may be that $PUV is ultimately reduced as customers experience reduced product reliability. This is why any selected initiative must be evaluated right across the value system before it is introduced, and feedback from across the system is vital so we can monitor the unfolding impact of the change.

Or, for instance, any short-term cost savings need to be balanced against any longer-term damage to the brand. Some initiatives will have a simple, one-way benefit without any potential compromises elsewhere in the system. Assuming there is time and the right resources to introduce the initiative, it should be adopted. But most initiatives will not have a simple unambiguous positive effect across the system. In these cases you have to judge whether the potential gains more than offset any potential losses, and only when you are confident that there is a potential net gain across the system is it worth proceeding.

Trials and experiments

As we mentioned in Chapter 4, significant change in an organisation typically occurs in two circumstances: a crisis, or a change of leadership, which is often preceded by a crisis.[44] This is not surprising as to change an organisation that is ticking along in an acceptable way is a daunting prospect. *'If it ain't broke don't fix it'* would be the way most people would think. The idea that managers will enact 'transformational change' outside of a crisis is frankly unlikely. We might go further and suggest that to introduce transformational change into an organisation could be construed as a dangerous experiment.

This is because of the emergent nature of the organisation. The particular pattern of interactions, skills, relationships and systems that you see around you has emerged over time. Behaviours that 'synergise' with the system tend to persist, those that don't tend to get squeezed out. You may recall ideas, reorganisations and mission statements that were introduced that seem to have faded from the scene, and there will be activities that were not deliberately designed or 'managed' into the system that work very well and persist. Therefore, if there isn't a crisis we need to proceed with some caution if we are to intervene in this emergent system.

We would suggest that you treat each initiative in the way a scientist might approach a test of a new idea or theory. You should *trial* the initiative in a small way if possible and make sure that you get the maximum learning from this trial or 'pilot test'. This means actively seeking high-quality *feedback* from all those involved in the trial. Be prepared for some aspects of the initiative not to work in the way you had expected or hoped. Also be prepared to accept that it might 'fail', that is, this initiative, or the way we have trialled it, is not right for our system at this time. This is an important 'mind set' issue. If managers act (and others expect them to act) as if they have all the answers, then we would guess that there are nowhere near enough trials and pilot tests going on. Why would a manager risk his reputation on some risky experiment? *If you approach the change as an experiment, as an opportunity to learn, the only 'failure' is if we didn't learn.*

Tracking initiatives

In Figure 12.5 we set out the dimensions of an initiative that can help us track its evolution. Firstly, we need to have a clear *description* of the initiative: what is involved in the change being proposed. The expected or hoped for *outcomes* of the initiative should also be set out which can help us figure out what *feedback* is required to monitor the impact of the changes on the wider value system. Some thoughts as to the *time frame* of the change process will help, that is, is it weeks, or months before we would expect to see some effects?

It will be necessary to identify, at least initially, the *resources* required to kick-start the change process, and who *owns* the initiative. If there are expected *synergies* with other initiatives, these could be set out and monitored and it would be essential to highlight potential *risks* associated with the changes.

Figure 12.5 An initiative checklist

But given the emergent nature of the system, we need to be alert to unexpected outcomes and unanticipated changes in the wider system which might lead to a rethink of the initiative. We may need to adapt or adjust it, in line with the feedback from the system, or to abandon it altogether.

The energy to change

Much has been written in the strategy field about the need for businesses to develop *dynamic capabilities,* which enable the business to build and reconfigure its asset base.[45] By embarking on the development of a live portfolio of initiatives that are guided by a clear competitive strategy, you will be building a particular dynamic capability. This is the ability to generate and continually evaluate and adjust a mix of initiatives, guided by a clear competitive strategy, which operate directly on the value processes of the business.

The first initiative will require a significant amount of *change energy.* The idea is new, it will need management support, and those involved will need to move out of some familiar routine ways of behaving. But once the initiative gets established, it requires a lot less energy to sustain it as the new practices become embedded into routine ways of working. One of the authors worked with a large aerospace company who wished to move from a functional organisation to a 'product centre' structure. The idea was that by reorganising into twelve semi-autonomous product centres, many of the problems of the unwieldy functional structure could be overcome. They pilot tested the new structure with one centre, which was located in its own 'shed' on the sprawling site. Over a year the new centre was set up, and began to operate. Naturally, there were teething problems, the main one being a lack of supervisory leadership capabilities, which were not required in the old structure as the supervisory role was in effect performed by a corrupted piece-rate system.

But as the team bedded-in and the centre began to perform well, curious employees from other parts of the site would stop by and talk to the staff in the centre. Then when the decision to roll out the structure across the whole site was taken, there was already a degree of goodwill amongst the employees to make it work. This is the advantage of pilot testing: it is a powerful, relatively low-risk vehicle to learn and adapt and it can signal that change is not only possible but can also be beneficial.

Less change energy is required to embark on the *next* initiative if the first one has been seen to be successful. There is less resistance for trialling something new. And when the third initiative gets underway, staff start to see these changes not as 'one-offs'; instead, this way of changing the organisation is now the new 'normal' way of continually adapting our business. Thus, the ability to generate an ongoing portfolio of initiatives itself becomes a high-level dynamic capability that gets embedded in the organisation.

We depict the roll-out of strategy initiatives in Figure 12.6. The first initiative requires a significant amount of change energy. If this is seen to be successful, then less change energy is required to launch the second initiative, and so on. The effect over time of this sequence of initiatives is to *layer* capabilities, one on top of another. The energy required to sustain them reduces as they become embedded in everyday practices. The additional benefit of the sequential introduction of strategy initiatives is to build a *change* capability, where change becomes the norm not the exception. In this way the firm can incrementally build its capabilities to thrive in the unfolding environment.

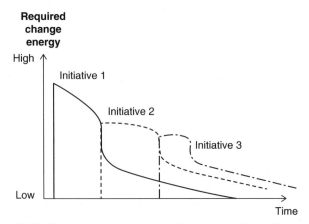

Figure 12.6 Change energy required for sequential initiatives

The impact of initiatives on the value creation process

Value is created by combining inputs with existing assets to create products and services. *Operations* activities are those where the firm has most influence. Relationships with suppliers and customers can be *influenced* by what happens in the value creation process, but the firm has no direct *control* over what suppliers or customers choose to do.

The value activities 'inside' the firm generate outcomes with respect to customers, costs and prices which we have summarised in Figure 12.7. Our seven *competitive strategies* operate on these activities to effect improvements in the flows of use values and exchange value. These improvements work their way through a number of variables which ultimately coalesce to produce a flow of profit.

A *value mechanism* is a causal link between two variables in the system. We have picked out the most important connections between these variables and the primary direction of causation is indicated by the arrows. Down the right side of the figure we have the critical variables in the *selling* process. $PUV is driven by the operations domain, that is, what we make, how well we align the

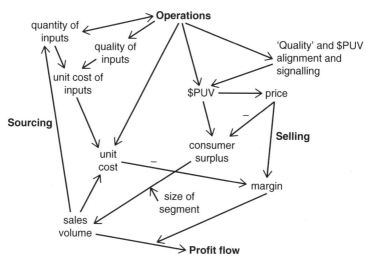

Figure 12.7 Change energy required for sequential initiatives

internal quality measures with what customers actually perceive as valuable product attributes and how well we are able to 'signal' the value of our products to potential customers.

$PUV, or 'willingness to pay' affects the prices we are able to charge, and $PUV less price determines consumer surplus. Note that the minus sign on the arrow between price and consumer surplus indicates that if price goes up, consumer surplus goes down, and vice versa. Consumer surplus or 'value for money' is what drives sales volume, moderated by the size of market or segment we are trying to serve. For example, if we offer a specialist product, although we might have the best solution on the market, and be the market leader, the market for these products may be very small.

Down the left side of the figure, we have critical variables in *sourcing*. How much we procure is affected by how much we make and how efficiently we make it. Efficiency is affected by the quality of inputs, for example, the skills of staff and the reliability of equipment. The quantities we procure may enable us to bargain with suppliers to reduce the costs of some inputs, and we may in addition have sourcing expertise which helps to reduce the costs of acquiring some inputs. Sales volumes affect unit costs, and average prices less average unit costs gives us the average margin. Sales volumes multiplied by margin drives the flow of profit.

The value mechanisms track the impact of changes in the value system on the flow of profits. The competitive strategy drives and shapes the selection of specific strategy initiatives which impact the value creation process. The above figure shows how any change in the three value processes has direct and indirect effects on these mechanisms. This is why we emphasise the need for feedback from across the system to enable us to track the impact of any initiative. In particular, we focus on the two critical outcomes: *unit cost* and *$PUV* later in this chapter.

The complexity of the value system is only hinted at in this figure; in reality, there will be many more intervening variables and interaction effects between them. This is a high-level abstraction from the system, but one that serves to illustrate the need for caution and high-quality and timely feedback when introducing any strategy initiative.

Force field analysis

Any particular strategy initiative will have positive and negative impacts on the system. In Figure 12.8 we suggest Lewin's 'force field' can be used to try to anticipate the impacts, positive and negative, on the firm's value system *prior to* embarking on the change.[46] Each arrow would represent a positive or negative 'force', and the length of each arrow can be used to represent the strength of each force. Of course, these will be largely subjective judgements, but they can be very helpful in framing discussions about any initiative, and they can help capture a variety of perspectives that people from different parts of the firm will inevitably bring. In the case depicted in Figure 12.8 the overall judgement would be that the initiative would add value, so it should be explored further.

Risks

As we have argued, the risk of introducing an initiative can be mitigated through pilot testing, feedback and learning. The big risk of any change is that it destroys value. This can occur where a change has unintended consequences, which may include the

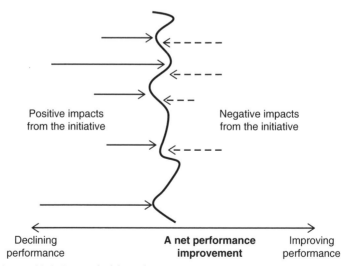

Figure 12.8 Force field analysis

inadvertent destruction of subtle sources of advantage, as we explain in Chapter 13. This is why we strongly advocate trialling initiatives in a low-risk way, if this is feasible, generating feedback and responding to what it tells us about the effects of the change.

The role of feedback

Feedback is critical to help identify the impact of initiatives. Adopting the perspective that all initiatives are experiments, feedback is the required data to judge whether an initiative is producing a positive outcome, a negative outcome or producing an otherwise unanticipated effect.

Without feedback, it is not possible to analyse outcomes against expectations and so learn and accordingly adjust, abandon or escalate an initiative. Given the importance of feedback, we would advocate putting in place a rigorous and well thought-out feedback *process.*

As explained earlier, it is impossible for any one person to fully understand a complex system, let alone the complex set of interaction affects that can result following an *intervention into* the system. However, despite this difficulty we believe it is important that managers invest in developing a deep knowledge of the firm value system, whilst appreciating that no one person can completely comprehend the entire system and certainly no one can control what happens in it.

With some degree of understanding of the system, a manager will be better placed to outline some predictions as to what an intervention might ideally produce, that is, a prediction that is in the realm of viable possibilities, and certainly be in a better position to observe the impact and identify changes to the system that result from an intervention. This ability is important if we are to identify outcomes, judge those outcomes against some predefined expectation, and so learn and take appropriate incremental action.

By proceeding in an incremental way, actively seeking feedback and responding accordingly, strategy initiatives can be successfully introduced. To manage this process, we need ongoing *feedback* particularly on customer PUV and unit costs. To generate this feed-back, we need a deep understanding of:

(a) who are the target customers

(b) what dimensions of product use value are important to them

(c) what signifiers do they use to judge PUV, signifiers being the cues customers use to evaluate products and services.

In the next section we explore customer value in some depth, as a deep understanding of customer-perceived value is the foundation for the successful introduction of any of the seven competitive strategies.

Unpacking perceived use value

Customers perceive use value in products and services. For exam-ple, in considering a car purchase one critical dimension of per-ceived use value is whether the car can actually get me from A to B. But there are other dimensions of value that may well be influ-ential in my ultimate choice of what car to buy. These might include less tangible dimensions of perceived use value like styl-ing, brand cachet and the ambience inside the vehicle. It is pos-sible to itemise these separate dimensions of perceived use value. This can be useful to help us analyse our product offerings and compare them to rival firm's offerings. In the John Lewis and NetJets case studies, we used this disaggregating technique to fig-ure out how each firm is creating value. Constructing *Dimensions of Use Value* charts is a valuable analytical step in building an understanding of how we might change the products or services we offer.[47]

However, whilst it can be useful to disaggregate the dimensions of product use value to enable us to analyse and compare products, customers do not make purchase decisions based on piecemeal comparisons of individual dimensions of use value. People make purchases of a product or service as a *gestalt* or complete offering. The individual dimensions of value are taken together as an inter-active whole. If we lose sight of the holistic nature of product pur-chase decisions, we run the risk of developing products which may appear to be offering superior value to customers on a dimension by dimension basis, but as a whole, as a *gestalt* the product is perceived to be unattractive.

We have stressed the importance of understanding who the customers are that we are trying to sell to, what their needs are and what they value. We also need to recognise that the customer may not be the *consumer* of the product or service, for example, a procurement manager buys computers that the designers use or a parent buys cakes for their daughter.

In Figure 12.9 we show how customer needs are determined, to some extent, by their perception of a possible product that will meet their needs, which may suggest to them a set of desired product attributes. These in turn may have attached to them *signifiers* of value, the criteria the customers use to evaluate different products that they can perceive. In Figure 12.9 the basic customer need is financial security in their retirement. The product that they identify that may meet this need is a long-term, fixed-rate bond. When considering alternative bonds, they may look for a variety of different dimensions of value: these might include a good rate, the security of the institution issuing the bond, whether their money will be invested in ethical companies and whether the product is simple to understand. They may also be interested in whether they have a degree of flexibility allowing them to cash in the bond as and when they choose.

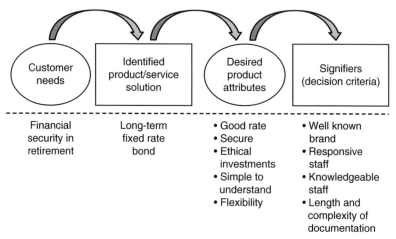

Figure 12.9 From customer needs through to signifiers

The *signifiers* that they may use in evaluating alternative products that they can perceive in the market place may be related to these desired product attributes, but they may well be *not* directly connected with these attributes. As we have shown in Figure 12.9, the signifiers could be 1) the 'brand' of the institution issuing the bond, 2) the attitude and responsiveness of the staff that they phone up, 3) the staff member's knowledge and how they demonstrate it and 4) they make inferences based on the length and complexity of the documentation that they have to complete. Therefore, it is important if we are striving to deliver more PUV that we need to understand not only the dimensions of perceived use value and how they interconnect in the customer's mind but also what *signifiers* customers use to evaluate these dimensions. If we don't understand the signifiers and communicate effectively with potential customers, no matter how good the products may be on some objective basis, we will not influence customer perceptions of our product's value.

Moreover, in developing our insights into the *needs, product solution, attributes* and *signifiers*, this may well provoke ideas about how else these needs might be met, or whether there might be better ways of signifying value. Working through these steps might generate possible initiatives which could be trialled and tested.

What stops us understanding customer PUV?

There are a variety of factors which can prevent us from forming a thorough understanding of customers and their needs. The first of these is where we don't really understand who our customer is. We have worked with organisations who, when asked 'who are your customers?' their responses indicate how unclear they are. One bank's executives when asked who their target customers were said, 'anyone who wants a mortgage'. Where firms are trading business-to-business, again there can be a tendency to form simplistic perceptions of the customer. On many occasions our clients have referred to their customers as firms or corporations. This just isn't good enough. You don't sell anything to corporations, you only sell to *people*. So you need to know who within the client organisation is the most influential person in choosing a supplier. *They* are the customer, not 'the corporation'.

A second problem that creates a barrier to insight is the common practice of *stereotyping* our customers. It is very convenient to refer to customers as homogeneous groups, for example, we sell to 'the small businessman'. This leads into our third source of problems, which is inappropriately homogenising the market. This is where we make inappropriate generalisations about customers as in, for example, 'customers want flexibility'. Well some do, many don't, or are certainly not willing to pay extra for it. We therefore need to understand different *segments* of demand. The market may segment by $PUV with some customers preferring particular product dimensions or attributes, whilst others don't rate these as important. Or even if customers value the same dimensions of $PUV, some customers may be much more price sensitive. For example, customers shopping at a discount supermarket like ALDI may well value the same dimensions of $PUV as someone shopping in a more 'upmarket' store, for example, Waitrose; but they can't afford to shop at Waitrose.

The next source of problems is in the mindset or the orientation of the executives of the firm. In some organisations, the prevailing and predominant perspective is a *'technical'* product orientation rather than a *customer* orientation. People talk about products, and the features of products; they rarely consider the motivations of the customer. In these firms, people get excited about product innovations, new technical features and presumably they assume that there are customers out there who are equally excited by these innovations.

Perhaps surprisingly we can make mistakes where we don't understand the *product set* that customers are comparing our offering with. On numerous occasions, we have encountered businesses that don't truly understand *who* they actually compete with. They operate on the basis that *they* choose who they compete with, where in fact they have no say in the matter. Sometimes they are shocked when market research reveals that they do in fact compete with firms that they never considered to be part of their market. But the most general failing here is a lack of interest, leading to a lack of effort in trying to understand who these customers might be, what their needs are and what signifiers they use.

This information can be gathered if we are prepared to put some effort in. Well-run focus groups are a good vehicle for understanding customers and the way they go about their purchasing behaviour. If you have a B2B relationship and have ongoing interactions between some of your staff and your client organisations' staff, then these can be used as opportunities to gather intelligence. The great advantage here is that these natural and informal interactions are much more likely to reveal the client organisations' true perceptions of what we are doing for them and what they think of rival firms. They are more likely to give honest feedback, and less likely to try to 'game' the interaction.

Connecting the firm's offer with customer needs

In Figure 12.10 we bring together the various high-level needs of the customer and the kinds of 'offerings' that a firm might put forward to meet those needs.[48] Starting from the centre of the figure, we would have some basic needs that can be readily met through the purchase of a product. It is the *functionality* of the

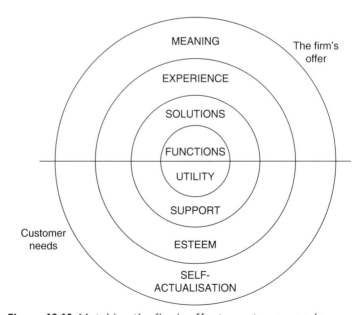

Figure 12.10 Matching the firm's offer to customer needs

product that the customer is interested in, for example, 'I need a new tyre to replace one that has a puncture'. The customer is concerned with whether the tyre will fit his car and will it be safe. Thus, the utility needs of the customer match the functionality offered by the tyre.

In the next concentric circle, the customer feels he needs support through the purchase and installation of the tyre. This is matched by the offering of a more complete *solution* to his needs. He schedules a time with the depot, takes his car with the slow puncture to the depot, where the fitter changes the tyre whilst he waits.

The next circle addresses less tangible needs that the customer might have, for example, for self-esteem, recognition, social acceptance, belonging. How might these needs be met through the purchase of a tyre? They could be met by a) involving the customer in a discussion of alternative tyre options, b) recognising his experience and preferences and commending him on his choice, whilst c) acknowledging his thanks and leaving him with a feeling of accomplishment, recognition and satisfaction. This might seem at first glance rather an unlikely scenario, but we know that customers can place great value on how they are treated during these seemingly routine encounters.

The outer circle juxtaposes Maslow's idea of 'self-actualisation' with the provision of *meaning* generated through interacting with the firm. Is this a credible outcome in our tyre purchase? Assume that through interactions between the customer and the depot salesperson, it becomes clear that the customer has concerns about the environmental impact of his car driving, and the disposal of the used tyre. Through a discussion with the salesperson, the customer is made aware of some 'greener' alternative packages and he settles on a more expensive but more environmentally sustainable combination of tyre choice and disposal. He leaves the encounter feeling that in some small way he has done the right thing and acted in line with his deep-seated values; *meaning* has been created for him through the interaction.

In Figure 12.11 we offer another perspective on the interactions between the firm and the customer. Here we differentiate between the exchange of products for cash and the co-creation of value

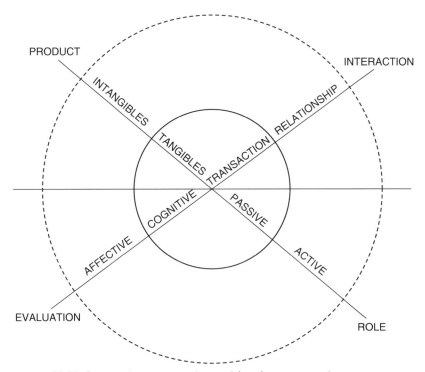

Figure 12.11 Comparing transactions with value co-creation

through ongoing interactions between firm and customer. In the inner circle, we see the transfer of tangible products for cash; there may be no need for any dialogue or direct contact between buyer and seller, for example, the deal is done online; the customer is essentially a passive recipient of the product, and largely cognitive processing is deployed to evaluate PUV and price.

In the outer circle here we have the *co-creation* of value where the customer is actively involved in specifying and even designing the product or service, through a sequence of interactions which could last months. Less tangible aspects of the service come to prominence and emotions as well as 'facts' play a large part in the interaction between firm and client.

Our tyre purchase example would be a B2C transaction where the customer is purchasing a tyre for his own use. But the same issues arise where the customer is buying for a family member or on behalf of a firm (B2B). The reason we say this is that *people* buy things, not firms. The less tangible benefits like recognition, self-esteem that may be generated through a purchase situation may be just as valuable to an individual in their role of, for example, Head of IT Procurement as they would be when they are buying something for their family or their own consumption.

Feedback on unit costs

To appropriately adapt the initiative, we also need cost information. *We can 'benchmark' against our current position.* The important point is the direction of travel. Are we *adding* PUV? Are we *reducing* unit costs through this initiative? And how do we ensure that we are cutting costs in ways which don't reduce customer PUV? Similarly, tracking the initiative through feedback can help us avoid adding to customer PUV by loading in excess costs which we cannot recoup through premium pricing.

There are various accounting techniques that can be utilised to help allocate costs down to the unit level. For example, activity-based costing (ABC) identifies activities in a firm and assigns the cost of activity to all end products or services according to the level of associated activities 'consumed'. The outcome of using ABC is to assign more indirect costs (overhead) into direct costs compared to conventional accounting allocation methods. In this way, a firm can more reliably estimate the true unit costs of its products and services.

The more accurate allocation of unit costs can improve decision making. ABC is predominantly used to support decisions concerning price, cost targets, process improvements, outsourcing options and product portfolios.

Usually, we can have some reasonable estimates of our costs, although it is never possible to unequivocally allocate some costs to specific products. But we are used to dealing with some ambiguity about unit costs. Often the important issue is to focus on *changes* to costs. So if we are reasonably comfortable that we measure the right cost components, then we can devote attention to how these components are changing as the initiative gets trialled and rolled out.

To summarise, *feedback* is essential to enable the system to adapt to changing circumstances, whether these changes were instigated by managers, or whether the changes emanate from the actions of competitors, customers or suppliers. To check that the system is 'on track' during the strategy change process, we emphasise the need for a continual flow of information about customer $PUV and costs.

Key performance indicators

Over the past decade, key performance indicators (KPIs) have been spreading through our organisations like a plague.[49] The idea of KPIs is that they provide an intervening measure and target which will, it is assumed, lead ultimately to profit flow. But here's the problem. If you set specific KPIs as *targets*, this assumes you *know* how profits are produced. Our view would be that in a complex open system, this is a questionable assumption to make.

A simple (and true) example might make this point. A sales team was set a monthly sales target, which is unremarkable, but, in addition all sales staff were given a target to be on the phone to customers and prospects for a minimum of two hours per day. The phone calls were monitored and logged. Lucy hit her monthly sales targets, but was fired because she didn't hit the two hour per day phone target. She was more comfortable contacting customers through emails with the occasional brief phone call. She felt customers were too busy to spend time chatting on the phone and felt embarrassed if she just 'kept them talking' just so she didn't hit the hours target.

The assumption of the sales director, based presumably on his past experience of selling, was that the more time one spent on the phone, the more sales were generated. The general point is this: specific KPIs and targets that are set 'from the top' reflect the assumptions executives have about how value is created and captured. They can also distort behaviours away from what *should* be done, they can encourage 'gaming' the system to hit the targets and they can lead to frustration and demotivation. The more your behaviour is monitored through KPIs, the more the message comes across that you are *not trusted* to behave appropriately.

Application 5: Mapping the value system

In Figure 12.12 we set out a simple structure that can be used to explore the *current value system*. The map is built by posing four questions:

- Why do we win business?
- What gives us a cost advantage?
- Why do we lose business we should win?
- What gives us a cost disadvantage?

By addressing these four questions, we can build an understanding of our current sources of advantage and disadvantage.

It is impossible to build a precise and comprehensive representation of any complex system, but by focusing on four critical questions we can build some shared understanding of how we think the system seems to operate. This can help us protect current sources of advantage from inappropriate changes to the system. What is not possible is to *predict* what the system might look like in the future. The primary role of the mapping process we outline is to *provoke useful conversation*.

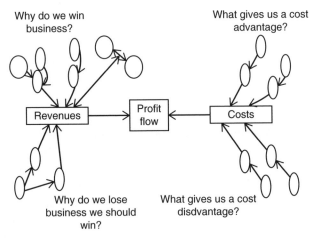

Figure 12.12 Mapping the value system

The map tries to summarise what the system looks like today. The purpose of the system is to generate a flow of profit. We generate profit only where the inflow of cash (revenues) exceeds the outflow of cash from the system (costs). The map enables us to focus attention on the primary sources of advantage that the business has.

The four questions in more detail are:

1. *Why do we win business?* When we are competing with other firms, on what basis are we able to secure the order? Is it through superior $PUV? Or are we offering equivalent products to rivals but we price lower than they do? And what seems to be the critical order-winning dimensions of $PUV?

2. *What gives us a cost advantage?* Do we have more efficient processes? Can we source cheaper components than rivals?

The mapping process should help in identifying the unique *strategic assets and capabilities* the firm has that give it competitive advantage (we explore strategic assets in depth in Chapter 13). The map also poses two questions that could generate possible initiatives:

3. *Why do we lose business we should win?* This question gets us to focus on the 'near misses', why didn't we get that order? We seem to be in a good position but somehow we weren't able to get over the line. The point of this question is that there may be relatively straightforward changes that could be made that would increase our 'hit rate'. By reflecting on these 'near misses', we can identify specific initiatives that could resolve some of these shortcomings.

4. *What gives us a cost disadvantage?* We will enjoy some cost advantages, but these may be outweighed by too many sources of cost *dis*advantage. We may be in a location where there are higher rents, local wage rates may be above the average, we may have too many support staff, or aging equipment. Again, by focusing on these sources of disadvantage, this may provoke some ideas for initiatives that might reduce the outflow of costs.

The steps are set out below. We suggest allowing 120 minutes for the activity.

Step 1 The team agrees on the business unit to be analysed. This could be the whole firm, or a division or a product group.

Step 2 Break into four sub-group: each sub-group tackles ONE of the four questions: Why do we win business? Why do we lose business we should win? What gives us a cost advantage? What gives us a cost disadvantage?

Step 3 Using post-it notes on a flip chart, the group generates ideas about the causes of advantage/disadvantage as appropriate. Try to separate the generation of these ideas from a subsequent evaluation. Thus, generate the ideas first, then go through the ideas and develop, amend or take out the idea.

Step 4 Look for causal links, that is, can we uncover the causes of us either having/not having advantage? In this way, the group can start to dig deeper and reveal underlying issues, assets and valuable capabilities.

Step 5 Reconvene as a group. Pin the sheet(s) on walls and have each group talk through their work.

Step 6 Agree a way of capturing these insights so they can be shared and recalled when exploring strategy choices.

The map is a loose structure that can be constructed through discussion using a white board, or by using 'post-it' notes. The circles would be causes of advantage or disadvantage, and it is often useful to pose the question 'why is this like it is?' In this way, the surface level or presenting source of advantage (or disadvantage) might be traced back to some underlying causes. And one or more of these causes could be enhanced or reduced accordingly through an initiative.

The map can also help to reduce the risks of introducing an initiative to, say, reduce costs which has a negative impact on a source of advantage. The map can be used as a reference when suggesting change initiatives and it can also be updated as the system evolves: it should be a 'live' map.

Application 6: Exploring strategy initiatives

To get used to thinking about change as a series of discrete strategy initiatives, we suggest taking the team through a 'trial run'.

Step 1 Choose a strategy.

Step 2 Familiarise yourselves with the *practices* associated with the chosen strategy. These appear at the end of each strategy chapter. For example, the *excellence* practices are reproduced in Figure 12.13.

Step 3 Agree a change in current practice that would start to shift the value system in the direction of the strategy.

Step 4 Work *individually* for five minutes to think about a possible initiative that could help embed the chosen practice.

Step 5 Share your ideas and choose **two** initiatives. Explore them as a team and then summarise them in the template in Figure 12.4.

Step 6 Discuss what feedback would be required to make sure the initiative is delivering the benefits required. This feedback could be quantitative, for example, a reduction in overhead costs over a time period, or it could be more subjective and qualitative, for example, through informal conversations with staff they report that they feel more involved in decision making.

EXCELLENCE: Practices

Culture

- *A culture wich values knowledge creation, sharing and retention and where insights into customers' needs are widely shared and valued*
- *Trust-based relationships which value professional expertise*

Structure

- *Specialisation of tasks to facilitate the building of deep expertise*
- *Decentralised structures that encourage decision making by those with the greatest expertise and who are closer to the problems and issues*
- *Strong coordination mechanisms to ensure specialised activities are integrated to deliver customer value*

Systems

- *Reward systems that recognise and encourage excellence*
- *Building strong brand and reputation which improves bargaining relationships with customers and suppliers*

Figure 12.13 Excellence practices

Strategy initiatives exercise

Chosen strategy:

Desired change in practices	Possible initiatives	What feedback is required?

Figure 12.14 Template for Initiatives exercise

Chapter

13

Strategic assets and capabilities

Firms consist of configurations of value-creating assets and capabilities and the competitive strategies guide initiatives that build capabilities. The successful embedding of a competitive strategy should create *strategic assets and capabilities* for the firm. ***Strategic assets and capabilities give the firm competitive advantage and they are difficult for rival firms to imitate.*** In this chapter we explore the assets and capabilities that combine to create and capture value. Some assets are obvious, for example, a brand name, but others are subtle and complex capabilities that are difficult to create and to protect. Whilst the 'upside' of a competitive strategy is the creation of additional sources of competitive advantage, the potential 'downside' is that the change processes involved in embedding the strategy may inadvertently destroy existing but often subtle sources of advantage. As we explained in Chapter 12, it is critically important that any strategy initiatives that we trial do not damage existing capabilities. Throughout the chapter, we draw heavily on the *resource-based view* of the firm.[50]

We explore the inner workings of the value system and uncover different categories of assets and capabilities. We identify what makes assets difficult to imitate, and we stress the importance of careful forethought and feedback from the system to try to ensure the strategy change processes do not damage any current sources of competitive advantage.

Tangible assets would include machinery, buildings and software and intangible assets would include brands, reputation, trust, customer switching costs, relationships and external networks. Some of these assets exist separately from people, so they can be moved or traded, but capabilities are embedded in the people that work in the business. Capabilities are made up of combinations of *routines*, people acting and interacting with assets and each other.[51]

Any business that is trading will have valuable capabilities. It might also have some disadvantages which reduce the profit flow the business can produce. The competitive strategies enhance or *augment* these capabilities to improve profit flow. We explained in Chapter 1 that managers cannot directly 'command' the development of the firm's capabilities, but they can *enable* their development by changing some of the firm's *practices*. And in the case study chapters, we set out some of the enabling practices associated with each strategy.

It's important that we understand the firm's current capabilities because some of them may well be subtle and complex and easily damaged or disturbed by any changes we make to the system. Developing a deep understanding about how the current value system operates can, at the very least, reduce the risks of destroying valuable capabilities. The first step in avoiding the inadvertent destruction of capabilities is to try to understand the current configuration of assets and capabilities that enable the firm to operate today. In Chapter 12 we introduced a simple mapping device to help elicit what helps us win business and/or have lower costs than our rivals. In this chapter we look more deeply at the assets and capabilities that help us be competitive. We begin by exploring the firm's current *routines*.

Routines: The engine of value creation

Routines are the bedrock of any organisation. By 'routine' we mean a *repeated performance* either by an individual or a collection of people interacting together. Some of these routine behaviours have been deliberately designed and trained into people. Others have emerged without any deliberate intervention by managers. All routines evolve and are a source of incremental change and improvement inside the organisation. However, if there are changes in the market environment of the firm, then existing routines may become less effective and at some point they may become 'core rigidities' which are damaging the firm's value processes.[52]

Routines have an *ostensive* aspect and a *performative* aspect.[53] The ostensive aspect is the basic structure of the routine. For example, consider the routine of dealing with a customer in a car-servicing facility. There is a general structure for this routine which includes greeting the customer, offering a seat and some refreshment, locating the paperwork, checking the work to be done and any other issues, handling the car keys, informing the customer when the car will be ready, etc. This *ostensive* structure is understood implicitly by experienced customer-service personnel, and it rarely alters significantly. The *performative* aspect is a particular enactment of the routine, that is, what I did with this customer this morning. Each time someone performs the routine, it will be slightly different, due to a whole raft of reasons, for example, time of day, the mood of the customer, the complexity of the service and repairs, etc. Thus, the *performative* aspect of the routine is the source of variation.

Where learning occurs, the individual becomes more skilled at the activity, they then become more effective and more efficient in how they perform. This process goes on continually within any organisation. At the more abstract *ostensive* level, you might perceive the organisation to be highly stable; however, at the *performative* level, there is continual evolution of activity. When we talk about the changes involved in introducing an initiative, we are talking about a rate of change in routines which is *faster* than these incremental emergent processes that would *naturally* occur.

Changes in the effectiveness of routines are strongly influenced by feedback. The quality and frequency of feedback affects the way a routine evolves and adapts. For example, consider a stand-up comedian embarking on his first ever five-minute routine in a comedy club. He has worked on the material for weeks, honing the language, the timing and sequence of the stories and one-liners. Naturally, he is nervous. He waits in the wings to be introduced by the MC. Unfortunately, when he gets on stage the lights are so bright that he can't see anyone beyond the first row of tables. He starts the routine.

Now consider two ways that this could go: 1) his first gag is received in silence, or 2) it gets a roar of appreciative laughter. What happens to the rest of the routine is driven by the feedback. In case 1, he tries his next gag, silence, and gets more nervous and ends up finishing the routine two minutes early, as his timings had allowed for laughter. In case 2, he never gets to finish the routine. His confidence builds, a heckler shouts a comment, he *ad libs* a response which the audience love, and he adjusts the tone and timing of the rest of his set accordingly.

The feedback is immediate and in case 1, unforgiving. The value being created is an entertained and amused audience. In case 1, regardless of the 'intrinsic' quality of the material and the talent of the comedian, he bombs and no value gets created. In case 2 the interactions with the audience, the immediate feedback and the ability of the comedian to react appropriately generated significant value. Thus, value creation is highly contextual, and feedback enables more value to be created. The more direct and immediate feedback is, the more likely it is that we can adapt and adjust our actions.

Some organisations become 'insulated' from feedback from customers. In these insulated systems, the 'operating core' of the business is essentially isolated from the external environment. Very little useful feedback from customers penetrates the operating core. In its place, we have routines developed in the past persisting, and where there is any change, it is provoked by top-down targets. The clear danger here is that the system drifts further from the changing market place, leading to reduced effectiveness and its ultimate demise.

In fairly stable environments, it is likely that the ostensive routines of most competing firms will look very similar. What this means is that the sources of advantage that a particular firm might have will come from the particular *performances* of these routines achieved by its members. Subtle differences in the way that they enact these routines may well be sources of advantage and if these subtle differences incorporate significant amounts of *tacit knowledge*, then it is very difficult for competitor firms to replicate these valuable routines. Tacit knowledge is often referred to as *know-how*, and it is built through experience. Tacit *routines* are collective performances of groups of people acting and interacting to create a product, solve a problem, respond to a client's needs, etc. We explore tacit knowledge later in this chapter.

Products and services are created through interactions between people and other assets. Interactions between people can take the form of complex routines, or alternatively, there may be little interaction in the value creation process. An example of the latter case would be an assembly line. Here employees primarily interact with equipment and components; they have little requirement to interact with each other, other than for social reasons. Their work is coordinated not through conversation or *mutual adjustment,* as it is formally referred to; their work is coordinated through them performing a sequence of standardised activities. Thus, the output from one stage of the process is passed on, maybe on a conveyor, to the employee in the subsequent stage.[54]

In some industries, non-human assets like equipment play a prominent role in the value creation process. In other more labour-intensive industries, like professional services, non-human assets play a relatively insignificant role.[55]

Assets and capabilities

For any firm to exist at all, it must have the required capabilities to survive in its market place. We refer to these as *entry assets* and capabilities. Typically, the current configuration of assets and capabilities in any firm is the outcome of a flow of plans, decisions and intentions, and surprises and luck. However we have arrived at the current situation, there must be sufficient positive *synergies* between this complex mix of assets and capabilities to enable the firm to persist.

In Figure 13.1 we suggest that any firm can be subdivided into five parts. We shall start with the *entry assets and capabilities* of the firm.[56] These refer to things like equipment, software, skills and capabilities that are required for the firm to operate within a particular market place. The point about entry assets is they are *equivalent* in their effect between competing firms. In other words, if one were able to look inside two closely competing firms, we would expect to see a lot of similarities between them. These entry assets and capabilities are valuable insofar as they help the firm operate within its chosen markets, but they are not in any way distinctive, they do not deliver any competitive advantages.

The *liabilities* and *disadvantages* destroy value. These may well be individuals who make little contribution to value creation; however, they still draw a salary. It could be that our products are good, but our reputation is poor, based on customer perceptions of problems we had in the past.

For an asset or capability to be classified as *strategic,* it has to simultaneously pass what have become known as the VRIN criteria. This acronym, derived by Jay Barney, stands for Valuable, Rare, Inimitable, and Non-substitutable.[57]

A *valuable* resource or capability increases relative customer-perceived use value, or it lowers the relative costs of the firm. In each case, when we talk about relative performance we are referring to the average or typical competitor for this particular firm. *Rare* just means it is not commonly found as a capability amongst this group of firms, and *inimitable* means that it is very difficult for rival firms to copy this capability or asset. The final criterion is *non-substitutability*. This means that the use value that this asset or capability contributes to the firm cannot be delivered in an alternative way.

There is not much inside any firm that would pass all of these criteria *simultaneously*. So we are focusing on a small subset of the firm's activities, assets and capabilities; however, this is a subset which is strategically critical.

There are two other parts to any firm. One is what we have described in Figure 13.1 as *future-orientated activity*. This refers to activity currently undertaken inside the firm but which is directed towards

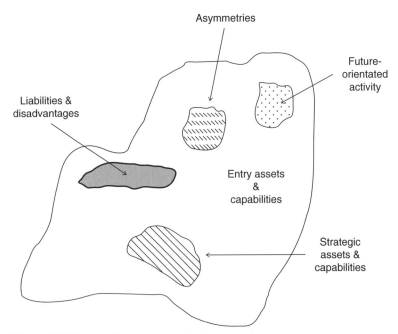

Figure 13.1 Strategic assets and entry assets

improving the firm's *future* performance. Typically, we would include research and development, training, market research or business development activity in this category. The problem is that these activities incur real costs today, for a hoped-for performance improvement in the future. The causal connection between investing in these activities today and the future bottom line of the firm is not clear or straightforward. Many of these activities are undertaken almost as an act of faith, or because the firm has always engaged in these activities, or because this is the norm in this industry. When a firm hits hard times, these are the budgets which typically are the first to be cut, because this delivers an immediate cost reduction. Therefore, they are very vulnerable to short-term performance declines.

An *asymmetry* is simply something the firm has that is *rare but not yet valuable*.[58] Often, firms have asymmetries purely through chance, but a change in the market environment or someone spotting a new opportunity to use the asset in a novel way can make this asymmetry extremely valuable. There is some evidence that luck plays a significant part in business success. This links well with our idea of initiatives and an exploratory approach to change. Introducing variations, pilot tests or trials is like entering a lottery. If you don't buy a ticket, you can't win the jackpot, and the more tickets you buy, the more chance you have of winning. Thus, you need to generate a sufficient number of trials and experiments in order to enable your organisation to probe the changing context, learn and adjust. In this way, you have a much better chance of thriving in an uncertain environment.

In some markets, the 'entry' level of capabilities may be orientated primarily to deliver a standard product efficiently. In other contexts, the entry capabilities might require some agility in the system to cope with changing customer demands. *The role of the competitive strategy is to augment these embedded capabilities with additional capabilities, which in combination can give the firm some advantage.* If these changes are successful, the augmented capabilities become *future* strategic assets for the firm.

As we have argued, any firm can explore any of our seven strategies. If an *adaptive* strategy is introduced into an existing 'low-cost' business, these combined capabilities may enable the firm to capture more value. Similarly, a set of existing capabilities may be delivering *excellence,* but not much in the way of *innovation.* Thus, an innovation strategy would start to *augment* the firm's capabilities. The point here is that the firm can gain advantage by being a *bit more* adaptive, or low cost or innovative compared to its close competitors. You don't have to innovate to the extent that, say Apple or Dyson have, you just need to be more innovative than close rivals (our Usain Bolt principle).

Categories of strategic asset

We now explore six categories of strategic asset. The purpose of this section is to alert you to the range of possible assets, and in this way we might reduce the risks of introducing changes which inadvertently damage or destroy strategic assets.[59]

Tangible assets

We begin with *tangible* assets, for example, the physical *location* of the firm. A retailer may have a prime site on a busy high street. Or it could be *equipment* that a firm has which gives it an advantage, but it cannot be equipment that the firm has bought, because other firms could easily buy the same kit. *Patents* are clearly unique and owned by the firm, although they can be traded. One other source of tangible assets may be *information* that the firm has. This is information rather than *know-how,* and it may pertain, for example, to the customers that the firm serves. This information may enable this firm to serve its clients or customers more effectively than rival firms who do not have access to it.

System assets

When we refer to *system* assets, we mean any deliberately created, explicit, codified set of procedures or processes that give the firm an advantage. Examples of system assets may be quality assurance processes, a cold-calling script, induction and training activities, systems for accessing and reusing past proposal documents.

Structural assets

We would suggest that the *structuring* of the organisation, that is, the choices that are made about how the overall task is subdivided and allocated between different people and groups, could be a source of advantage. For example, choices about how to *group* people may give the firm an advantage, if co-locating these individuals encourages a more rapid and informal flow of information between them. There may be structural advantages in reducing layers of hierarchy, which might enable the firm to be more responsive and it may also encourage more initiatives from individuals closer to the operating core of the business. If we choose to have some staff *specialising* in a particular activity, this should build expertise that may become a source of advantage.

Knowledge assets

Knowledge assets and capabilities come in a variety of forms. We may have a very gifted designer, engineer or salesperson. These special individuals may enable the firm to add value in unique ways to its customers, or they may help the firm to operate more efficiently. However, one of the problems with individual technical know-how as a strategic asset or capability is that it is highly mobile; this know-how can move to a rival firm.

Polanyi succinctly defines *tacit knowledge* as 'we know more than we can tell'.[60] A simple example would be a tacit skill like riding a bicycle. Most of us know how to do this, but if you have tried to teach a child to ride a bicycle, you realise that there is a lot of information that you've not passed on to them. The reason for this is not any malicious intent on your part, it's because many of the things you do when you ride a bike are tacit, in other words, they are things that you do *automatically,* for example, when you turn a corner you don't just move the handlebars, you shift your weight as well.

The point about tacit knowledge as a source of advantage is that it is very difficult for rival firms to replicate. If we cannot explain how we produce the skilled performance of an activity, it is virtually impossible for a rival firm to reproduce it. *Tacit knowledge*:

- *is at the heart of the value creation process*
- *can only be built through doing, through experience*
- *cannot be transferred from one person to another*

Tacit *routines* are a *collective performance* involving a group or team of people interacting with each other, and they pervade the entire value system.[61] The point about these routines is that they have not been specified or prescribed by managers; these have evolved through time and through experience. Embedded tacit routines can deliver advantages, and when we often refer to culture as a source of advantage, it is often these embedded routines that we are referring to.

The intuitive understanding or insight of a specific entrepreneur is clearly a knowledge asset.[62] Some entrepreneurs are able to sense or 'read' changing market circumstances and are able to discern, ahead of rivals, what the market is moving towards. Most entrepreneurs may find it quite difficult to explain to other people how they generate these insights. Therefore, these sources of advantage are likely to remain inimitable.

There is an additional source of knowledge-based advantage which we would call *knowledge architecture*. This can refer to different things but the specific meaning we have here would be a shared understanding of 'who knows what' inside the firm. What this means is that everyone knows what everyone else knows about, that is, they don't all have the same knowledge but they are aware of the knowledge that their colleagues possess. This may be a source of advantage. For example, if a client or customer asks a salesperson for a specific service or problem to be solved, a shared understanding of the breadth of knowledge possessed by the employees in the firm will enable the salesperson to identify the relevant expert who can help the client. Incidentally, like many other knowledge-based assets, knowledge architecture as a source of advantage is vulnerable if there is high staff turnover.

Relational assets

Relational assets include trust-based relationships that the firm has either with its clients or with its suppliers. At a minimum, where the firm has established these trust-based relationships with external stakeholders, they are able to transact business at a lower cost. For example, it may not be necessary for highly detailed and specified contracts to be drawn up between the parties, a handshake would be enough. We would argue that trust-based relationships between the managers and staff are also a source of advantage. Where there is trust, there is no need to invest in control and monitoring systems, for example, no need for target setting around KPIs.

The firm's reputation, for example, a reputation for reliability or on-time delivery, is clearly a source of advantage and should help the firm win more business. The term 'brand' is often used quite loosely, but here we refer to what a brand name or logo *evokes* in the customer's mind. Others have defined brand far more broadly than this, but we would suggest these broader definitions of brand would incorporate some other relational assets that we have identified separately.

Where a firm has been able to establish long-term and favourable contracts with customers or suppliers, these can be enduring sources of advantage. *Switching costs*, the costs that customers or suppliers incur if they move away from the existing relationships that they have, can be a source of advantage insofar as they tend to lock customers into their existing suppliers. Just to be clear, what we mean by a switching cost is a cost over and above the price of the product or service concerned that the customer might incur, for example, if they were to switch their suppliers. A good example would be an airline like Ryanair which has an all-Boeing fleet deciding to shift to a mixed fleet of Boeing and Airbus aircraft. In addition to the costs of the new aircraft, there would be costs involved in training staff to operate with the new equipment, stocking of spares, changing ground-based facilities, etc.

There is a great deal of focus in the human resource management literature on the importance of human capital. Our view is that human capital takes many different forms, some of which we have already covered, for example, special know-how. But there is a form of human capital that can be really valuable but quite specific to the individual that has it, and that is social capital. Social capital which might include the personal reputation of the individual, that individual's network of colleagues inside and outside the organisation that they can call upon, and there may well be a set of obligations and favours that that individual has accumulated over time. These things taken together may well make a specific member of staff highly effective and which might translate into a source of advantage for the firm that employs them.

However, like much human capital, social capital tends to be highly *context specific*. What this means is that an individual can exercise and create value from their social capital within this context: if they were to move to another part of the organisation, they might find that this form of human capital is not easily transferrable.

Cultural assets

We have mentioned that culture can be a source of competitive advantage, and we would suggest that where there is a pervading culture within an organisation, then this culture may be a source of advantage over and above the other manifestations of culture that we have covered so far. For example, the employees within the firm may display a culture of professionalism. The values of professional behaviour may have been inculcated in them from when they joined, through various means, some formal, for example, training and induction processes, some informal, for example, the examples set by role models inside the firm. A culture of professionalism can, at its most basic, reduce the firm's costs of staff supervision. People know instinctively how to behave; they don't need someone standing over them to tell them this. A culture of professionalism might also enable the firm to operate on clients' premises, where individual members of staff may operate without supervision.

Whilst entry assets and capabilities might be relatively easy to understand, strategic assets and capabilities are often subtle and complex. The reason for delving into these subtle sources of advantage is to alert us to the possible impact of any particular initiative or change we might undertake. As we have explained, if we are alert to these critical but less obvious aspects of the value creation processes, we are more likely to introduce changes with sensitivity to these unique and valuable idiosyncrasies in the system.

Sources of inimitability

For a strategic asset or capability to be an *enduring* source of advantage, it not only has to be valuable over time but also has to be difficult to copy or imitate. There are four primary sources of inimitability. The first of these is *causal ambiguity*.[63] Put simply, this means that a competitor cannot understand how we do what we do. The links between actions and outcomes, or means and ends, is opaque or ambiguous to them. Therefore, they don't know what it is they should be trying to replicate. Causal ambiguity can come about just through the sheer complexity of the way our firm creates value.

Whilst causal ambiguity is a barrier to imitability, it also can create problems *within* the firm. We have encountered circumstances where new managers are introduced into the organisation from elsewhere, where they themselves do not fully understand how the firm creates value. Perhaps this is not surprising when we realise that if the firm's sources of competitive advantage were obvious, the chances are that rival firms would already have replicated these. So there is a potential danger where managers are not too familiar with the subtle operations of the firm. We will revisit this issue later in this chapter.

The second source of inimitability is *path dependency*.[64] Some of the more complex assets that we have identified above, for example, a culture of professionalism, may have taken the firm years to build up. Therefore, if a rival firm wishes to replicate this particular source of advantage, it may well take them just as long. There isn't necessarily any causal ambiguity, but for a competitor to replicate the asset or capability, they would need to travel down the same developmental pathway that we followed. It may actually not be possible to recreate this pathway due to circumstances that existed in the past not being present today. Moreover, even if the rival firm could embark on this developmental process, it may take a considerable time. And whilst they are doing this, we will not stay still and wait for them to catch up.

Our third source of inimitability is *asset configuration*. In Figure 13.2 we have identified two different sources of advantage. In Case A we have the straightforward situation where the firm possesses a strategic asset or capability which is valuable, unique and inimitable. In this case, it is the combination of the unique asset with other entry assets that enables the firm to gain and sustain advantage. As long as the unique resource remains valuable and inimitable, the firm's source of advantage will endure.

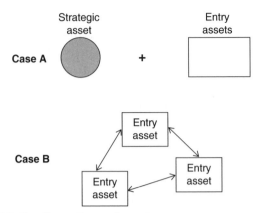

Figure 13.2 Configurations of assets

In Case B we have a situation where the firm does not have any unique or special assets per se, but what it does have are *unique interactions* between entry assets and capabilities. Here the source of advantage is the *interaction between* these assets rather than the assets themselves. An example would be a professional soccer team where the players have played alongside each other for many years. They are able to build up an understanding, as well as strong feelings of loyalty and commitment to each other which may give them an advantage. This team may not possess any outstanding star players, but they have created a *collective capability* which makes them successful on the pitch.

Alternatively, let us assume that this highly effective team has at its hub a particularly skilled midfield player, who could be classified as a unique strategic asset (as in Case A). Let us also assume that a rival but poorly performing team has decided to buy this star. Once that player has transferred to his new team, his personal ability remains the same. However, his new team mates may not be able to benefit from the special skills that he has; therefore, although *he* hasn't changed, his effectiveness on the pitch has been severely reduced. Thus, the interactions between the configuration of players in his new team are not sufficient to give the team any competitive advantages.

A Case B example would be easyJet. When you look at what easyJet has done, like Ryanair it has essentially replicated the model of South West Airlines. In fact, none of the practices that easyJet employ could be argued to be complex or impossible to imitate, for example, the demand-based fare structure, eliminating travel agents' commissions, encouraging internet booking, a paperless reservation system, flying one kind of aircraft, eliminating business class, operating only short-haul point-to-point, charging for in-flight food, getting flight attendants to clean the plane, outsourcing noncore activities, for example, check-in, baggage handling, a no-frills HQ based in Luton, no secretaries. But these cannot account for the cost advantage that the airline enjoys over most of its rivals. What delivers advantage is the combination or *configuration* of these relatively easy to comprehend individual practices. Value is created through the interactions between them rather than the practices taken in isolation.

Asset imitability

In Figure 13.3 we have arranged our six categories of strategic asset. Over time, we would expect tangible assets, structural assets and system assets would be more likely to be imitated by rival firms. The reason being that the barriers to imitability that these assets have are likely to be *lower* than knowledge, relational or cultural assets. This means that if we are to understand what gives a firm

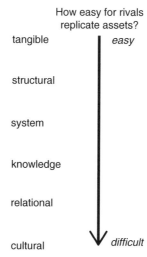

Figure 13.3 Asset imitability

sustainable competitive advantage, it is less likely to be coming from the tangible, structural or system assets, and more likely to stem from knowledge, relational and cultural assets.

This poses a severe managerial challenge. It is far easier to manage tangible, structural and system sources of advantage. These sources of advantage are easier to comprehend, and they can be more readily changed or improved. But, if all it takes is for a disgruntled employee to leave with a particular piece of software, then our source of advantage may well walk out with that individual. The asset categories in the lower half of Figure 13.3, knowledge, relational and cultural, are much more difficult to manage, they are more difficult to comprehend, and they are much more difficult to create.

When strategic assets become entry assets

Strategic assets and capabilities, that is, those that give a firm competitive advantage, do not stay strategic and valuable forever. As soon as a rival firm is able to imitate or replicate this source of advantage then, by definition, it is no longer unique to the firm. In this way, imitation redefines strategic assets as *entry* assets.

Some strategic assets become redundant if what they are helping to produce is no longer valued by the market place. For example, we may well have the most efficient diesel engine-producing plant in the world; the problem is the market for diesel cars is in rapid decline. But here we want to focus on the *mutilation* or inadvertent destruction of strategic assets by *managers*. We hinted at this problem earlier on in the chapter. Our point is that if managers do not truly understand the often subtle sources of competitive advantage that their firm has, they may well inadvertently destroy them.

An example would be a producer of specialist high-performance cars. This firm was acquired by a very large multinational car manufacturer. As a way of reducing costs, the workers on the production and assembly lines were required to wear the same uniforms as all the other employees in the other car plants. Common overalls procured from the same supplier in the quantities that the corporation required gave them a significant cost saving. When this fed through to this subsidiary producing high-performance sports cars, they

STRATEGIC ASSETS AND CAPABILITIES

too experienced a small reduction in their operating costs. However, there were unintended consequences from this improvement in cost efficiency. The first was damage to customer perceptions of value. Customers were encouraged to visit the car plant to see their car in various stages of production. Unfortunately, when some customers visited the plant what they saw were people wearing overalls branded with the logo of the acquiring corporation, not the logo of the specialist sports car manufacturer.

But if anything, the damage internally was much greater than this. Staff formerly perceived themselves to be different from the larger volume car assemblers; they saw themselves being special and one of the ways this difference was manifested was through the 'branded' workwear that they were used to wearing. Changing what they wore literally changed their identity. This, along with other changes severely damaged their morale and motivation.

Competitive strategies and strategic assets

The successful pursuit of a clear competitive strategy should help to create strategic assets and capabilities. But because strategic assets are often subtle and complex, and because value is created through *interactions* between assets and know-how, we need to be careful when we introduce any strategy initiative not to damage these existing sources of advantage. This chapter explored strategic assets generally, which should enable you to assess the asset base in your own organisation. The minimum benefit that can be gained from developing a deeper insight into the assets of the business is that you can try to ensure that you don't inadvertently destroy these sources of advantage as you introduce initiatives.

But because the firm is a complex system, the effects and impacts of any changes we make cannot be known in advance. If the ultimate impact of a strategy initiative is that the system becomes more profitable, then the likelihood is that some new strategic assets and capabilities have emerged in the system. Some of these may be obvious, for example, a new and successful product is launched, others will be subtle and may be diffused through the system in the form of changed attitudes, or more effective coordination between activities.

When we introduce a strategy initiative, we must be careful not to *disrupt, diminish* or *destroy* existing sources of advantage that we have. To be clear, a competitive strategy is merely an idea. It can only create value if it impacts on the value system. Thus, for a strategy to have impact, it must cause some change in *action*. One *deliberate* way we suggest that the system could be changed is through strategy initiatives, but if the strategy is well understood and there is consensus that this is the right way to go, people's actions may be influenced more pervasively and thus the strategy impacts the system in a more *emergent* way.

In Figure 13.4 we depict the value system at Time 1, with its attendant cost, revenue and cash flows. Assume a choice of competitive strategy, and an initiative introduced into the system to assist in shifting the system in the desired direction. The initiative provokes a change in action which 'invades' the system and it will have some positive and negative interaction effects with the existing elements in the system. If the initiative has a positive impact on cash flow, that is, the flow at T2 is greater than at T1, then we can say that the initiative has created value. Identifying the impact of any initiative is difficult, but if we are able to get good quality and timely feedback from the system, we are more able to attribute the changes in cost and revenue flows to the strategy initiative.

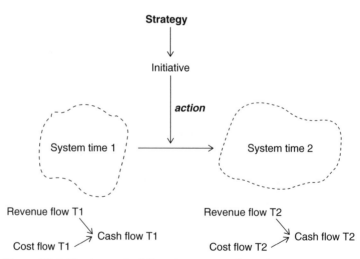

Figure 13.4 The impact of the strategy on the value system

Valuing strategic assets

In the resource-based view of the firm (RBV), 'resources' (our *strategic assets*) are valuable and inimitable. There is an assumption in the RBV that these inimitable assets can be identified, and in a sense that their value contribution can be isolated from the wider system. We take a different approach. Whilst we recognise the importance of idiosyncratic assets and capabilities, we also acknowledge that they can only be 'valued' as part of the wider value system. Their value consists in the unique quality the assets have as *use values*, and the *synergistic interaction effects* these assets have with the rest of the system, and how the value system as a whole interacts with the wider environment. Their value derives from their uniqueness, but this value is highly context-specific and embedded in the system.

An initiative that generates a positive cash flow has created a valuable change in the system. This change could take the form of a more efficient routine, an improvement to a product, a targeted marketing campaign, improvements in the way we source key components, etc. The impact of the initiative, if positive, creates some form of additional value or surplus from the system. Thus, the outcome of the initiative is a systemic change which generates more value.

Whether these enhancements to the system can be readily identified or not is an empirical question. Some improvements will be immediate and obviously attributable to the initiative; others may work their way through the wider system causing subtle but valuable adjustments to working practices that collectively contribute to the flow of surplus.

In Figure 13.5, we depict the firm's value system at two points in time. At *t1*, the assets and capabilities of the firm are *interacting* with the wider environment in the process of value creation. These assets are only valuable in relation to the wider environment; they have no value independent of these interactions. Thus, the value of any asset is determined by its deployment in a particular context at a point in time.

The way we have drawn the value system at *t2* suggests that it is the same as it was in *t1*. The implication is that the firm is operating in an identical way as it did in *t1*. However, the wider environment at

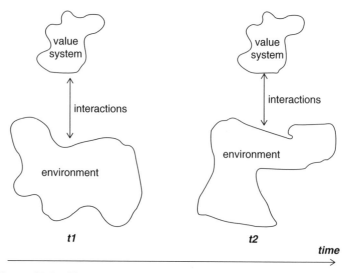

Figure 13.5 Effects of environmental change

t2 is different to *t1*, thus the interactions will be different in *t2*, thus the value of the assets in the firm will inevitably change from *t1* to *t2*, even though the firm remains 'stable' during this time period.

Thus, the value of assets and capabilities is contingent upon the specific deployment of them, how they configure and interact and how they relate to the changing context.

Identifying strategic assets

Application 7: The strategic asset audit

We need to understand the assets and capabilities the firm currently has which provide some competitive advantage. Advantage would stem from our ability to offer superior customer PUV or from being able to operate at lower costs than rivals. If we are aware of these often subtle sources of advantage, this should enable us to:

(a) select a more appropriate competitive strategy and

(b) make sure we don't destroy sources of advantage through any changes we introduce into the value system.

The first technique that can provide an overview of the asset base of the business is the *strategic asset audit*.

The audit takes a top-down view of the business and it tests out assets against Barney's VRIN criteria. There are two ways of conducting the audit, both have their merits. In both approaches, you first need to agree the business unit you are choosing to analyse. This could be a single product, a group of products, a 'strategic business unit' or an entire corporation. Then you can either get members of the team to do their own audit and then share the different analyses, or work simultaneously as a team and build consensus as you go. The advantages of the 'individuals first' approach is it generates more diversity, challenge and debate. The benefit of the group approach is that it is often a swifter process, but it relies to some extent on members of the team feeling able to challenge others and disagree.

Step 1 Decide the business unit you are analysing.

Step 2 Working as individuals, identify *three* strategic asset candidates (5 mins).

Step 3 Share the lists and record on a flip chart. From this long list, agree on *ten* asset candidates.

Step 4 As group then evaluate each asset candidate against the VRIN criteria, and score it.

Step 5 Total the rows and classify the *ten* assets.

Step 6 Discuss the implications of the audit: Any surprises? Problems? Over-dependence on specific individuals/groups? And can any of these assets be leveraged to generate more value?

The six steps are summarised in the box. We now expand on these steps.

The team uses the six categories of asset that we developed in the chapter as prompts (tangible, structural, system, knowledge, relational and cultural) and lists potential strategic assets ('asset candidates') in the left column of Figure 13.6. Then work across the row, testing out each asset candidate against the VRIN criteria.

How does it add value? Does it give you a PUV advantage? Or a cost advantage? We use a simple scoring system (0–5) to judge the

Strategic asset audit

Asset candidate	How does it add value?		Rare? (5)	Inimit -able? (5)	Non- substitute -able?(5)	Total (25)	+ Category	Where can it be leveraged?
	? PUV (5)	1 Costs (5)						

Figure 13.6 Strategic asset audit

extent to which the criteria is fulfilled. For example, if the asset was a brand name, we might conclude that it gives us a significant advantage in customer PUV (score 5), and because of strong brand awareness, we typically get to appear on most client's shortlists when they are looking to place an order. This reduces our selling costs relative to our rivals, so we might score a 2 for 'lower costs'. Typically, most assets *either* give us a cost advantage *or* a PUV advantage.

We then move on to the next column 'rare'. To our knowledge, is this asset unique? If it is, we score it 5; if some rivals have something similar then it gets a lower score. Then we test out how imitable the asset is. A test question would be: *'how likely is it that this asset could be copied by a rival in the next 2 years?'*

If the answer is 'very likely', it gets a low score. If the answer is 'impossible', it gets a 5.

The non-substitutable test is tricky. We are posing the question: 'can the use value or benefit of this asset be delivered in another way?' Take our brand example. The brand name is legally protected, so it cannot be copied. But, a rival firm may have their own established brand name, which does the same job as ours. If this was the case, then the non-substitutable score would be zero.

When you have evaluated one asset, total the score, and then move to the next one. In this way, your scoring will more likely be consistent across the range of assets. Our experience is that when teams compare their firm's assets, they are often surprised that what they initially thought were highly valuable and rare assets turn out to be less valuable, and *vice versa*. We also suggest categorising each asset (*tangible, system,* etc.). Again teams are often surprised that the enduring sources of advantage are in the more intangible categories of *relationships, know-how* and *culture.*

This 'top-down' audit is a useful way of generating some understanding of the assets you currently have. A complementary 'bottom-up' technique is cause mapping.

Application 8: Cause mapping

Cause mapping, in our application here, is a way to dig deeper inside the business to surface often subtle sources of advantage. We have trialled various versions of the cause mapping technique over the years. We have varied the starting point of the map, the process of generating the map and who is involved in the process.

What is common to all these approaches is that it reveals what we refer to as **strategic detail.** In most mature market settings, most firms are endowed with very similar configurations of assets and capabilities. This comes about through imitation over time, often driven by suppliers and employees moving between competing firms. However, despite this tendency to 'isomorphism', there will still be persistent differences between firms that account for their differential performance. The mapping process can reveal these subtle variations in asset endowment and practices.

You can start the map with either a critical incident like winning a recent contract, or something broader like 'profit flow' or 'success'. To build the map, the team keep posing the same question: 'What causes that?' In Figure 13.7 we have started with a critical incident – in this case, it was a construction company that won a competitive contract to build a bridge. The client made it very clear that

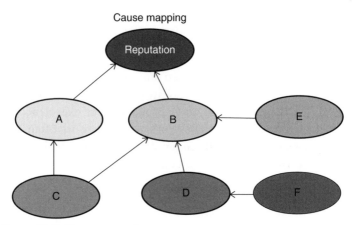

Figure 13.7 Cause mapping

they won not because of price, but because they have a reputation for on-time completion, a critical requirement in this very large and complex project.

To build the map, start by asking 'what causes us to have this reputation?' The team surface two main causes (A and B). We then ask 'what causes A?' which yields C, which also contributes to B, as does D. We then move on to ask, what causes D, which is E, and so on. The steps are summarised below. Allow 90 minutrs for the activity to maintain momentum and energy.

Step 1 Agree a 'critical incidence' of success, for example, the recent winning of a big order.

Step 2 Discuss the reasons why the order was won. Choose the most important explanation, this starts the map. A white board is useful, if not post-it notes on a flip chart will do.

Step 3 By repeatedly posing the question, 'What causes this?', build out from this start point.

Step 4 At a suitable point (due to time or a loss of energy in the room), pause the mapping process and take stock. What have we learned? Are there any inimitable sources of advantage that have been revealed? How might we build on these and protect them?

What we have learned from many teams using the technique is as follows:

1. To build a 'rich' map takes time and energy.

2. Often, the top team does not know enough detail so it is useful to involve staff closer to the action in the mapping process.

3. Once you get three steps away from the starting point ('reputation' in our example), you start to uncover useful intelligence. These may be strategic assets, but either way this digging process reveals important *detail*.

4. Ninety percent of the sources of advantage that mapping reveals are PEOPLE: particular individuals with special know-how, high-performing teams, personal contacts and relationships, reputations, etc.

5. If you do several maps around different incidences of success, you can triangulate across them. If this reveals that the same people keep cropping up in different maps, they are strategic assets.

In Figures 13.8–13.10, we have maps that have different starting points. Figure 13.8 starts from 'success' and it was created by a firm in the pensions industry. (We have anonymised the actual firms.)

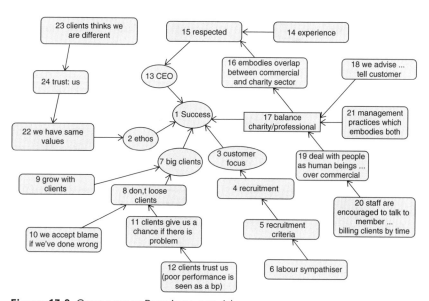

Figure 13.8 Cause map: Pensions provider

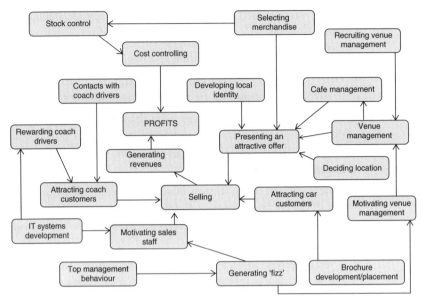

Figure 13.9 Cause map: Jewellery retailer

Figure 13.8 was constructed by a jewellery retailer and the map starts with 'profits'.

Figure 13.10 is a stripped-down version of a bigger map that was created by a firm that grows turkeys. This revealed the firm's

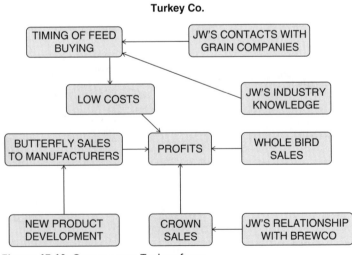

Figure 13.10 Cause map: Turkey farm

dependence on 'JW' the founder, whose personal relationship with the buyer for their main customer ensured their continuing flow of orders, and his tacit knowledge about the industry, built over decades, enabled him to anticipate how future grain prices were likely to move. In this highly competitive industry, this know-how gave them a slight but significant cost advantage.

Application 9: Combining the asset audit and cause mapping

The advantage of the audit is it enables us to unpack the firm's value system to reveal strategic assets. What the audit does not do is show how these assets and capabilities combine together in the value creation process. Often, it is the *combination* of assets that is critical, and the *interaction effects* between them. The audit cannot represent these, but a map can. In the last example, we have a map created by a team from a publisher of 'in-house' magazines. They first did the audit, which revealed the critical strategic assets, then they arranged these into a cause map, which better represented how the value system operates (see Figure 13.11).

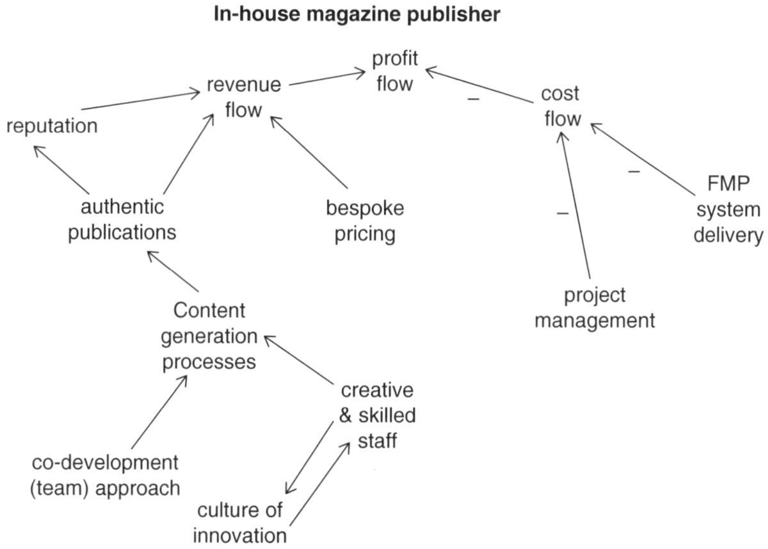

Figure 13.11 In-house magazine publisher: Map of strategic assets

Step 1 As a group, discuss the outcome of the asset audit and agree the set of strategic assets. Typically at this stage additional assets are suggested which did not appear in the audit.

Step 2 Using a flip chart or white board, capture each asset on a post-it note and spread them across the white board.

Step 3 Looking across these assets, are there clear connections between some of them? Most important would be the synergy benefits that arise due to assets co-existing. Draw lines indicating these synergistic connections.

Step 4 Work through all the assets checking for possible strong linkages with complementary assets. This process typically reveals that there are important asset/skills that are not yet on the map. Add them and create the required links. Try to avoid connecting everything with everything, focus on the critical synergies.

Step 5 This is a collectively created 'model' of the firm's value system, which needs to be captured, so take picture of it!

Part

5

Corporate strategies

Chapter

14

Synergy strategies and scope choices

The competitive strategies we have explored thus far (*specialisation, adaptive, low cost, innovation, excellence, no-frills,* and *targeting*) operate at the level of the single business. This could be a 'stand-alone' small- or medium-sized enterprise, or it could be a strategic business unit (SBU) that is part of a larger corporate structure. The most straightforward circumstance is where the firm makes one product and sells it into one geographic market. Although single-product firms are not unusual, most firms of any size tend to have a portfolio of products, and they look to serve several markets. In this chapter we look at what strategy means in the multi-business context. How can a corporation add value to an acquisition? There must be a reason for combining different businesses together. Typically, the argument is that combining businesses will create value through various forms of synergy. Thus, the first part of the chapter explores different *synergy strategies,* and the second part considers the vertical *scope* of the business, focusing on the *make vs buy* decision.

The multi-business context

In Figure 14.1 we have a very simplified corporate structure. At the top of the figure, we have the corporate centre in charge of two business units. Strategies that span across more than one line of business, we refer to as *synergy strategies.*[65]

There must be a reason for combining A and B in one structure. That reason must be to do with creating value for shareholders by either reducing the overall costs of those businesses or by boosting net revenues across the businesses. A synergy strategy must deliver one or other of these outcomes.

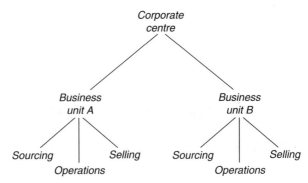

Figure 14.1 A corporate structure

However, there are no structures, systems and culture which can deliver *all possible* synergies. Typically to deliver any synergy requires a specific set of organisational arrangements. Often corporate structures emerge through *acquisitions*. If the corporation understands the synergy benefit that they are pursuing through an acquisition, and if they have the requisite structures, systems and culture to ensure that the target firm will be properly integrated into the corporation, then it is more likely that value will be created. Where we have problems and hence why most acquisitions fail is because those arrangements are not in place and it is not clear what synergies the corporation is trying to deliver.

Seven synergy strategies

We have identified seven distinct *synergy strategies* (SSs), which each require a particular configuration of structure, systems and culture. Value creation at corporate level requires the identification of how extra value will be generated from this mix of SBUs. As there is no single configuration of structure, systems and culture that will deliver all possible synergies, the selection of a synergy strategy must inform all activities at *corporate* level.

We now explore these seven synergy strategies, starting with enhanced efficiency through centralisation.

Centralisation

The centralising strategy involves the consolidation of support functions (see Figure 14.2). What is 'support' is defined in relation

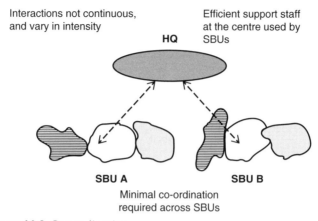

Interactions not continuous, and vary in intensity

Efficient support staff at the centre used by SBUs

HQ

SBU A

SBU B

Minimal co-ordination required across SBUs

Figure 14.2 Centralisation

to the 'core' functions. As a guide, support functions are loosely connected to the core activities and some of them could potentially be outsourced.

The advantages of consolidating these activities at the centre are 1) it can reduce SBU 'overhead' costs, especially where these specialised functions are underutilised at SBU level, and 2) it may be feasible to employ specialists at the centre who can deliver more effective services to the SBUs.

In Figure 14.2 we depict the Centralisation SS. The SBUs can be quite varied in their products, technologies and markets, all that is required for them to 'fit' this configuration is that they can get cost savings from using the centralised functions. There is minimal requirement for the SBUs to coordinate with each other, and interactions between the SBUs and the support staff at the centre are likely to be episodic rather than continuous.

Scale

The difference between the *centralisation* strategy and the *scale* strategy is that the latter refers to the *core* functions of the SBUs. In the scale SS, the core functions of the SBUs are combined and managed from the centre. These might be operations, marketing, R&D and procurement. Consolidating these functions delivers significant scale advantages which the SBUs can benefit from as they are able to deliver products to their customers at lower costs.

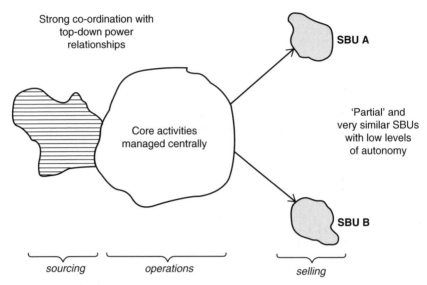

Figure 14.3 Scale

As indicated in Figure 14.3, the configuration that delivers the *scale* strategy is dominated by these centrally managed core functions. There is a need for strong and continuous coordination between the centralised functions and the SBUs. The power is clearly at the centre and the SBUs have severely limited strategic autonomy. Typically, the scope of the SBUs' strategic autonomy may be restricted to decisions about sales and service in their local markets.

Bargaining power

Corporates can create value by coordinating or centralising the bargaining interactions between SBUs and suppliers. Clearly, this coordination only works where SBUs buy from the same suppliers, so the SBUs must be similar in these respects. Coordinating how we *sell* may also enable us to bargain more effectively with customers. Examples might be P&G who through large acquisitions such as Gillette has enhanced its bargaining power over the likes of Wal-Mart, Tesco, etc.

Knowledge transfer

Figure 14.5 depicts the *knowledge transfer* strategy. Here the corporation adds value to the SBUs through the identification, codification

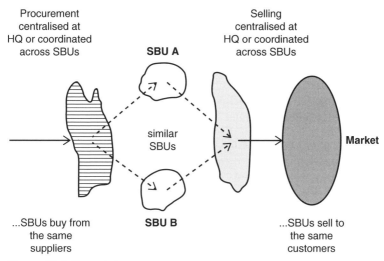

Figure 14.4 Bargaining power

and transfer of knowledge. In this SS, the SBUs need to be similar insofar as they can benefit from 'best practices' developed in other SBUs. The role of the centre is to be able to understand what are better practices, and to do this they need *detailed understanding* of SBU operations. Otherwise, they run the risk of attempting to leverage practices that do not fit a particular SBU's operations.[66]

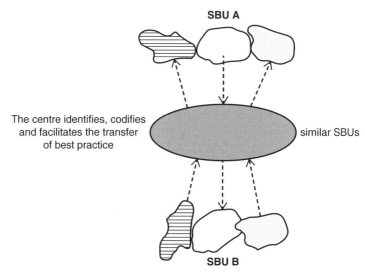

Figure 14.5 Knowledge transfer

The knowledge transfer SS can deliver both efficiency and effectiveness benefits. We can leverage knowledge to enhance product quality and to lower costs. The centre needs to foster a climate where SBU staff feel comfortable interacting and sharing with the centre staff, and with their counterparts in other SBUs. Acquisition targets would be firms where value can be added by transferring knowledge *from* them or *to* them.

Tacit know-how, embedded in people, resists codification which makes it difficult to capture and transfer this form of knowledge. Thus, there are limits to knowledge transfer due to what Szulanski refers to as its 'stickiness'.[67]

Knowledge integration

The knowledge integration SS is probably the most difficult to deliver and sustain, and as a consequence, it is not found in many corporations. The corporation adds value by creating a climate where SBU employees feel comfortable in sharing their expertise on cross-SBU development projects (Figure 14.6). By integrating complementary knowledge in project teams, the corporation fosters innovations. These may be new product ideas, or new practices, processes, etc. There is an element of risk in these projects as there

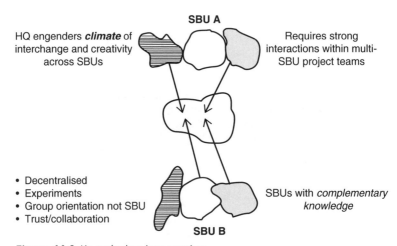

Figure 14.6 Knowledge integration

is no guarantee that they will create value. An experimental culture supports the project teams, and individual team members see their primary loyalty to the *corporation,* rather than to the SBU that they currently operate within.

Cross-selling

Cross-selling leverages the relationships that SBUs have with their customer base. The benefits of cross-selling are increased sales without necessarily increasing the costs of selling and marketing activity. For cross-selling to occur, the SBUs must have similar customers, who would be interested in products or services from other SBUs. Cross-selling will only occur if staff in one SBU see some benefit in promoting products from another SBU to their customers. The extra value takes the form of enhanced sales revenues.

Problems with cross-selling include a lack of trust, or arguments over which SBU gets credited with the sale. The role of the centre is to create a climate that encourages cross-selling behaviour. One possible way to avoid conflict is to credit both SBUs with a sale. The 'double counting' can be dealt with when SBU P&L's are consolidated.

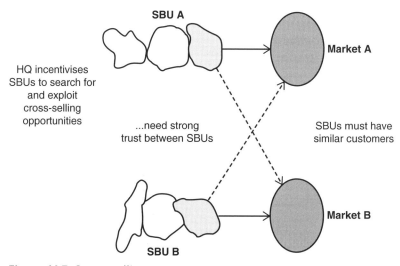

Figure 14.7 Cross-selling

Decentralisation

In unpredictable environments, enabling SBUs to respond to the particular contexts they operate in can create more value. By decentralising, the centre is allowing the SBUs to carve out their own pathway, and it may lead to the SBUs becoming more dissimilar, and hence more unrelated to each other. Where we have a mix of unrelated SBUs, the role of the HQ is to set tough financial targets, to decide capital allocations and to monitor SBU performance. As there are few synergies to be had, there is no requirement for the SBUs to interact with each other. The centre would likely have infrequent but regular interactions, for example, quarterly meetings where the focus of the conversations will be almost exclusively on SBU performance. Typically, SBU metrics are P&L focused, and SBU executives will have their remuneration tied in some way to these performance measures. (see Figure 14.8)

If we are clear about the *synergy strategy* (SS), then we are able to answer three other key questions which are fundamental at corporate level. We can figure out:

● the role of the HQ or centre in delivering this synergy

● the role of the business units in delivering the synergy

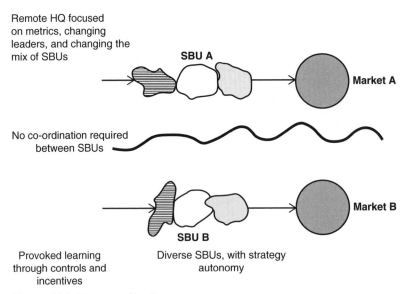

Figure 14.8 Decentralisation

- what the relationship should be between the centre and the business units.

In the absence of clarity around the synergy strategy, these three dimensions, that is, the role of the centre, the role of the business units and the relationships between them, are determined by essentially *political processes*, they are not driven by a well-understood strategy. We would suggest that the executives at the corporate centre decide the primary synergy strategy. Once this is clear, then the answers to these three questions can be worked through.

Most corporate executives we have met are looking to pursue *multiple synergies*: they would like to get the benefits of two or more of the synergies we have identified. We have tried to point out that to deliver one synergy benefit well requires a focus on developing a particular kind of corporate structure, with its appropriate systems and culture. Where we attempt to pursue more than one source of synergy simultaneously, there is a real danger that we end up delivering none of the hoped-for benefits. Staff are unsure about what they should be focusing on, and ambiguous structures and conflicting KPIs emerge which further confuse and demotivate staff.

However, in the same way that our competitive strategies can be 'layered' (see Chapter 12), it is possible to layer synergy strategies *over time*. We can pursue one SS for a time, get the right systems and structures in place and embed the appropriate routines. Then there may be an opportunity to introduce another source of synergy, as long as the required changes to the corporation do not disturb the synergy benefits we have already embedded.

Case study
LeaseCo: Pursuing sequential synergy strategies

We can take as an example of sequencing synergy strategies, the case of LeaseCo, a business that rents out specialised construction equipment (this is a real business, but we have disguised it). LeaseCo operates across most countries in the EU as well as the Middle East. It procures the equipment from manufacturers and rents it to construction and building maintenance firms. One of its challenges is that the construction industries are quite different across the markets it serves. Some country markets are dominated by a few large corporate customers; others are fragmented with many small and medium-sized firms. Also the market for leased equipment is very localised; generally, it becomes prohibitively expensive to transport this equipment more than a 50 miles radius from a depot. Moreover, in some markets the firm competes with a few large players; in others, it faces smaller firms but who nevertheless have large local market shares.

LeaseCo has exploited the *bargaining power* SS which centralises equipment purchasing. This was introduced in 2007. In 2010 the executives decided to try to *transfer knowledge* about maintaining the equipment; this was easier to do as most of the leased equipment was sourced from the same supplier, as a result of the bargaining power strategy. The 'best practice' in equipment maintenance was found in the UK business and these practices were shared across all the depots. It was easier to identify where the best practices were because of an earlier initiative to standardise how costs were reported.

In one of the Belgian depots, a small team came up with a patented safety system, which significantly reduced the number of operative injuries. This innovation was initially developed locally, and only when there was a requirement for additional capital expenditure did the corporate HQ get involved. This system is now offered on all the relevant equipment across the markets LeaseCo serves. Spreading the safety system was made easier as it required minimal adaptations to the standardised equipment and depots were keen to adopt it as it was seen to be a valuable differentiator when negotiating with clients.

So far so good. Building on the successes in transferring maintenance knowledge, the executive decided to introduce a standardised pricing system across all the depots. However, this has been abandoned as it reduced the ability of local depots to adapt their pricing to the local market conditions.

Because the attempt to standardise pricing failed, LeaseCo is now introducing an initiative which is designed to build the capabilities of local staff to research and respond appropriately to local market conditions.

This realisation that local depots need to be given some freedom and discretion to effectively operate in their particular markets goes against the preferences of some of the senior management for exerting centralised control over the depots. But through trial and error, over time the corporation has discovered where it is appropriate to have standardised processes, for example, maintenance; where it is OK to centralise processes, for example, procurement; and where it is necessary to decentralise, for example, pricing. This differentiated approach is the right way to go.

The market-facing activities around building a local presence and having a flexible approach to pricing can only be achieved if depots are given the freedom and are able to develop the skills to respond locally. But there are substantial benefits to be derived from centralising procurement, and through embedding the same maintenance practices across all depots. These activities do not need to vary across localities, and they give each depot cost advantages which enable each depot to price competitively. Whilst the patented safety system is a standardised 'bolt-on' addition, which continues to be developed in LeaseCo's newly established R&D group, gaining regulatory approval for the system has required a team approach between the R&D group and staff on the ground who know how to operate with their local regulatory authorities.

Thus, there is a necessary and value-creating mix of embedded synergy strategies, some of which are about centralising activity (R&D, procurement), some are looking to standardise processes across the depots (equipment maintenance) and some are about enabling local adaptation (pricing). These have been developed *over time* and *feedback* has enabled the synergy practices to evolve and adapt along the way.

Diversifying and decentralising

We should not assume that corporate strategies are only orientated around the potential for synergies. With risk-spreading diversification, the idea is to collect businesses which are *unrelated*. Thus, when we aggregate the net revenues across all of the business units, some would be in growing markets, others in markets that were less attractive, then overall we might be able to show some steady growth. Whereas one SBU might be experiencing tough times, there might be compensating business units that are doing well.

The synergy strategies are a way for a corporate structure to add value to its portfolio of SBUs. Where the corporation has a mix of unrelated businesses, it is difficult for the HQ to add value. However, the more diverse the portfolio of SBUs, the more feasible it becomes for each SBU to select its *own* SBU-level competitive strategies, for example, adaptive, low cost, innovation, excellence, no-frills. This is because the more autonomous and independent the SBUs are, the less likely there will be for conflicts to emerge between their operations.

Decentralisation is a way of dealing with a horizontally diversified portfolio of business units. Choosing to acquire unrelated businesses is a choice to extend the *horizontal scope* of the corporation. There are similar choices to be made about the *vertical scope* of any business, summarised in the 'make or buy' decision which we explore later.

The costs of synergy

Costs are incurred when implementing a synergy strategy. Some of these costs are relatively easy to identify in advance of the changes, others are not. Identifiable costs might include:

- redundancy, relocation and training
- coordination costs: meetings, travel
- control costs: measurement, incentives, monitoring
- acquisition costs: transaction costs, bid premium
- the loss of goodwill where acquired brands are eliminated.

But there are other costs that might be difficult to estimate or anticipate before the changes are made. These might include:

- loss of SBU accountability
- loss of market focus
- destruction of complex, causally ambiguous sources of advantage
- reduced supplier or customer confidence
- lowering morale of those impacted by changes
- reputational damage
- diseconomies of scale.

In Figure 14.9 we indicate that as much effort should be put into assessing the likely *costs of synergy* as is typically exerted when justifying an acquisition or corporate restructuring in pursuit of synergies. Then perhaps the success rate of acquisitions might be improved.

Before embarking on the pursuit of a synergy strategy, we should have some idea of the 'size of the prize': how much extra value do we estimate the SS could generate? Then we would need to consider the changes in the system that would be necessary to deliver

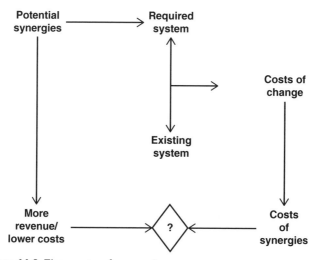

Figure 14.9 The costs of synergies

these synergy benefits. We could then try to estimate the costs of the required changes. Complexity means we can only make rough estimates of likely costs and benefits; therefore, we should only proceed if the potential benefits substantially outweigh the likely costs.

Comparing the seven synergy strategies

In Figure 14.10 we locate each synergy strategy in a space described by four dimensions: 1) SBU Similarity, 2) SBU Strategic Autonomy, 3) Co-ordination across SBUs and 4) Co-ordination between Corporate HQ and SBUs. We can see that each of the seven synergy strategies occupies a different space in this figure. This means that each strategy requires a specific configuration of these four parameters.

This reinforces the argument we set out earlier: there is no single configuration of structure, systems and culture which will deliver

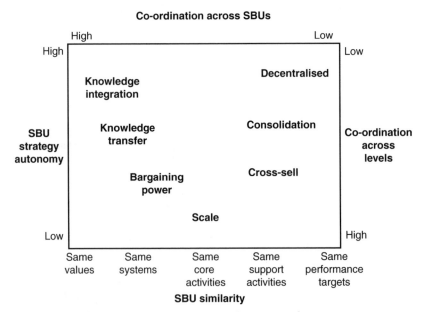

Figure 14.10 Comparing synergy strategies across four dimensions

every possible strategy. Corporate executives need to choose which strategy to focus on, and they need to develop the appropriate structures, systems and cultures.

But as we have argued, over time, once the required organisation has 'bedded in' it may be possible to try to further develop the corporation to deliver additional strategies. For example, it would be feasible to begin with the decentralisation strategy, which is relatively easy to implement as it does not require any consolidation of SBU activities, and then later to augment this by centralising some support functions. Thus, it is feasible to shift to closely related configurations in Figure 14.10. What is not feasible is to jump from, for example, *decentralisation* to *knowledge integration*, as the two required configurations are too dissimilar.

The default system

Where there is little clarity about how the corporate centre is creating value, the 'default' configuration is likely to be *decentralisation*. This is because it is most likely that in this structure the centre will be measuring SBU P&L performance. In the absence of any other influences on SBU behaviour, these P&L targets will drive SBU activity.

Strategy alignment across organisational levels

The seven *competitive strategies* that we introduced in Part 1 of this book operate at the level of the individual SBU. In this chapter we have explored seven *synergy* strategies which potentially add value at the corporate or multi-business level. In this section we explore the relationships between these two sets of strategies. In particular, we are looking at the extent to which the strategies align across the different organisational levels.

In Figure 14.11 we juxtapose both sets of strategies, with the synergy strategies along the top of the figure and the competitive strategies arranged down the left side. If the corporate centre is pursuing *scale, bargaining power* or *centralisation*, then these synergy strategies would align well with the competitive strategies *low cost* and *no frills*. Thus, if SBUs are pursuing *low cost* or *no frills*, the culture,

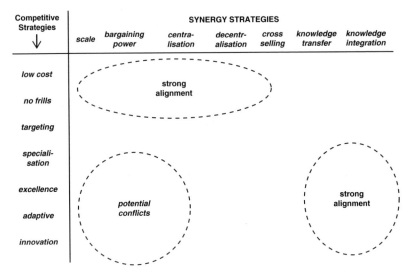

Figure 14.11 Alignment between competitive strategies and synergy strategies

systems and controls being promoted from the corporate centre would fit with the culture, systems and controls being developed at the SBU level.

However, the same set of synergy strategies would result in potential conflicts if SBUs are pursuing product *specialisation, excellence, adaptive* or *innovation*. For example, *innovation* typically involves investments in R&D, there are risks involved and some investments will not pay off. If the corporate centre is imposing tough profit targets, and if the culture being promoted is one of cost reduction and centralisation, then staff at the SBU level will feel they are being driven to behave in conflicting ways.

In contrast, the bottom right of the figure indicates strong alignment between the competitive strategies of *excellence, innovation* and *adaptive* and the corporate-level synergy strategies associated with the transfer and creation of *knowledge*. Thus, there would be a strong feeling of congruence or 'fit' between intentions at both corporate and SBU levels.

Potentially, *decentralisation* would align with any competitive strategy choice an SBU makes. However, typically the decentralised synergy strategy adds value by setting tough performance targets for SBUs. If these are *short-term* targets, this may provoke SBUs to pursue cost-orientated strategies, for example, low cost. In which case, the pressures for short-term performance may squeeze out longer term investments in R&D.

We now consider the *vertical scope* of the business.

Vertical scope: Make vs buy?

All firms operate within a wider value system. A firm may buy materials from upstream producers, like component parts, and then assemble these into a completed unit and then sell them downstream to a retailer. We can consider the extended value system as a *sequence* or network of firms that are linked together, and ultimately the last firm in the chain sells a product or service to the final consumer. The management team has choices about the *vertical* and *horizontal* scope of the firm. By *vertical* scope we mean choices about whether to buy a component or a service, or to make it or do it ourselves. It also includes whether we should distribute our products ourselves or rather have somebody else do that for us. These are the fundamental decisions about vertical scope.

A highly integrated firm would find itself engaged in nearly all the processes involved in value creation, from gathering raw materials at one end of the system and then selling the product to the final consumer at the end of the pipeline. In the past, oil companies like Shell were fully integrated, engaging in exploration, extraction, transportation of crude oil, refining, running terminals and operating pipelines and finally retailing gasoline. Now the value system of most oil majors is more fragmented.

The decision to '*make*' rather than '*buy*' is usually based on an efficiency argument. If we have a capability advantage, then it makes sense for us to make the component inside the firm. If we don't, it might be more efficient for us to procure this as an input into our value creation processes. However, choices of vertical scope are constrained by the *coordinating mechanisms* involved. Where we procure discrete and separate components, it is easy to see that we would have the choice as to whether we would buy it or whether we should make it. This component can be identified, specified, transported, priced and stored, before it enters our system.

However, some activities may interact frequently and intensively with our core processes, which may make it very expensive or even impossible for us to procure this as a bought-in service. Where we have strong and frequent interactions in the value creation process, it is almost impossible to conceive of how that particular activity could be bought-in rather than performed in-house.

But where we can specify what we want, and we can assess whether the supplier has provided what we want, it becomes a lot easier to write contracts and to monitor their performance against our requirements. Where the firm has activities which produce discrete, measureable outputs or services, then there is the option to outsource this activity, that is, to buy it rather than to make it. However, where it is not possible to do this, where there are strong and ongoing *interactions* involved in performing a service that we are considering, then this probably rules out any simple outsourcing option.

Vertical scope choices

Changing the vertical scope redefines your suppliers and customers. Assume a car manufacturer buys in gearboxes. If it extends the scope of the system by manufacturing gear boxes, the car maker now has to deal with the suppliers of gear box components. Similarly, assume the car maker uses franchised dealers to sell the cars, but a decision is taken to extend the scope downstream and operate the sales processes 'in house'. Thus, whereas previously the car maker had the dealers as customers, now it has to develop capabilities to sell directly to the final consumer.

In Figure 14.12 we set out some of the vertical scope choices facing our car maker. A is the current situation. B has the system extending *upstream* where the car maker decides to produce its own gear boxes (our case study SpaceX chose to extend its scope upstream). C has the system extending *downstream* where the car maker decides to sell directly to the final customer. In D we have a choice to *reduce* the vertical scope. Here, the decision is taken to focus on what are seen to be the real strengths of the business, assembling cars and

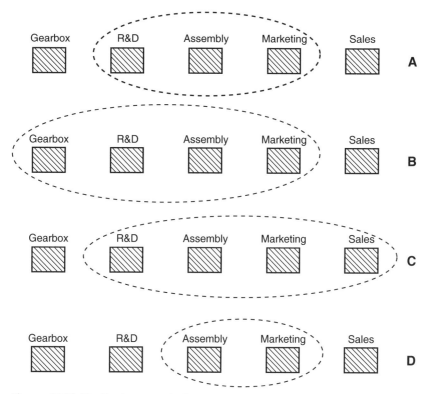

Figure 14.12 Vertical scope choices

marketing them, and to outsource most of the R&D activities to specialist engineering design companies (our case study Bavaria Yachts chose this option).

A firm could decide to exit from retailing and outsource product assembly and manufacture completely. Good examples here would be Nike who doesn't manufacture clothing and apparel, and Apple who outsources all manufacturing.

As well as redefining who are the customers and suppliers in the system, changing vertical scope also presents challenges in dealing with new actors in the wider value system. Take the case of a helicopter manufacturer who chose to focus on assembly and outsourced the manufacture of the gearbox. Initially, the relationships with the 'new' gearbox supplier went well. But over time, as engineers who knew about gearboxes left or retired, the assembler

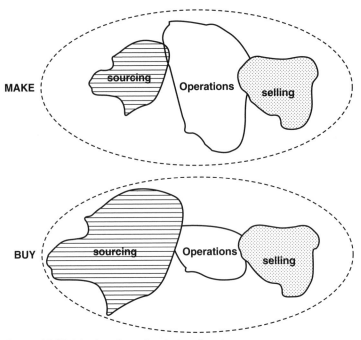

Figure 14.13 Moving from 'make' to 'buy'

realised that the skills to manage relationships with the gearbox supplier had eroded. In effect, there was no one left in the firm who really understood the gearbox; hence, the firm became overdependent on the gearbox manufacturer. This is problematic, as the gearbox is the most critical component in a helicopter.

Moving from manufacturing gearboxes to buying them in from a supplier redefines the roles of the value processes. Outsourcing the gearbox increases the role and significance of *sourcing* and reduces the relative role and significance of *operations* in the overall system. This is represented by the relative sizes of sourcing and operations in Figure 14.13.

Extending vertical scope

Any decision to replace a market-based or contractual relationship with suppliers upstream or customers downstream should be made on the basis of this move enhancing firm value creation. For example, where a firm is unable to source from a market the exact components that it requires in the quantities and at the times that it really needs them, it may well choose to manufacture these components itself. Similarly, where the firm is unable to secure the appropriate space in retail outlets, or if it is unhappy with the way its products are merchandised to the final customer, it may well choose to set up its own retail outlets. What is almost certain, however, is that the firm will not possess the capabilities to successfully manufacture components on the one hand or to run retail stores on the other. So these capabilities will either have to be developed, or more probably, they will have to be acquired.

Assembling the required capabilities to operate a successful retail chain may in itself be beyond the capabilities of the current management team and, similarly, the capabilities required to assemble and configure a successful component manufacturing plant may again be beyond the capabilities of the current management. Unsurprisingly, therefore more often than not these moves to extend the vertical scope of the firm are undertaken through the *acquisition* of firms that already have the required complex bundle of know-how and assets.

A check list of questions concerning vertical scope would be:

- Is it cheaper to do this activity in-house?
- Is the activity easily separable from the core activities of the firm, or is it strongly interconnected?
- What are the transactions costs of buying it in, which include the costs of searching, writing and enforcing contracts, quality assurance, coordinating with in-house activities?
- What are the costs of doing it 'in-house' which includes the costs of managing and coordinating, equipment costs, training, etc.?
- How does making it or buying it affect the firm's flexibility?

Application 10: Exploring two synergy strategies

In our experience in most multi-business organisations, there is a lack of clarity about the corporate strategy. Executives often explain that they are pursuing several sources of synergy simultaneously. As we have explained in this chapter, the problem with this is each

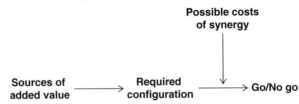

Figure 14.14 Synergy strategy exercise

source of synergy requires *particular* structure, system and culture *configurations* for the added value to be realised. Trying to deliver three or more synergies from the existing configuration is likely to be ineffective, due to conflicting priorities and KPIs and the inevitable compromises that result.

In Figure 14.14 we set out a process that can be used to evaluate a possible synergy strategy.

Step 1 As a group, choose a feasible synergy strategy.

Step 2 For each strategy, discuss 1) the sources of extra value that you think could be realised, for example, cost saving, revenue generation, 2) try to put a rough quantitative estimate on these sources of added value.

Step 3 Guided by the synergy configurations explained in this chapter, try to rough out what the organisation would look like if the synergy strategy was successfully introduced.

Step 4 Any synergy will involve some costs. Using the list of possible synergy costs as a prompt identify what might be the TWO most significant sources of additional cost.

Step 5 Based on the costs, and the possible benefits come to a judgement about whether this synergy strategy is worth exploring further, or whether it should be ditched (the Go/No go decision).

Step 6 Repeat the process for the next synergy strategy.

Bibliography

Aldrich, H. (1979). *Organizations and Environments*. Englewood Cliffs: Prentice Hall.

Allen, P. (2001). 'A complex systems approach to learning in adaptive systems', *International Journal of Innovation Management*, 2 (2): 149–180.

Allen, P. and Boulton, J. (2011). 'Complexity and limits to knowledge: the importance of uncertainty', in Allen, P., Maguire, S. and McKelvey, B. (Eds.), *The Sage Handbook of Complexity and Management*. London: Sage.

Allen, P., Strathern, M. and Baldwin, J. (2007). 'Complexity and the limits to learning', *Journal of Evolutionary Economics*, 17: 401–431.

Ambrosini, V. (2003). *Tacit and Ambiguous Resources as Sources of Competitive Advantage*. Basingstoke: Palgrave.

Ambrosini, V. and Bowman, C. (2001). 'Tacit knowledge: Some suggestions for operationalization', *Journal of Management Studies*, 38: 811–829.

Ambrosini, V. and Bowman, C. (2009). 'What are dynamic capabilities and are they a useful construct in strategic management?' *International Journal of Management Reviews*, 11 (1): 29–49.

Ambrosini, V. A. and Bowman, C. (2010). 'The impact of causal ambiguity on competitive advantage and rent appropriation', *British Journal of Management*, 4: 939–953.

Ambrosini, V., Bowman, C. and Collier, N. (2009). 'Dynamic capabilities: an exploration of how firms renew their resource base', *British Journal of Management*, 20 (1): S9–S24.

Amit, R. and Schoemaker, P. J. H. (1993). 'Strategic assets and organizational rent', *Strategic Management Journal*, 14: 33–46.

Ansoff, H. I. (1965). *Corporate Strategy*. New York: McGraw-Hill.

Argenti, J. (2012). The Beneficiary Doctrine. http://www.argentisys.com/admin/guides/standard-new/the-knowledge/index.html

Arthur, W. B. (1994). *Increasing Returns and Path Dependence in the Economy*. Michigan: University of Michigan Press.

Barney, J. (1986). 'Strategic factor markets: Expectations, luck, and business strategy', *Management Science*, 32: 1231–1241.

Barney, J. B. (1991). 'Firm resources and sustained competitive advantage', *Journal of Management*, 17(1): 99–120.

Barney, J. (2001). 'Is the resource-based "view" a useful perspective for strategic management research? Yes', *Academy of Management Review*, 26 (1): 41–56.

Boulton, J. (2012). 'Strategy for a complex world', in Verity, J. (Ed.), *The New Strategic Landscape: Innovative Perspectives on Strategy*. Basingstoke: Palgrave Macmillan.

Boulton, J. and Allen, P. (2007). 'Complexity perspective', in Jenkins, M. and Ambrosini, V. (Eds.), *Advanced Strategic Management: A Multi-Perspective Approach*. Basingstoke: Palgrave Macmillan.

Boulton, J., Allen, P. and Bowman, C. (2015). *Embracing Complexity*. Oxford: Oxford University Press.

Bowman, C. (1999). 'Action-led strategy and managerial self-confidence', *Journal of Managerial Psychology*, 14 (7/8): 558–568.

Bowman, C. (2003). 'Formulating strategy', in Faulkner, D. and Campbell, A. (Eds.), *The Oxford Handbook of Strategy*. Oxford: Oxford University Press.

Bowman, C. and Ambrosini, V. A. (2000). 'Value creation versus value capture: towards a coherent definition of value in strategy', *British Journal of Management*, 11 (1): 1–15.

Bowman, C. and Ambrosini, V. A. (2001). 'Value in the resource-based view of the firm: a contribution to the debate', *Academy of Management Review*, 26 (4): 501–502.

Bowman, C. and Ambrosini, V. A. (2003). 'How the resource based and dynamic capability views of the firm inform competitive and corporate level strategy, *British Journal of Management*, 14 (4): 289–303.

Bowman, C. and Ambrosini, V. (2010). 'How value is created, captured and destroyed', *European Business Review*, 22 (5): 479–495.

Bowman, C. and Collier, N. (2007). 'A contingency approach to resource creation processes', *International Journal of Management Reviews*, 8 (4): 191–211.

Bowman, C. and Faulkner, D. (1994). 'Measuring product advantage using competitive benchmarking and customer perception', *Long Range Planning*, 27 (1): 119–132.

Bowman, C. and Faulkner, D. (1997). *Competitive and Corporate Strategy*. London: Irwin.

Bowman, C. and Hird, M. A. (2014). 'Resource-based view of talent management', in Sparrow, P., Scullion, H. and Tarique, I. (Eds.), *Strategic Talent Management*. Cambridge: Cambridge University Press.

Bowman, C. and Schoenberg, R. (2008). 'From customer understanding to strategy innovation: practical tools to establish competitive positioning', in Galavan, R., Murray, J. and Markides, C. (Eds.), *Strategy, Innovation and Change*. Oxford: Oxford University Press.

Bowman, C. and Schoenberg, R. (2010). 'Value creation in corporate acquisitions', *Advances in Mergers and Acquisitions*, 9: 153–175.

Bowman, C., Schoenberg, R. and Collier, N. (2013). 'Strategies for business turnaround and recovery: a review and synthesis', *European Business Review*, 25 (3): 243–262.

Bowman, C. (2015). 'The role of technology in the creation and capture of value', *Technology Analysis and Strategic Management*, 27 (2): 237–248.

Bowman, C. and Swart, J. (2007). 'Whose human capital? The challenge of value capture when capital is embedded, *Journal of Management Studies*, 44 (4): 488–505.

Bunge, M. (2003). *Emergence and Convergence: Qualitative Novelty and the Unity of Knowledge.* Toronto, Canada: University of Toronto Press.

Christensen, C. (1997). *The Innovator's Dilemma.* Harvard, USA: Harvard Business Review Press.

Coff, R. W. (1999). 'When competitive advantage doesn't lead to performance: the resource-based view and stakeholder bargaining power', *Organization Science*, 10 (2): 119–213.

Cohen, W. M. and Levinthal, D. A. (1990). 'Absorptive capacity: a new perspective on learning and innovation', *Administrative Science Quarterly*, 35 (1): 128–152.

Collis, D. J. and Montgomery, C. A. (1995). 'Competing on resources: strategy in the 1990s.' *Harvard Business Review*, 73 (4): 118–128.

D'Aveni, R. (1994). *Hypercompetition.* Free Press.

Dierickx, I. and Cool, K. (1989). 'Asset stock accumulation and sustainability of competitive advantage', *Management Science*, 35: 1504–1511.

Duncan, R. (1976). 'The ambidextrous organization: Designing dual structures for innovation', in Killman, R. H., Pondy, L. R. and Sleven, D. (Eds.), *The Management of Organization*, 1: 167–188. New York: North Holland.

Eisenhardt, K. and Martin, J. (2000). 'Dynamic capabilities: What are they?' *Strategic Management Journal*, 21: 1105–1121.

Eisenhardt, K. and Sull, D. (2001). 'Strategy as simple rules', *Harvard Business Review*, 70 (1): 106–116.

Feldman, M. S. and Pentland, B. T. (2003). 'Reconceptualizing organizational routines as a source of flexibility and change', *Administrative Science Quarterly*, 48 (1): 94–118.

Follett, M. P. (1926). 'The giving of orders', *Scientific Foundations of Business Administration*, 29–37.

Freeman, R. E., Harrison, J. S, Wicks, A. C., Bidhan, L. P. and de Colle, S. (2010). *Stakeholder Theory: The State of the Art.* Cambridge: Cambridge University Press.

Gell-Mann, M. (1994). 'Complex adaptive systems', in Cowan, G., Pines, D. and Meltzer, D. (Eds), *Complexity: Metaphors, Models, and Reality*. SFI Studies in the Science of Complexity, Proc. Vol. XIX, Addison-Wesley.

Grant, R. (1991). 'The resource-based theory of competitive advantage: implications for strategy formulation', *California Management Review*, 33: 114–135.

Grant, R. (1996). 'Toward a knowledge-based theory of the firm', *Strategic Management Journal*, 17: 109–122.

Gray, D., Micheli, P. and Pavlov, A. (2014). *Measurement Madness*. UK: Wiley.

Helfat, C. E., Finkelstein, S., Mitchell, W., Peteraf, M., Singh, H., Teece, D. and Winter, S. (2007). *Dynamic Capabilities: Understanding Strategic Change in Organizations*. London: Blackwell.

Katz, D. and Kahn, R. L. (1966). *The Social Psychology of Organizations*. New York: John Wiley & Sons.

Khalifa, A.S. (2004). 'Customer value: A review of recent literature and an integrative configuration', *Management Decision*, 42 (5): 645–666.

Kim, C. and Mauborgne, R. (2005). *Blue Ocean Strategy: How to Create Uncontested Market Space and Make the Competition Irrelevant*. Boston: Harvard Business School Press.

Koller, T., Goedhart, M. and Wessels, D. (2015). *Valuation: Measuring and Managing the Value of Companies*. Sixth Edition. Wiley.

Lawrence, P. and Lorsch, J. (1967). 'Differentiation and integration in complex organizations', *Administrative Science Quarterly*, 12: 1–30.

Lepak, D. P., Smith, K. G. and Taylor, M. S. (2007). 'Value creation and value capture: A multilevel perspective', *Academy of Management Review*, 32 (1): 180–194.

Leonard-Barton, D. (1992). 'Core capabilities and core rigidities: A paradox in managing new product development', *Strategic Management Journal*, 13: 111–125.

Lewin, K. (1951). *Field Theory in Social Science*. New York: Harper and Row.

Lindblom, C. E. (1959). *The Policy-Making Process*. Englewood Cliffs, NJ: Prentice Hall.

March, J. G. (1991). 'Exploration and exploitation in organizational learning', *Organization Science*, 2 (10): 71–87.

McGrath, R. (2013). 'Transient Advantage', *Harvard Business Review*, 91 (6): 62–70.

McGregor, D. (1960). *Human Side of the Enterprise*. New York: McGraw-Hill.

Miles, R. E. and Snow, C.C. (1978). *Organizational Strategy, Structure, and Process.* New York: McGraw-Hill.

Miller, D. (2003). 'An asymmetry-based view of advantage: towards an attainable sustainability', *Strategic Management Journal*, 24 (10): 961–976.

Miller, D. and Friesen, P. H. (1984). *Organizations: A Quantum View.* Englewood Cliffs, New Jersey: Prentice Hall.

Mintzberg, H. (1979). *The Structuring of Organizations: A Synthesis of the Research.* Englewood Cliffs, New Jersey: Prentice-Hall.

Mintzberg, H. and Waters, J. A. (1985). 'Of strategies, deliberate and emergent', *Strategic Management Journal*, 6 (3): 257–272.

Mintzberg, H., Ahlstrand, B. and Lampel, J. (2005). *Strategy Safari: A Guided Tour through the Wilds of Strategic Management.* Canada: Pearson Education.

Nelson, R. and Winter, S. G. (1982). *An Evolutionary Theory of Economic Change.* Cambridge, MA: Harvard University Press.

Nonaka, I. H. (1994). 'Dynamic theory of organizational knowledge creation', *Organizational Science*, 5: 14–37.

Nonaka, I. and H. Takeuchi (1995). *The Knowledge-Creating Company, How Japanese Companies Create the Dynamics of Innovation.* Oxford: Oxford University Press.

O'Reilly, C. A. and Tushman, M. L. (2004). 'The ambidextrous organization', *Harvard Business Review*, 82: 74–81.

Parmigiani, A. and Howard-Grenville, J. (2011). 'Routines revisited: Exploring the capabilities and practice perspectives'. *The Academy of Management Annals*, 5, 413–453.

Pentland, B. and Feldman, M. (2008). 'Designing routines: On the folly of designing artifacts, hoping for patterns of action', *Information and Organization*, 18: 235–250.

Peteraf, M. (1993). 'The cornerstone of competitive advantage: A resource-based view', *Strategic Management Journal*, 14: 179–191.

Pfeffer, J. (1981). *Power in Organizations.* London: Harper Business.

Pfeffer, J. and Salancik, G. R. (1978). *The External Control of Organizations: A Resource Dependence Perspective.* New York: Harper and Row.

Polanyi, M. and Sen, A. (2009). *The Tacit Dimension.* Chicago: University of Chicago Press.

Porter, M. E. (1980). *Competitive Strategy: Techniques for Analysing Industries and Competitors.* New York: Free Press.

Porter, M. E. (1985). *Competitive Advantage: Creating and Sustaining Superior Performance.* New York: Free Press.

Priem, R. L. (2007). 'A consumer perspective on value creation', *Academy of Management Review*, 32 (1): 219–235.

Prigogine, I. and Stengers, I. (1984). *Order Out of Chaos: Man's New Dialogue with Nature*. London: Flamingo.

Quinn, J. B. (1980). 'Strategic change: Logical incrementalism', *Sloan Management Review*, 19: 7–21.

Raisch, S., Birkinshaw, J., Probst, G. and Tushman, M. L. (2009). 'Organizational ambidexterity: Balancing exploitation and exploration for sustained performance', *Organization Science*, 20 (4): 685–695.

Ramírez, R. (1999). 'Value co-production: intellectual origins and implications for practice and research', *Strategic Management Journal*, 20: 49–65.

Ries, E. (2011). *The Low-cost Startup: How Today's Entrepreneurs Use Continuous Innovation to Create Radically Successful Businesses*. USA: Crown Publishing.

Schmidt, J. and Keil, T. (2013). 'What makes a resource valuable? Identifying the drivers of firm idiosyncratic resource value', *Academy of Management Review*, 38 (2): 206–228.

Schoenberg, R., Bowman, C. and Ambrosini, V. (2011). 'Should acquiring firms pursue more than one value creation logic? An empirical test of acquisition performance', *British Journal of Management*, 22 (1): 173–185.

Smith, B. and Raspin, P. (2008). *Creating Market Insight: How firms create value from market understanding*. London: John Wiley & Sons.

Stacey, R. (2010). *Complexity and Organizational Reality*. London and New York: Routledge.

Sweeney, J. C. and Soutar, G. N. (2001). 'Consumer-perceived value: the development of a multiple item scale', *Journal of Retailing*, 77 (2): 203–220.

Szulanski, G. (1996). 'Exploring internal stickiness: impediments to the transfer of best practice within the firm', *Strategic Management Journal*, 17: 27–43.

Taleb, N. N. (2007). *The Black Swan: The Impact of the Highly Improbable*. New York: Random House.

Tetlock, P. E. and Gardner, D. (2015). *Superforecasting: The Art and Science of Prediction*. London: Random House.

Teece, D. 2007. 'Explicating dynamic capabilities: The nature and microfoundations of (sustainable) enterprise performance', *Strategic Management Journal*, 28 (13): 1319–1350.

Teece, D., Pisano, G. and Shuen, A. (1997). 'Dynamic capabilities and strategic management', *Strategic Management Journal*, 18: 509–533.

Thompson, J. D. (1967). *Organizations in Action*. New York: McGraw Hill.

Tranfield, D. and Starkey, K. (1998) 'The nature, social organisation and promotion of management research: Towards policy', *British Journal of Management*, 9 (4): 341–353.

Treacy, F. and Wiersema, F. (1995). *The Discipline of Market Leaders.* Addison-Wesley.

Tuli, K. R., Kohli, A. K. and Bharadwaj, S. G. (2007). 'Rethinking customer solutions: From product bundles to relational processes', *Journal of Marketing*, 71 (3): 1–17.

Tushman, M. L. and O'Reilly, C. A. (1996). 'Ambidextrous organizations: Managing evolutionary and revolutionary change', *California Management Review*, 38: 8–30.

Vargo, S. L. and Lusch, R. F. (2004). 'Evolving to a new dominant logic for marketing', *Journal of Marketing*, 68: 1–17.

Wernerfelt, B. (1984). 'A resource-based view of the firm', *Strategic Management Journal*, 5: 171–180.

Wilcox King, A. and Zeithaml, C. (2001). 'Competencies and firm performance: Examining the causal ambiguity', *Strategic Management Journal*, 22: 75–99.

Zahra, S. A. and George, G. (2002). 'Absorptive capacity: A review, reconceptualization, and extension', *Academy of Management Review*, 27: 185–203.

Zeithaml, V. A. (1988). 'Consumer perception of price, quality and value: A means-end model and synthesis of evidence', *Journal of Marketing*, 52: 2–22.

Zollo, M. and Winter, S. G. (2002). 'Deliberate learning and the evolution of dynamic capabilities', *Organization Science*, 13 (3): 339–351.

Notes to chapters

[1] This chapter builds on complex systems thinking. The original ideas were developed by Prigogine (1984) and Gell-Mann (1994). Other contributions that informed our thinking come from Boulton (2012), Boulton et al. (2015), Boulton and Allen (2007), Allen et al. (2001, 2007, 2011), Stacey (2010), Arthur (1994) and Bunge (2003).

[2] Boulton et al. (2015).

[3] See Mintzberg and Waters (1985) and Mintzberg et al. (2005).

[4] Eisenhardt and Sull (2001).

[5] In this chapter we build on contributions to the theory of value creation and capture from Bowman and Ambrosini (2000, 2001, 2010), Bowman (2015), Coff (1999), Lepak, Smith and Taylor (2007), Porter (1985), Sweeney and Soutar (2001), Vargo and Lusch (2004) and Zeithaml (1988).

[6] Collis and Montgomery (1995), Bowman and Ambrosini (2001), Priem (2007).

[7] Bowman and Faulkner (1994, 1997), Bowman and Schoenberg (2008), Sweeney and Soutar (2001) and Zeithaml (1988).

[8] Ansoff (1965), Kim and Mauborgne (2005), Treacy and Wiersema (1995) and Porter (1980, 1985).

[9] Porter (1980, 1985)

[10] Treacy and Wiersema (1995).

[11] Kim and Mauborgne (2005).

[12] Christensen (1997).

[13] Ansoff (1965).

[14] D'Aveni (1994).

[15] Teece (2007) and McGrath (2013).

[16] Ries (2011).

[17] Taleb (2007).

[18] Tetlock and Gardner (2015).

[19] Bowman and Ambrosini (2000), Coff (1999) and Lepak et al (2007).

[20] Katz and Kahn (1966).

[21] Bowman (2003).

[22] Koller, Goedhard and Wessels (2015).

[23] Freeman et al. (2010).

[24] Ramirez (1999).

[25] Porter (1980).

[26] Pfeffer and Salancik (1978) and Pfeffer (1981).

[27] Argenti (2012)

[28] Mintzberg (1979), Mintzberg, Ahlstrand and Lampel (2005) and Quinn (1980).

[29] Nelson and Winter (1982), Feldman and Pentland (2003) and Pentland and Feldman (2008).

[30] Bowman and Swart (2007).

[31] Barney (1986), Dierickx and Cool (1989).

[32] Mintzberg and Waters (1985).

[33] Bowman (1999).

[34] Here we build on the idea of organisations as configurations of strategy, structure and processes developed by Miles and Snow (1978), Mintzberg (1979), Miller and Friesen (1984) and Aldrich (1979).

[35] Lindblom (1959).

[36] Thompson (1967).

[37] Duncan (1976), March (1991), Raisch, Birkinshaw, Probst and Tushman (2009) and O'Reilly and Tushman (2004).

[38] See Bowman, Schoenberg and Collier (2013) for a review of turnaround strategies.

[39] Tranfield and Starkey (1998).

[40] This is an edited extract from BBC Radio 4's *Today* Programme broadcast on 21 February 2017.

[41] Aldrich (1979), Bowman and Collier (2007), Lawrence and Lorsch (1967), Miles and Snow (1978), Mintzberg (1979) and Miller and Friesen (1984).

[42] Cohen and Levinthal (1990) and Zahra and George (2002).

[43] McGregor (1960).

[44] Bowman (1999).

[45] Teece, Pisano and Shuen (1997), Eisenhardt and Martin (2000), Zollo and Winter (2002), Helfat et al. (2007), Ambrosini and Bowman (2009) and Ambrosini, Bowman and Collier (2009).

[46] Lewin (1951).

[47] Bowman and Faulkner (1994) and Bowman and Schoenberg (2008).

[48] This section draws heavily on Tuli, Kohli, and Bharadwaj (2007) and Khalifa (2004).

[49] Gray, Micheli and Pavlov (2014).

[50] This chapter draws extensively on the resource-based view of the firm: Wernerfelt (1984), Barney (1986, 1991, 2001), Amit and Schoemaker (1993), Collis and Montgomery (1995), Dierickx and Cool (1989), Grant (1991,1996), Peteraf (1993), Bowman and Ambrosini (2003), Bowman and Hird (2014) and Schmidt and Keil (2013).

[51] Feldman and Pentland (2003), Pentland and Feldman (2008) and Parmigiani and Howard-Grenville (2011).

[52] Leonard-Barton (1992).

[53] Feldman and Pentland (2003).

[54] Mintzberg (1979).

[55] Bowman and Swart (2007).

[56] Bowman (2003).

[57] Barney (1991).

[58] Miller (2003).

[59] Bowman (2003).

[60] Polanyi and Sen (2009), Ambrosini (2003) and Ambrosini and Bowman (2001).

[61] Ambrosini (2003), Ambrosini and Bowman (2001) and Nelson and Winter (1982).

[62] Grant (1996).

[63] Wilcox-King and Zeithaml (2001) and Ambrosini and Bowman (2010).

[64] Dierickx and Cool (1989).

[65] Bowman and Ambrosini (2006), Bowman and Schoenberg (2010) and Schoenberg et al (2011).

[66] Schoenberg et al (2011).

[67] Szulanski (1996).

Index

Page numbers followed by *f* indicate figures.